IT IS
FINISHED

IT IS FINISHED

A 40-DAY PILGRIMAGE
BACK TO THE CROSS

CHARLES MARTIN

W PUBLISHING GROUP

AN IMPRINT OF THOMAS NELSON

Published in Nashville, Tennessee, by W Publishing, an imprint of Thomas Nelson.

Published in association with The Christopher Ferebee Agency.

Thomas Nelson titles may be purchased in bulk for educational, business, fundraising, or sales promotional use. For information, please email SpecialMarkets@ThomasNelson.com.

ISBN 978-1-4003-3886-3 (audiobook)
ISBN 978-1-4003-3885-6 (ePub)
ISBN 978-1-4003-3883-2 (HC)
ISBN 978-1-4003-4197-9 (ITPE)

Library of Congress Control Number: 2023938998

Printed in the United States of America

23 24 25 26 27 LBC 5 4 3 2 1

FOR THE KING

All we like sheep have gone astray; we have
    turned—every one—to his own way;
and the LORD has laid on him the iniquity of us all.

                                        –ISAIAH 53:6

For all have sinned and fall short of the glory of God,
and are justified by his grace as a gift,
through the redemption that is in Christ Jesus,
whom God put forward as a propitiation by his blood,
to be received by faith.
This was to show God's righteousness,
because in his divine forbearance he had passed over
    former sins.
It was to show his righteousness at the present time,
so that he might be just and the justifier of the one who
    has faith in Jesus.

                                        –ROMANS 3:23–26

Blessed is the man whose strength is in You, whose
    heart is set on pilgrimage.

                                        –PSALM 84:5 NKJV

CONTENTS

CONTENTS

PART 2: WHY BLOOD WAS THE ONLY
WAY TO SETTLE OUR DEBT

CONTENTS

CONTENTS

PART 3: BUT WHY JESUS' BLOOD?

CONTENTS

CONTENTS

WHY TAKE A 40-DAY PILGRIMAGE
BACK TO THE CROSS?

The road is well-trafficked and sits just outside the city walls. Out where they burn the trash. The soldiers have lit a small fire and pass the wineskin one to another. They slap each other's backs. Bragging about the scourging. And admiring the clothes.

Days after riding into Jerusalem on a donkey, the conquering, triumphant King who raised Lazarus to life is being taught a lesson. Humiliated. Cursed. Hung on a cross. Naked before the world. Passersby spit at Him. Mock Him. Remind Him of all the stupid things He said leading up to this moment.

"After this, Jesus, knowing that all was now finished, said (to fulfill the Scripture), 'I thirst.'"[1]

What scripture? Psalm 69: "For my thirst they gave me sour wine to drink."[2] Jesus is now the subject of jokes. Gambling. The song of drunkards.[3]

The soldiers mock Him and gamble for His clothes. "A jar full of sour wine stood there."[4] Some have remarked the soldiers mixed the vinegar with water to sterilize it for drinking. Offering it to Him as an act of mercy. Maybe, but I don't think so. Given their general attitude toward Jesus, I think the vinegar had another use. "So they put a sponge full of the sour wine on a hyssop branch and held it to his mouth."[5]

In A.D. 33, the Roman army was the largest the world had ever known; and a large army has to be fed; and a fed army has to go to the bathroom, which can cause problems if they're not careful. Sickness, for starters. So how did one keep so large an army clean? During the first century, vinegar was an effective and commonly used cleanser—for everything. Both astringent and antiseptic. In lieu of toilet paper, soldiers were issued vinegar, a stick, and a sponge and instructed as to how to clean their backsides. This sponge-on-a-stick was called a *tersorium*.

How does the King go from triumphant parade where people lay down their cloaks before Him to feces-laced vinegar shoved into His mouth?

"When Jesus had received the sour wine, he said, '*Tetelestai*,' and he bowed his head and gave up his spirit."[6]

Tetelestai.

If you were VP of marketing for Jesus, Inc., how would you broadcast the message? How would you get the word out that the answer to the problem of all mankind, the consummation of the ages, the One to make propitiation and satisfy the wrath of God, has come? Seems like a glistening throne, inhabited by a golden, yoked deity with twelve-pack abs and ridiculous biceps throwing lightning bolts with accuracy, framed by hundreds of millions of angels singing at the tops of their lungs and surrounded by other rulers who have cast their crowns at His feet and plastered their faces to the floor, would do a much better job of attracting the masses than hanging a mangled, naked man on a bloody cross and shoving a filthy sponge down His throat.

And I'd wager you wouldn't kill the messenger.

I write fiction for a living, and rule number one in writing a series is don't kill your protagonist. So how is the death of Jesus a good idea? How does that make any sense at all? And how are we to make sense of something that doesn't make much sense?

For two thousand years, people have written and talked about the life and death of Jesus of Nazareth more than any other man who's ever died. We've seen "John 3:16" billboards and heard people say, "I'd like to thank my Lord and Savior Jesus Christ" or "I'm saved." "Born again." "Jesus Christ saved me from my sins." Further, the instrument of His execution has become a symbol. Something hung around necks, displayed on walls, erected on sidewalks. And if you listen to those who have written or spoken on the subject—or better yet, read the words of the dead man Himself—His death has something to do with you and me.

But what? What's the connection? Who'd He save? From what? And maybe most importantly, why? What does the death of a man two thousand years ago have to do with you and me? Right here, right now.

If the death of Jesus means something, then I think the doorway to a better understanding is one word. Spoken by Jesus with His last breath, just before He gave His Spirit to His Father. The mushroom cloud rising out of the kingdom of darkness was ignited by one word. *Tetelestai*—"It is finished"—may be the most significant word ever uttered across the stratosphere. The single most important statement in all of human history. Spoken by the innocent and dying only begotten Son of God. *Tetelestai* is a stake driven into eternity, which stands there still, and the kingdom of darkness is powerless against it.

+

Let's jump to the other side of the Cross. Twenty-three years later. To a day and time when people were still alive who had seen it. Eyewitnesses. In A.D. 56, Paul wrote a letter to the church in Corinth. Corinth was a leading commercial city in its day, centered on the city's chief deity, Aphrodite (Venus), the goddess of love, where over one thousand prostitutes served in the temple dedicated to her. So extensive was their service that "to Corinthianize" meant to practice prostitution. Given its access to trade and markets, the city was a leading influencer in philosophy and reason, with no shortage of stoic prognosticators. Twenty-three years after Jesus' death, Paul told the church in Corinth, "For Christ did not send me to baptize but to preach the gospel, and not with words of eloquent wisdom, lest the cross of Christ be emptied of its power. For the word of the cross is folly to those who are perishing, but to us who are being saved it is the power of God. . . . For Jews demand signs and Greeks seek wisdom, but we preach Christ crucified, a stumbling block to Jews and folly to Gentiles, but to those who are called, both Jews and Greeks, Christ the power of God and the wisdom of God."[7]

Question: How is the Cross of Jesus Christ, the merciless death of a Galilean carpenter, both the power and the wisdom of God?

In the very next chapter, Paul doubled down, saying, "I decided to know nothing among you except Jesus Christ and him crucified."[8] Why did the greatest theologian and evangelist and writer the world has ever known summarize his own ministry in two words: "Christ crucified"? Why not Christ feeding the five thousand? Or Christ healing the paralytic? Or Christ turning the tables over in the temple? Or Christ raising Lazarus?

Why focus on His crucifixion? His death?

Twenty years after Jesus' death, Paul also wrote a letter to the church in Galatia, a church that we might describe as Spirit-filled, even charismatic, containing eyewitnesses to Jesus' crucifixion. To those people, Paul said, "Foolish Galatians, who has bewitched you, before whose eyes Jesus Christ was publicly portrayed as crucified?"[9] Translation? "What happened to your focus? You stood there and watched this man bleed and die. You heard the word come out of His mouth. What has happened to you since? Why have you taken your eyes off this man and His cross?"

The Cross is the sole basis for God's total provision for us. Period. Everything He did, does, and will do for us and in us, He does through the Cross and the shed blood of His only Son. There is no path back to Him that does not go through the Cross. Paul told the Romans, "He who did not spare his own Son but gave him up for us all, how will he not also with him graciously give us all things?"[10] With and through Jesus, the Father grants us all things—and first on the list is a path back to Himself. Without Jesus, we receive nothing. And no way back.

So why spend forty days going back to the Cross? Why take this pilgrimage?

Because, while "it is finished," He is not. His work on the Cross was perfect. Complete. Absolute. And because of it and through it, He continues working in and through us. The Cross is the singular basis of Christ's total defeat of satan[1] and his kingdom. satan had no response then and has none now. There's nothing he can do about it. his defeat was complete, everlasting, and irrevocable. And while satan can't change what happened on that Friday, he has been working ever since to hide what happened there. To obscure the work of the Cross. To avert our eyes. This is why Paul told

---

1. I realize this breaks long-held rules of grammar and punctuation, but I don't capitalize satan. he's not due the honor. Not in his name and not in his pronoun. And not at the beginning of a sentence.

the Galatians they'd been "bewitched." Even though they were Spirit-filled eyewitnesses to the death and resurrection of Jesus and even though God was actively doing miracles in their church, they'd taken their eyes off the Cross. Some power of darkness had obscured the work of the Cross, and they were focused on something else.

If Paul were alive today, I think he'd take one look around and say, "See my letter to the Galatians." We are no different. We are too easily bewitched and routinely take our eyes off the Cross. Off Jesus Christ crucified. God, in His mercy, has provided one path back to Himself, and that path is through the Cross. The Father delivered the Son to the Cross, and in return, the Cross became the symbol of our deliverance and the enemy's defeat. Our job is to "believe in him who raised from the dead Jesus our Lord, who was delivered up for our trespasses and raised for our justification."[11]

Throughout history, there have been two primary responses to the death of Jesus: mock, spit, curse, beat, scourge, and crucify, or fall at His feet and cry out, "My Lord and my God."

A third response is indifference, which is simply a variation on the first.

From the onset, let me pose a question. And in asking, I'm not poking you in the chest. I'm hoping to wrap an arm around your shoulder, come alongside, and walk with you. Pilgrims, headed in the same direction: What will you do with this man, Jesus? Shove a sponge in His mouth, or bow?

Over the next forty days, I want to return here. Every day. To look up from a different angle and ask the Father to reveal to us: What does this mean? What did You do here that I so easily forget and take for granted? What do I not realize about me that You've never forgotten? I am coming back here because I know me and I need to be reminded what the Cross has done in me. Done to me. Done for me. Again and again.

God seldom works *through* without first working *in*, *to*, and *for*.

My encouragement is to press in. Look up. See it again for the first time. Let the blood of Jesus, which flows fresh from the Cross on Calvary, do for the first time, the tenth time, or the ten thousandth time what only the blood can do in you and to you. No matter how many times I or we have been here, we never graduate from the Cross. This doesn't mean it's the final destination. It's not. For which I thank God. There is an empty tomb just over this hill, but the path leading to it runs through this Cross.

Without this Cross, there is no tomb. No "He is risen." No "firstborn from among the dead." No Savior with the keys of death and hell dangling from His belt. No Alpha and Omega, Beginning and End. Before we can celebrate where He is not (i.e., the tomb) and why He is not there, we need to backtrack to where He's been, how He got there, and what His presence there accomplished.

My hope is that each of these devotions is about a cup of coffee long. Maybe two. And that they stand as road signs to Jerusalem. I'm hoping to retell one slice of the story each day, focusing on one thing at a time. If I were to describe my posture, it would be a fellow traveler, sojourner, locking arm in arm, walking with you, and then letting you listen as I fall on my face and cry out. Hoping you join me.

At times, it won't be pretty, and it might hurt. You won't like what you see. But when you tire and begin counting the cost of returning one more time to that splintery, blood stained reminder, just remember what it cost Him to hang there.

Personally, no matter how long I sit at the foot of the Cross and stare up, I cannot fathom why He would do that. For me. I simply can't wrap my head around this question: When each of us has gone astray, turned our own way, why did God the Father lay on Him—Jesus—the iniquity of us all?[2] I know the answer intellectually. It swims around my head. "For God so loved the world." I'm praying for both of us that during these forty days, it migrates down into our hearts and takes root there. So that we "know-that-we-know" it. Because while I know in my head the love of God came on a rescue mission for you and for me, I think if that knowing were to sink down into my heart, it might shake a few things loose. Might change me. And I'd be more like Him, which is my heart's desire. And His.

Paul ended his letter to the Galatians with this: "But far be it from me to boast except in the cross of our Lord Jesus Christ, by which the world has been crucified to me, and I to the world."[12] Boast in the Cross? Really?

This Cross was and is God's solution—His remedy—to our problem. Seems rather drastic, doesn't it? I mean, is it really worth all that? What's the big deal?

To answer this, you and I need to know our own need. To see the problem anew. Clearly. You and I will never be grateful for the Cross until we know how desperately we need it.

Jesus told His disciples, "If anyone would come after me, let him deny himself and take up his cross daily and follow me."[13] Herein lies the tension of all mankind. The self is the seat of our will, the place where we decide what we want. By definition, it is selfish and antithetical to the selfless nature of Christ. The self is a rebel; it cannot be tamed or improved, and it exists—24/7/365—in total enmity to God. To suggest otherwise is to mock the Cross. The only remedy

---

2. And that word "iniquity" not only means rebellion but includes all of the evil consequences due to us for our rebellion. This makes no sense.

is to put it to death. Crucify it. This means that for each of us there's an execution in our future. Something and someone is going to be put to death. So what is our cross? It's different for each of us, but in my experience it is the place where our will and His will collide. The place where we surrender our will to His. Totally. Without qualification. Without reservation. Without revocation. Where we die. It is why Paul said, "I have been crucified with Christ."[14] And, for the record, it's not a one-and-done. This denying, taking up, following, and dying is a daily thing.

Hence, our journey in this book.

According to Paul, the Cross is offensive.[15] Why? Because it is both a mirror of and a magnifier into our self. Our sin. It is the X-ray that diagnoses the break in us and our need for surgery. To the world, those without the mind of Christ and the Spirit of God, the Cross is folly and foolishness. What Isaiah called a stumbling block.[16] But to us who are being saved, it is the power and wisdom of God.

Here at this Cross, Jesus—through the spirit of Holiness—is going to show you some things about yourself you may not like. Some things might leave a bitter taste. You might be tempted to look away. Don't. Press in. Pull back the veil. His desire is to expose the ugly in us in order to reveal the pure and beautiful and Holy in Himself. Why? The next forty days are my attempt to answer this question.

I pray throughout this journey that you and I come face-to-face with both the weight of our need and the depth of the problem. I pray that we are undone by the truth of us. And I pray that we simultaneously experience the limitless joy of what Christ accomplished for us.

Paul told the church in Corinth, "For I decided to know nothing among you except Jesus Christ and him crucified."[17] **Paul was and is** arguably the greatest thinker and writer in the history of thinking and writing, and yet after everything, he came to this singular decision: only the Cross.

Have you ever wondered why?

WALK WITH ME BACK TO THE CROSS

Smell the burning trash, and sweat, and blood, and human waste. Now look up. Look at the bleeding man hanging there on the middle cross.[3] According to the Bible, that man is the only and innocent Son of God. He's moments from dying. Listen to the gurgle. The labored breathing. See the mangled, hamburger body. Now listen to Him speak.

"*Tetelestai.*"

What will you do with Him?

The answer to this question will change everything about everything for everyone for all time.

---

3. If you're a believer, a follower of Jesus, and you're well versed in this story, please don't get too tripped up when I say He's hanging there. You and I both know that while He did at one time, He's not now. He is risen. I am attempting to walk people to the Cross who've never considered the fact that He did hang there. I am doing so in the same mindset as the writers of the Gospels who used the historical present tense with verbs, which our translators convert to the English past tense to conform to modern usage. Greek authors frequently used present tense for "heightened vividness, thereby transporting their readers in imagination to the actual scene at the time of occurrence" (Schuyler, NASB Bible "Explanation of General format," p. ix.). I'm hoping to walk in their shoes, or better, stand on their shoulders.

Pray with Me

King Jesus, I know that shortly before his death, Paul wrote to the believers in Ephesus from a Roman prison because he knew they were asking the same question. What would they do with You? How would they, how could they, come to know the answer to this mystery hidden for ages? He answered it this way, and it is my prayer too: "I pray that the God of our Lord Jesus Christ, the Father of glory, may give you [me] the Spirit of wisdom and of revelation in the knowledge of him, having the eyes of your [my] hearts enlightened, that you [I] may know what is the hope to which he has called you [me], what are the riches of his glorious inheritance in the saints, and what is the immeasurable greatness of his power toward us [me] who believe, according to the working of his great might that he worked in Christ when he raised him from the dead and seated him at his right hand in the heavenly places, far above all rule and authority and power and dominion, and above every name that is named, not only in this age but also in the one to come. And he put all things under his feet and gave him as head over all things to the church, which is his body, the fullness of him who fills all in all."[18]

Jesus, I know that wisdom and revelation into this mystery only come from God the Father. Please reveal that truth to me. Holy Spirit, help me. Please. I need You. Show me, reveal to me, what You want me to see about me, and You. And keep me, daily, from the enemy who would blind me to the Cross and to my King. King Jesus, You— and You alone—are my Lord and my God. I choose You. I want to know You and You crucified because I have a feeling that if I did, it would change me. Please bring me face-to-face with both the weight of my need and the depth of the problem. I give You permission, here and now, to make me undone by the truth of me. Help me deny myself, lay down my will, die willingly, and follow where You lead. Lastly, I pray that You allow me to experience the limitless joy of what You and You alone accomplished for me on this splintery wooden stake of execution. I believe that at the end of this journey, this pilgrimage, is a joy I have seldom, if ever, known. So bring it. I'm in. Because while I am headed to a merciless crucifixion, an inconceivable resurrection follows. In Jesus' name.

AND GOD RESPONDS

"For the word of the cross is folly to those who are perishing, but to us who are being saved it is the power of God. For it is written, 'I will destroy the wisdom of the wise, and the discernment of the discerning I will thwart.' Where is the one who is wise? Where is the scribe? Where is the debater of this age? Has not God made foolish the wisdom of the world? For since, in the wisdom of God, the world did not know God through wisdom, it pleased God through the folly of what we preach to save those who believe. For Jews demand signs and Greeks seek wisdom, but we preach Christ crucified, a stumbling block to Jews and folly to Gentiles, but to those who are called, both Jews and Greeks, Christ the power of God and the wisdom of God. For the foolishness of God is wiser than men, and the weakness of God is stronger than men. For consider your calling, brothers: not many of you were wise according to worldly standards, not many were powerful, not many were of noble birth. But God chose what is foolish in the world to shame the wise; God chose what is weak in the world to shame the strong; God chose what is low and despised in the world, even things that are not, to bring to nothing things that are, so that no human being might boast in the presence of God. And because of him you are in Christ Jesus, who became to us wisdom from God, righteousness and sanctification and redemption, so that, as it is written, 'Let the one who boasts, boast in the Lord.'"[19]

PART ONE

The Origin Story of What Jesus Finished at the Cross

DAY 1

"Jesus of Nazareth, The King of the Jews."

JOHN 19:14–19

"Now it was the day of Preparation of the Passover. It was about the sixth hour. He said to the Jews, 'Behold your King!' They cried out, 'Away with him, away with him, crucify him!' Pilate said to them, 'Shall I crucify your King?' The chief priests answered, 'We have no king but Caesar.' So he delivered him over to them to be crucified. So they took Jesus, and he went out, bearing his own cross, to the place called The Place of a Skull, which in Aramaic is called Golgotha. There they crucified him, and with him two others, one on either side, and Jesus between them. Pilate also wrote an inscription and put it on the cross. It read, 'Jesus of Nazareth, the King of the Jews.'"[1]

It's 3:00 P.M. on Friday, April 3, A.D. 33. The town of Jerusalem.

It's dark and has been for three hours. As if someone has blocked out the sun, which is strange since it's the middle of the afternoon. Jerusalem is bustling with people. Jews have come from all around to observe Passover. Many have walked days just to get here.

Just outside the city walls, Roman soldiers are executing three criminals along a common, well-traveled road. While their crimes are unknown, their sentence is obvious: death by crucifixion—a practice started by the Persians some six hundred years ago[2]—where they attach, or hang, a man by his hands and feet along a vertical pole topped with a crossbar. It looks like a "T." Once hung, gravity exerts downward pressure on the man's body, which stresses his lungs, decreasing lung capacity and, hence, his ability to breathe. To take a breath, he must push up with his feet and pull up with his arms, producing a slow, painful death. There's nothing quick about it. But what the Persians started, the Romans perfected, which is why these three men are hanging on this road—where they can be seen. A warning to squash future rebellions by dissuading those who would start them.

Crucifixions were known to take all day. Records indicate thirty-six hours to nine days.[3] With each passing hour, fluid builds up in the man's lungs, causing a slow death. He is caught between a desire to breathe and the decreasing ability to push and pull, and as that ability decreases, the man drowns. Suffocates. This form of death is considered one of the most painful ways to die.

Improving on the Persian model, and to prolong both the torture and the agony, the Romans made one addition called a "sedile," or "mercy seat." It's a sharp peg of wood driven into the vertical post between the man's legs just below butt-level. To avoid puncture, the man arches himself out away from the vertical post, allowing him less leverage to lift himself. When he tires, the only option is to rest, or sit, on the "seat."

But there is nothing merciful about it. In addition to the excruciating pain, many lost bladder and bowel control, further increasing their shame.

Despite artistic portrayals to the contrary, crucified criminals were hung at eye level. This allowed passersby to see the excruciation.

The naked bodies. The shoulders popped out of joint. They could smell the feces and urine. Hear their cries. Proximity to the dying allowed them to spit. Mock. Remind them of all the foolish things they said and did in this life and how that futile attempt had brought them to this point. How they were getting what they deserve.

These three men will die. Right here. Today.

During His life on earth, the man on the middle cross claimed to be the Son of God. A claim punishable by death. This is *the* question. Given that claim, He now hangs below a sign written in Greek, Hebrew, and Latin that says: "JESUS OF NAZARETH. THE KING OF THE JEWS." The religious elite milling around want to rewrite it to say, "This man *says* He is King of the Jews," but Pilate wrote what he wrote, and he's not changing it.

Whatever the truth, and whoever this man is, He is struggling, and He looks anything but kingly. And if this really is God's Son, why on earth would God let this happen to Him? The soldiers hung Him on this cross with a nail through each wrist, then they spread the man's legs around the vertical post and nailed through the side of each heel.[4] There were two reasons for this: a high concentration of nerves, equaling greater pain, and fewer blood vessels, meaning he couldn't bleed out before the torture had time to set in. It also made pushing up and pulling that much more painful as the condemned did so against tearing flesh.

The man looks unnatural. Almost unrecognizable as a man. Prior to hanging Him here, someone got ahold of Him with a cat-o'-nine-tails. A scourge. Tipped with bone, glass, or nails. Which when slung at His body, wrapped around, embedding into His flesh. When ripped backward again, it removed chunks of the man's neck, back, face, and sides. He's hamburger. Shredded.

Proving he is the most evil of men.

During the course of His agony, the man says seven things, most of which are strange. He forgives His torturers. Says something to His mother and another man, but it does little good as she is inconsolable. He speaks to the criminal at His side. Then, for the first and only time, He speaks about Himself, saying He's thirsty. He cries out for His Father, asking why He has left Him there to die. Alone. Forsaken. Finally, with His last breath, He bows his head and gives up His Spirit.

But just prior to giving up His Spirit, He utters a single word. Just one word. It echoes off the rocks and the ears of those milling about. Judging by the looks on their faces, they know the word but pay little attention to it. The babbling of a dying man.

Tetelestai.

A simple word. It means, "It is finished." Something has come to an end. Concluded. Accomplished. Given its tense in the Greek, it's also translated as "It is perfectly perfect" or "It is completely complete." A verb tense that carries with it the promise that whatever happened is happening still. Throughout time. For all eternity. Once-and-for-all kind of stuff. It was finished then and is still being finished now, continually. The word is well-known, as it was used frequently by first-century bankers. When noting that a debt obligation had been fulfilled, they would write or stamp *"Tetelestai"* on the debt ledger. "Paid in full."

According to the dying man, something has been accomplished or completed. Something was made perfect. But what? The only thing finished is Him. The fact is this: His rebellion failed. He lost. Rome won. Looks like He should've kept His mouth shut.

Which gives rise to the question: Who is this man? Why is He dying? What horrible crimes did He commit? Further, what did He finish? And why would this tormented man speak *"tetelestai"* as His last word?

DAY 1

Walk with Me Back to the Cross

How is the shed blood of a man two thousand years ago relevant here and now? What could it possibly have to do with you and me? And what is finished?

Pray with Me

Lord Jesus, whenever I hear someone downplay, denigrate, or doubt the life, death, and resurrection of Jesus the Christ, I cringe. I want to pull them aside and say, "Hey, walk with me up to the Cross and let's look together at Jesus." Then I pray like crazy that You will do in them whatever You did in the centurion, the thief, and me.

For the record, I believe the story of You is true. Completely. You were and are the Son of God who came here on a rescue mission—better yet, a prisoner swap—and died for a rebel like me. You paid a debt I could not pay in ten thousand lifetimes, but the story does not and did not end there. God the Father, through the power of the Holy Spirit, raised the Son—You—to life. Meaning, You're alive. Right now. Ruling and reigning. The King ruling over the kingdom sitting on the throne.

God the Father's answer to the problem of mankind, my problem, was Your premeditated and brutal death. His only begotten Son. But while that is horrible, it was no haphazard plan thrown together on the spur of the moment because God was caught off guard by man's utter depravity. God planned this very thing—the execution of His Son—since before He created light, darkness, the heavens, the earth, time, and me.

Billions of people have died on this earth, so please show me,

7

reveal to me, what does the shed blood of one man two thousand years ago have to do with any of us? Why do six hours on a Friday get so much airtime throughout human history? Paul himself told us it was a "*mystery hidden for ages and generations but now revealed to his saints.*"[5] **In another letter, he called it** "*the unsearchable riches of Christ . . . according to the eternal purpose that he has realized in Christ Jesus our Lord.*"[6]

The mystery, the unsearchable riches, and the eternal purpose, what today might be called "the best God can come up with," was and is a dead Jesus. How is this so? Please unpack that for me. In Jesus' name.

AND GOD RESPONDS

"He is the image of the invisible God, the firstborn of all creation. For by him all things were created, in heaven and on earth, visible and invisible, whether thrones or dominions or rulers or authorities—all things were created through him and for him. And he is before all things, and in him all things hold together. And he is the head of the body, the church. He is the beginning, the firstborn from the dead, that in everything he might be preeminent. For in him all the fullness of God was pleased to dwell, and through him to reconcile to himself all things, whether on earth or in heaven, making peace by the blood of his cross. And you, who once were alienated and hostile in mind, doing evil deeds, he has now reconciled in his body of flesh by his death, in order to present you holy and blameless and above reproach before him, if indeed you continue in the faith, stable and steadfast, not shifting from the hope of the gospel that you heard, which has been proclaimed in all creation under heaven."[7]

DAY 2

"I am the light of the world."

JOHN 9:1–7

"As he passed by, he saw a man blind from birth. And his disciples asked him, 'Rabbi, who sinned, this man or his parents, that he was born blind?' Jesus answered, 'It was not that this man sinned, or his parents, but that the works of God might be displayed in him. We must work the works of him who sent me while it is day; night is coming when no one can work. As long as I am in the world, I am the light of the world.' Having said these things, he spit on the ground, and made mud with the saliva. Then he anointed the man's eyes with the mud."[1]

Jesus is making mud pies.

He's done this before—to this man. He made these eyes. But in this moment, He's finishing, or completing, the job. Making them perfect. Science tells us there are over two million working parts to the human eye.[2] So while we see Jesus spitting and making mud, there's much more going on here. This is Handel, Mozart and Bach, Michelangelo, da Vinci, Rembrandt, Milton, Shakespeare, plus the entire NASA team rolled into one. In the blink of an eye.

"Then he anointed the man's eyes with the mud and said to him,

'Go, wash in the pool of Siloam' (which means Sent). So he went and washed and came back seeing."[3]

One minute he cannot see. Blind as a bat. Shuffling his feet while his hands feel the walls. Then he meets a man who makes a mud pie, packs it on his face, tells him to wash, and *whammo*! Now he can see. For the first time ever. I imagine the man screaming at the top of his lungs, "I can see! I can see!" I find the next part comical, and I think Jesus did too.

"His neighbors and those who had formerly seen him begging asked, 'Isn't this the same man who used to sit and beg?' Some claimed that he was. Others said, 'No, he only looks like him.' But he himself insisted, 'I am the man.'"

"'How then were your eyes opened?' they asked. He replied, 'The man they call Jesus made some mud and put it on my eyes. He told me to go to Siloam and wash. So I went and washed, and then I could see.' 'Where is this man?' they asked him. 'I don't know,' he said. They brought to the Pharisees the man who had been blind. Now the day on which Jesus had made the mud and opened the man's eyes was a Sabbath. Therefore the Pharisees also asked him how he had received his sight. 'He put mud on my eyes,' the man replied, 'and I washed, and now I see.'"[4]

The man is beside himself. *What is wrong with these people? I was imperfect. Now I see perfectly. Don't you get it?* But the Pharisees aren't interested in his eyes. Or the fact that he can see. Instead, they ask, "Where is this man?"

Which is the wrong question. Let's back up.

"Then the Lord God formed the man of dust from the ground and breathed into his nostrils the breath of life, and the man became a living creature."[5] The verb "formed" paints a picture of a potter or sculptor. God kneeling down, squinting one eye, rubbing His chin, rolling up His sleeves, and playing in the dirt. Delighting in the thing in His hands. Pretty soon a shape comes together. Shoulders. Hips. Legs. Feet. Wrinkles. Freckles. Hands. God is meticulous. Taking His time. He's not in a hurry. He's laughing, smiling, considering, delighting. A touch here. A touch there. A nose. A finger. An ear. Finally, an eyeball. He needs it to be roundish, so He spits in the dust, makes mud, rolls it into an oblong ball, and then gently places it into the man's skull where he covers it, or protects it, with a lid.

But man is not yet alive. Sizing up His perfect creation, He smiles. It's time. Like a kid blowing out candles on a birthday cake, God takes as deep a breath as He can, filling His lungs, then presses His lips to our lips and nostrils and breathes out—filling us with the *ruach* of God.

The very breath of God. Meaning, our first breath started in His lungs.

Our lungs expand, and we blink, becoming a living, breathing soul. In that moment, we are perfect in every way.

Stop right there—that Edenic place of perfection was and is His intention for us. Always has been. The heart of God for us is expressed in that moment. Perfect union. Perfect relationship. Perfectly perfect.

How do I know? John 17. One of the most amazing dialogues in Scripture. An intimate conversation between the Father and the Son.

This is Jesus talking with the Father hours before He goes to the Cross:

"I do not ask for these only, but also for those who will believe in me through their word, that they may all be one, just as you, Father, are in me, and I in you, that they also may be in us, so that the world may believe that you have sent me. The glory that you have given me

I have given to them, that they may be one even as we are one, I in them and you in me, that they may become perfectly one, so that the world may know that you sent me and loved them even as you loved me. Father, I desire that they also, whom you have given me, may be with me where I am, to see my glory that you have given me because you loved me before the foundation of the world. O righteous Father, even though the world does not know you, I know you, and these know that you have sent me. I made known to them your name, and I will continue to make it known, that the love with which you have loved me may be in them, and I in them."[6]

There's a lot here. Too much to digest over a single cup of coffee. But notice a few things with me. Jesus' desire is that we "may become perfectly one." Perfectly one. Where do we see that? Don't miss the word "perfect." The root Greek word is *teleo*. Same root word for *tetelestai*. Why is this Jesus' desire? It's simple. "That the love with which you have loved me may be in them, and I in them."[7] This is why we were created. To reveal and return us to the Father so that we might know His perfect love and be in perfect relationship.

This is also the reason for Jesus. That we might know that perfect love.

When sin entered, the perfect became imperfect. And God did not then, and does not now, like that. In fact, He hates it. The word used to describe that hatred is *wrath*.

In the garden, having eaten the forbidden fruit, Adam and Eve knew they had messed up, so they ran and hid. But watch what happened. "And they heard the sound of the Lord God walking the garden in the cool of the day, and the man and his wife hid themselves from the presence of the Lord God among the trees of the garden."[8]

Maybe we've trivialized this with Sunday school puppets and

felt boards, but God appeared in the garden *searching* for Adam and Eve. Calling out. Closing the distance. He initiated the search. The rescue.

Eden may well be beyond my ability to comprehend, but my guess is this: In Eden we (mankind) got to do what we wanted (save one thing: "Don't eat from that tree"), when we wanted, however we wanted, without sin or guilt, with no consequences, all while in the presence of God and the sound of His voice. His laughter. His participation.

When we made mud pies, God's hands were dirty too.

Now look at the moment sin entered. Pull away the vines. Look down through the trees. The serpent tucks tail and slithers back into the grass. Adam and Eve are attempting to hide. God leans around a tree and asks an amazing question. And it's not because He doesn't know the answer. It's not like He got caught off guard and lost his prized creation in the garden. He's asking for their benefit. Gently allowing reality to set in. "But the Lord God called to the man and said to him, 'Where are you?'"⁹

Adam hears the question "Where are you?" and while they've played hide-and-seek before, this is different. Adam doesn't answer, because for the first time in his short life, he doesn't know.

God voices the question because Adam and Eve need to know that for the first time ever, they have a problem. A big one. They are lost, hiding, and feebly sewing fig leaves together in an attempt to cover a mess way bigger than a fig leaf. A single spark has ignited a forest fire, and within seconds their entire world is ablaze. Adam and Eve didn't just choose a forbidden fruit. They chose a rival kingdom. And a rival king. At the root, their choice, their desire, was to be independent from God. (Which is also our root problem. It's the result of the snakebite, the venom in our veins.) And God, in His love, is about to let them live out their choice—while doing everything to return them to Himself. Including eventually sacrificing His Son. "For God so loved the world, that he gave . . ."[10]

Their Edenic life has been fractured, they are powerless to save themselves, and they don't possess the remedy. If Adam and Eve know anything in that moment, they know this: they can't undo what they've done. Can't fix what's broken. And what's broken is their once-perfect relationship with God.

That's the reason for God's question—which Adam and Eve filter through their newly acquired knowledge of good and evil.

Rather than bend them over His knee, God expresses His kindness, goodness, mercy, and grace; and out of His love for them, He asks, "Where are you?" Because to answer, they need to know their need. They need to see where their feet are standing. Which, judging by the hasty patchwork of fig leaves, they're starting to understand.

Adam and Eve's choice to eat forbidden fruit was outright rebellion. Defiance. A desire for independence. In doing so, they chose a rival king and kingdom. The kingdom of darkness. And so the rescue mission began. Paul wrote to the Colossians: "He [Jesus] has delivered us from the domain of darkness and transferred us to the kingdom of his beloved Son, in whom we have redemption, the forgiveness of sins."[11]

Back to the man born blind.

Jesus heals the man born blind, and while the man is ecstatic and jumping around like a kid on a pogo stick, the religious rulers are in an uproar because Jesus healed on the Sabbath. They are indignant. "Where is this man?"

But that's the wrong question.

Jesus healed the man "that the works of God might be displayed in him."¹² *The* work of God is standing before them. Making mud. Perfecting eyes. The blind see. Where the man once saw only darkness, now he sees light. And yet the self-righteous Pharisees are clueless. Blind as bats. They have no idea they're standing three feet from the promised Savior of the world.

From the garden to Jerusalem to this page, God has sought man. Closed the distance. Come searching. And in healing the blind man, restoring his sight, turning darkness to light, Jesus is asking a silent yet in-your-face question: "Where are you?"

And according to the narrative, only one man knows: the man with the new eyes.

WALK WITH ME BACK TO THE CROSS

The offer of this Cross is unlimited forgiveness. Salvation. Deliverance. Redemption. Ransom. Justification. Sanctification. Righteousness. Holiness. Perfection. Intimacy with the Father. Coheirs with Jesus. It's a shameless existence of mud pies, hide-and-seek, dancing barefoot, and belly laughter with the God of the universe. It's immeasurable. Priceless. Beyond comprehension. If we truly understood it, our fuzzy little heads would explode.

And yet despite the ridiculous nature of the offer, the offer stands. But so does the question. And Jesus is not asking for His benefit. He knows the answer. And the remedy.

Before we can receive the unmerited grace of God, Jesus meets us with the same question God asked Adam and Eve in the garden. And when He asks, He is bringing attention to both our location and condition: "Where are you?" It's a question of kingdoms.

Before we start sewing fig leaves together, let's be honest—where we are is in dire need. Without this Cross, we are lost. Dead. Prisoners in an evil kingdom. And we are powerless to fix this mess.

PRAY WITH ME

King Jesus, I don't know that I can entirely wrap my head around the garden. It's difficult to imagine a perfect world. I've seen too much of this one. It's like asking a fish to describe fresh water when all he's ever known is salt. But I can imagine Your intention. Your wish. And while I'm finite and You are infinite, I can play the slideshow of You fashioning me from the dust. Making a mud pie with delight on Your face. I know You crafted me out of love, and Your intention was to share Yourself with us. But then sin entered. And the perfect became imperfect. Mankind chose a king that was not You. I know that hurt Your heart. It hurts mine to say it. I'm so sorry. But ever since, You— because You love us with an inconceivable love—have sought to return us to You. We were created for Eden. Your kingdom. For walking with You in the cool of the evening. And when I dig down, I sense the long- ing. I look around me and scratch my head and know something is not right. I was created for something and someplace else.

In the garden, You asked Adam and Eve, "Where are you?" And when I read Your Word, I hear You asking me the same question. But I think the question is bigger than my location. You know where I am. I think Your question has more to do with condition. In asking, "Where are you?" You're asking both, "What is your location?" and "What is your condition?" Without You, my location is housed in the kingdom of darkness, and my condition is imperfect, dead in my sin, lost, a slave held captive in a rival kingdom, and yet deeply desiring a way back to You but totally unable to do anything about it. Jesus,

I'm so sorry that my nature—and often my decisions—is defiance, rebellion, and choosing my own way. Desiring independence from You, I have "gone astray." Forgive me please. When I look around, I know that where I am is not where I want to be. I want to be with You, but I can't get there on my own. I need You to do for me what I cannot do. Please come, Lord Jesus.

AND GOD RESPONDS

"I will not leave you as orphans; I will come to you."[13]

"For you formed my inward parts; you knitted me together in my mother's womb. I praise you, for I am fearfully and wonderfully made. Wonderful are your works; my soul knows it very well. My frame was not hidden from you, when I was being made in secret, intricately woven in the depths of the earth. Your eyes saw my unformed substance; in your book were written, every one of them, the days that were formed for me, when as yet there was none of them. How precious to me are your thoughts, O God! How vast is the sum of them! If I would count them, they are more than the sand. I awake, and I am still with you."[14]

DAY 3

"I am not."

JOHN 18:15–18, 25–27

"Simon Peter followed Jesus, and so did another disciple. Since that disciple was known to the high priest, he entered with Jesus into the courtyard of the high priest, but Peter stood outside at the door. So the other disciple, who was known to the high priest, went out and spoke to the servant girl who kept watch at the door, and brought Peter in. The servant girl at the door said to Peter, 'You also are not one of this man's disciples, are you?' He said, 'I am not.'"[1]

Every time I read this I want to skim quickly. Rip off the Band-Aid. Because I know what's coming. One of the more painful pictures in all of Scripture.

"Now the servants and officers had made a charcoal fire, because it was cold, and they were standing and warming themselves. Peter also was with them, standing and warming himself. Now Simon Peter was standing and warming himself. . . . So they said to him, 'You also are not one of his disciples, are you?' He denied it and said, 'I am not.' One of the servants of the high priest, a relative of the man whose ear Peter had cut off, asked, 'Did I not see you in the garden with him?' Peter again denied it, and at once a rooster crowed."[2]

One of Jesus' best friends denies Him as He heads to a sham trial and brutal execution. Is there anything more painful? Of all the events in Jesus' life, all the lessons, why start with this one? Why start here?

Because we are all Peter. We have all denied Jesus. Ten thousand times over. To deny that we've denied Him is to deny Him. Again.

John stated that "grace and truth came through Jesus Christ."[3] So while it is true that we are all Peter, it is also true that there is more mercy in Jesus than sin in us. If you remember anything I write in this book, remember that there is more mercy in Jesus than sin in us. As improbable as it seems, the Cross of Jesus is the mercy of God. And His grace covers every sin. Back to Peter.

When pressed, Peter made a choice, and that choice was not Jesus—but he wasn't the first man to do this. Denying Jesus started long ago.

Let's back up. All the way.

"Then God said, 'Let us make man in our image, after our likeness. And let them have dominion over the fish of the sea and over the birds of the heavens and over the livestock and over all the earth and over every creeping thing that creeps on the earth.' So God created man in his own image, in the image of God he created him; male and female he created them. And God blessed them. And God said to them, 'Be fruitful and multiply and fill the earth and subdue it, and have dominion over the fish of the sea and over the birds of the heavens and over every living thing that moves on the earth.'"[4]

God sizes us up, nods, admires His handiwork, then He leans over us, takes a ginormous deep breath, places His lips to our mouth and nose, and exhales—filling our chest with air that first started in Him.

We were dead, then we became alive. And the initiation for all that started and ended with Him. Why? Because He loves us with a love we can't fathom.

Notice the pronouns and the verbs. He formed and He breathed. What did we do? Not one thing other than receive—which He allowed us to do. All that we have, all that we are, including our next thought and breath, come from Him alone. We didn't do anything to cause it, didn't do anything to create it, didn't do anything to initiate it. Dust can do nothing of its own initiative. It's just dust. We were dead and He made us alive. We were blind and now we see. Who can boast before God?

Back to the garden. God cuts Adam and Eve loose to run and play in the fields of the Lord, and they do. Perfect bliss. Perfect world. Perfect everything. *Just don't eat from that tree.*

Things are Edenic for about five minutes when a strange serpent shows up. Eve often gets a bad rap because the serpent deceived her first, but my question is, How'd he get in? What was Adam doing when the serpent slithered up to Eve? I want to tap him on the shoulder, "Dude, you had one job." Why didn't Adam tell him to shut his mouth when he questioned the goodness of God? Why didn't Eve say, "Excuse me, you'll have to take that up with my husband. I don't talk to strange snakes." I don't know—I just know they didn't, and we are no different.

"Now the serpent was more crafty than any other beast of the field the Lord God had made."[5] This is it. The turning point. The point in time when sin entered. This is the moment everything went to hell in a handbasket.

Adam failed to defend God's garden and allowed the serpent to deceive Eve. As a result, they ate the forbidden fruit, "the eyes of both were opened, and they knew that they were naked. And they sewed fig leaves together and made themselves loincloths."[6] Notice when sin enters, man's knee-jerk is to cover it by his own ability, to get back to a right standing before God by his own work. It's called "works-based righteousness." Or self-righteousness. And it's not possible. Never has been. The truth is, yes, we are saved by works. Just not ours. We are saved by Jesus' finished work on the Cross, which is a gift of grace. One we cannot earn. The only thing we bring to the equation is our sin and the need for the finished work.

Remember the famous evangelical elevator question: "If you died tonight, do you know where you'd spend eternity?"

"Well, yes."

"How do you know?"

"Well, because I . . ."

Stop right there. The moment we answer this question by voicing pronouns in the first or second person, we've lost sight of the truth. *We*, you and I, can't get back to good. *We* can't do anything to return to a right standing before a good and Holy God. *We* are powerless to bridge the gap and get ourselves out of this mess. Only He can. This is why we are lost and in need of rescue. Of saving. It's not what *we* can do. It's what He's done. Period. We are identified not by our scars of hard work and pulling ourselves up by our bootstraps but by His scars of self-sacrifice—a life laid down. Big difference. Our response to the question should start with "Because He . . ."

Pronouns matter. When Adam and Eve heard the sound of God walking in the garden, they hid themselves.

I tend to think this broke God's heart. Until now, Adam and Eve heard Him and came running. Two kids turning the corner. The sound of footy pajamas slapping hardwood floors. Arms flinging. Smiles and eyes wide. Launching themselves. Jumping into His arms. Legs wrapped around His waist. "Daddy!" A sticky mess of syrup, butter, and pancakes all around. But not today. Today, it's crickets. Not a sound. Something is amiss.

Sin has entered. Man has fallen.

But rather than thundering and scattering lightning bolts from on high, God steps off His throne, walks across the garden, and asks an amazing question: "Where are you?"

Adam answers, "I heard the sound of you in the garden, and I was afraid."[7] And so fear entered the world—the first emotion on the heels of sin, which finds its expression in hiding. In separation from God. God then confronts Adam with a second question— "Who told you that you were naked?"—and Adam points the finger and blames both God and his wife. "The woman whom you gave to be with me, she gave me fruit of the tree, and I ate."[8] And so blame and denial enter the world. Along with deflection. And lying. "I'm a victim." "You gave her to me, and she did it."

God turns first to the serpent and says, "Because you have done this, cursed are you above all livestock, and above all beasts of the field; on your belly you shall go, and dust you shall eat all the days of your life."[9] From this moment, a curse enters the world. The curse of sin. Prior to this moment, mankind was in perfect relationship with God. Now that relationship has been fractured by sin. In other words, by rebellion. Failure to obey. A singular desire to be independent of the God who made us. And the ripple effects are many and still echoing through eternity. Because we are descendants of Adam and Eve, and every child born to them was born outside the garden, every child since the garden is a born rebel. Hell-bent on mutiny. Rebellion is the essence of our nature. Every single one of us is a wretched, black-hearted sinner deserving of an eternity in hell. Paul later described us as "dead in our trespasses."[10] From this moment on, all of mankind is snakebitten, and the poison flows in our veins. Which raises the questions: Are we forever doomed to an eternity apart from God? Is there a way back? A remedy? Can what was severed become unsevered? Can the broken become unbroken?

Is there an antivenom?

Adam and Eve's first action was to cover up. Fig leaves. But fig leaves only cover their shame. And not very well, as we will soon see. Further, leaves do nothing to deal with the presence of sin, the effect of the sin, or the consequences of the sin. And they do nothing to keep out the cold.

God responds to the serpent. "I will put enmity between you and the woman, and between your offspring and her offspring; he shall bruise your head, and you shall bruise his heel."[11]

The NIV Bible says, "He will crush your head, and you will strike his heel."

Theologians call this the "protoevangelium"—the first gospel. It's the first time redemption is promised in the Bible. In this moment, God has already masterminded the plan, developed the antivenom, and set His rescue in motion. But He's no clockmaker God who winds it up, sets it loose, and says, "Good luck. Hope it pans out." He's still the Potter. Intimate with every detail. Nothing is lost. Nothing gets past Him. From this moment, He is going to pour out His love on mankind to bring us back to Himself.

This is why He told the nation of Israel after He delivered them from Egypt, "You yourselves have seen what I did to the Egyptians, and how I bore you on eagles' wings and brought you to myself."[12] Again, pronouns. *I* did, *I* bore, and *I* brought. He did everything. They watched. And don't miss the last four words: "brought you to myself." This was His desire in the garden, and it is His desire now. The will of the Father is to return us to Him. And it's never changed. Jesus says so: "For this is the will of my Father, that everyone who looks on the Son and believes in him should have eternal life, and

I will raise him up on the last day."[13] Restored into perfect relationship with the Father was then, and is now, the destination. It's also the reason for Jesus: "I am the way, and the truth, and the life. No one comes to the Father except through me."[14]

How will it be accomplished? How will perfect relationship be restored? Especially, when we, like Adam and Eve, can do *nothing* to get it back. We were meant, designed, and created to know what God smells like. The color of His eyes. The strength of His biceps when He hugs us. The breadth of His shoulders when He sets us on them. The calluses on His hand as He holds ours. The tenderness of His lips when He smothers our faces in kisses.

But, here, outsides the garden, we have one fundamental, insurmountable, no-getting-around-it problem. We have no access. No way to get there. You and I are standing on the rim of a canyon. God the Father on the other side. Ten thousand miles between us. Bottomless pit below us. Our deepest longing is to stand on the other side—with Him. To be restored. Hug His neck. Hold His hand. Laugh. Dance. Cling. Stand in that perfect love. But there is no bridge. No way to cross the chasm. It's completely impossible.

Everything after Genesis 3:15, after the Protoevangelium, flows out of it; and without it, there is no rest of the Bible because there'd be nothing to talk about. Charles Simeon said, "This one verse is the sum and summary of the whole Bible."[15] And though He's not mentioned by name, it's the first we hear of Jesus coming and what He will do. Jesus is the seed of the woman—the promised serpent crusher. This is why Paul ended his letter to the Romans with these words: "the God of peace will soon crush [s]atan under your feet."[16]

After addressing satan, God turned His attention to Adam and Eve. "And the Lord God made for Adam and for his wife garments of skins and clothed them."[17]

Notice the initiation. *God* made and *God* clothed and *God* covered. Adam and Eve stood there and watched. Like a fitting at the tailor. I'm hammering the point to show the boundless love of God and the extent to which He goes and will go to return us to Himself.

But notice, too, the flip side of that equation. Skins. Where'd they come from? Obviously, the back of some animal—which meant something had to die. Blood was shed. And it was shed at the hand of God—to cover sin. Then God took that covering and placed it over Adam and Eve. An act of unmerited mercy. But while He is merciful, He is also just. And His justice requires sin be atoned for. Paid for. Which the spotless, innocent animal did with its life.

Because God is merciful He did not require Adam and Eve to make payment. Instead, He made the payment on their behalf. Do I understand why God chose this death-for-life requirement? This eternal payment for sin? No. Will I ever? Probably not on this side of the grave. Could He have chosen some other way? I have no idea. The point is this—in the economy and kingdom of God, the shedding of blood is required for the payment of sin. Period. In His kingdom, something died so that something might live. It's the first time we see an exchange. Death for life. This is why the writer of Hebrews later said, "Without the shedding of blood there is no forgiveness of sins."[18]

"But," you may respond, "that's not fair."

Hold it. You want fair? Fairness is the trap of your and my enemy, and honestly, we don't want what's fair. If God used fair as the plumb line, we'd get what we deserve, pay for our sin ourselves, and we'd already be dead and wouldn't be having this conversation. You and I would just be a stain on the earth where our souls once stood. The enemy wants us focused on fairness. While God is not. He's focused on our holiness, without which we cannot step into His presence.

The only way back is atonement. The only way back is through the blood.

All children born outside the garden—all of us—are wretched, evil-hearted, sin-infused rebels, hell-bent on mutiny. Dead in our sins. Slaves held captive in the kingdom of darkness. That's our condition from before the womb. "All we like sheep have gone astray; we have turned—every one—to his own way; and the Lord has laid on him the iniquity of us all."[19]

WALK WITH ME BACK TO THE CROSS

Jesus' death on the Cross was not a haphazard, last-ditch effort pieced together in a frenzy when God realized things were out of control. No Hail Mary, hope-this-works pass. It was premeditated. Planned. Ages before it happened. And not only did He set it in motion, but every action that led to that moment was sifted through the sovereign hand of God the Father, who—through the Spirit—offered the Son before the foundation of the world and then saw it through in what we call real time.

In Matthew 9, while Jesus was reclining at a table surrounded by tax collectors and sinners, the Pharisees asked, "Why does He eat with them?" Jesus overheard and answered their question, "Those who are well have no need of a physician, but those who are sick. Go and learn what this means: 'I desire mercy, and not sacrifice.' For I came not to call the righteous, but sinners."[20] The writer of Hebrews said, "Let us then with confidence draw near to the throne of grace, that we may receive mercy and find grace to help in time of need."[21] Because of His mercy and grace, we sinners can draw near in need.

On the night Jesus is betrayed, Peter says "I am *not*" His. At the same time, Jesus is quite literally standing in Peter's place, in our place, saying, "*I am* yours." Big, big difference. The "I am not" sin we see in Peter was first birthed in Adam and Eve. A result of the snakebite. The poisoning from the venom lie. And though He had every right, God did not obliterate Adam and Eve when they sinned. Nor did He Peter. Nor does He us. The offer is mercy. And it begins with His first question: "Where are you?"

Because He has always come looking for us.

Pray with Me

Jesus, I know in my own life, You have never moved away from me; but I, in my sin, have always moved away from You. I've denied You time after time. And yet no sooner do I sin than You in Your mercy always come looking for me. You close the distance and cross the chasm I can't. And when You do, rather than kill me dead on the spot—which is Your right—You ask me, "Where are you?" You do this because You love me and You know that before I can comprehend the Cross and what You purchased for me, I need to know my need of You. It's ground zero. You're asking for my benefit. Not Yours. You know where I am; I'm the one who's lost.

Jesus, I know, now more than ever, that I need You. That You alone can rescue me from my sin that so easily separates me from You. And while I know that my sin has separated me from You, I'm sure I don't know the totality of it. I want to pray a dangerous prayer, so please help. And I do this with fear and trembling. Please reveal to me the truth of me and the depth of my need for You. I want to know—how bad is it, really? I have a tendency to think I'm really not that bad, when in reality, without You and this Cross, I'm just a dead man walking. I think if

I had a clear view of me, I'd probably never get off my face. So please be merciful in how much of me You show me because I'm not sure how much of me I can take in one dose—but I'm asking, would You please show me the depth of my need for You? I know it may sound like a ridiculous question, but I need to know how much I need You because if I had a better understanding of just how wretched, selfish-hearted, and hell-bent I am, it would help me to understand how far You came to rescue me and what was required of You in the rescue.

And while we're here talking about me, I'm really sorry for all my stuff—my sin, rebellion, disobedience, and defiance—that has separated me from You. And if I've never told You, I am so grateful that You reconciled me to Yourself, not counting my sins against me.²² I know that when You ask me, "Where are You?" You are asking for my good. The truth is, I am not where I want to be. My heart's desire is to be with You and You alone, in Your kingdom, and to be submitted to Your lordship, Your righteous reign, Your sovereign dominion. So please just know that despite my childish attempts to sew fig leaves and then deflect and blame and play the victim, I want to be with You. Please come and find me. In Jesus' name.

AND GOD RESPONDS

"And you, who once were alienated and hostile in mind, doing evil deeds, he has now reconciled in his body of flesh by his death, in order to present you holy and blameless and above reproach before him, if indeed you continue in the faith, stable and steadfast, not shifting from the hope of the gospel that you heard, which has been proclaimed in all creation under heaven, and of which I, Paul, became a minister."²³

"For this reason I bow my knees before the Father, from whom every family in heaven and on earth is named, that according to the riches of his glory he may grant you to be strengthened with power through his Spirit in your inner being, so that Christ may dwell in your hearts through faith—that you, being rooted and grounded in love, may have strength to comprehend with all the saints what is the breadth and length and height and depth, and to know the love of Christ that surpasses knowledge, that you may be filled with all the fullness of God."[24]

"You yourselves have seen what I did to the Egyptians, and how I bore you on eagles' wings and brought you to myself."[25]

DAY 4

*"Behold, the Lamb of God, Who Takes
Away the sin of the world!"*

JOHN 1:29–34

"The next day he saw Jesus coming toward him, and said, 'Behold, the Lamb of God, who takes away the sin of the world!'"[1]

Seems a strange way for John the Baptist to introduce the King of all kings. The God of Angel Armies. The only begotten Son of God. Why a lamb? Why not a lion? Or a gorilla? Or Tyrannosaurus rex?

John continued, "This is he of whom I said, 'After me comes a man who ranks before me, because he was before me.' I myself did not know him, but for this purpose I came baptizing with water, that he might be revealed to Israel."[2]

"I came baptizing . . . that he might be revealed." This is the point of John's life in eight words. To reveal Jesus. Can I say the same? Can you? Can we reduce our *raison d'etre*, our reason for being, to something so simple? So selfless? So sacrificial? So other-focused?

If you feel small, don't. Jesus said, "Among those born of women there has arisen no one greater than John the Baptist. Yet the one who is least in the kingdom of heaven is greater than he."[3] Which means there's hope for us.

"And John bore witness: 'I saw the Spirit descend from heaven like a dove, and it remained on him. I myself did not know him, but he who sent me to baptize with water said to me, "He on whom you see the Spirit descend and remain, this is he who baptizes with the Holy Spirit." And I have seen and have borne witness that this is the Son of God.'"[4]

The Charles Martin paraphrase reads: "God told me to tell you that His Son is here. And that's Him."

Adam and Eve's problem is that while their sin had been covered with fig leaves, it still exists. Beneath the covering. Which means it hasn't been ultimately dealt with. So God in His mercy sheds the blood of an innocent animal, sews clothing, and covers Adam and Eve. A temporary solution that does not permanently deal with the ultimate problem.

Given their choice to sin, God escorts Adam and Eve out of the garden. This means every child born in the history of the world has been born outside of the kingdom of God and into slavery. Slaves to sin. No longer perfect. Separated from God. Dead. Every sin and all the consequences due to it had to be paid for. In full. For all mankind. For all time. We know God's heart for us is to bring us back to Himself. He tells us: "I . . . brought you to myself."[5] It is God's heart for us that the love with which He, God the Father, loved Jesus may be in us and Jesus in us.[6] We also know Jesus said, "I am the way, and the truth, and the life. No one comes to the Father except through me."[7]

Question: If the destination is the Father, how does God bring sinful man back? How does He deal with—atone for—all sin and not just cover it? How does He wipe the slate clean permanently? How does He snatch us back out of the hand of the devil?

We like to compare ourselves to others, noting how our sin is not as bad as this or that person's. How we're not on death row, not sentenced to life behind bars, not . . . you get the point. (For those of you who are, hang in there. And please revisit day 3. There's more mercy in Jesus than sin in us. Because without Jesus, we're all on death row.) This propensity is called the "sin of comparison." But the comparison is flawed. The question is not one of degrees of sin or comparative "badness"—that I'm somehow better or worse than you because I've done more or less good or bad things—but one of percentage dead. Can you be 90 percent dead? No. That makes you 10 percent alive, which is alive. If you're dead, you're 100 percent dead. Not *kind of* dead. Not sort of dead. Not pretty much dead. And according to God, all of us are dead in our sin until He makes us alive in Christ. So the question is not: How do bad people become good? There are no good people. The question is: How does God raise dead people to life?

The writer of Hebrews reminded us that "without the shedding of blood there is no forgiveness of sins."[8] How so? And why? "For the life of the flesh is in the blood, and I have given it for you on the altar to make atonement for your souls, for it is the blood that makes atonement by the life."[9] Okay, but what kind of blood? Will any blood do? No. For "it is impossible for the blood of bulls and goats to take away sins."[10] So whose blood and what altar will satisfy the wrath of God? Whose blood will God accept as payment for sin?

The disciple John, late in his life, was exiled to the island of Patmos where God revealed to him what was to come. In that revelation, John recorded this very question: "Who is worthy?"[11] But to his great dismay and sadness, no one in heaven or on earth or under the earth was found worthy. So John wept loudly because all of mankind hung in the balance. Then an elder tapped him on the shoulder and said, "Weep no more; behold, the Lion of the tribe of

Judah, the Root of David, has conquered, so that he can open the scroll and its seven seals."[12]

Enter Jesus.

WALK WITH ME BACK TO THE CROSS

See that man hanging there? That shredded, hamburger of a man, drowning in His own lung fluid. Blood dripping from His toes, painting the earth below like the mercy seat of old. Here hangs the innocent Lamb of God who has taken away the sin of the world. Yours and mine. Past tense. Paid in full.

"For freedom Christ has set us free."[13]

The execution of the only innocent man to ever live, God's only Son, is God's permanent solution to the problem of your and my sin. Jesus Christ crucified is God's answer to the how-much-does-He-love-me-and-how-far-will-He-go-to-rescue-me question. Paul explained to the Corinthians in twenty-one of the most powerful words ever strung together: "And because of him you are in Christ Jesus, who became to us wisdom from God, righteousness and sanctification and redemption."[14]

Because of Him.

Okay, but why? What reason could He possibly have for willingly enduring the Cross?

This is Jesus again, in His last few words before His arrest, praying to the Father about us: "The glory that you have given me I have given to them, that they may be one even as we are one. I in them and you in me, that they may become perfectly one, so that the world may know that you sent me and loved them even as you loved me."[15]

The root of the word "perfectly one" is the same root word as *tetelestai*.

PRAY WITH ME

Jesus, these are the words of Your servant John in his revelation. Please let me pray them as my declaration. My proclamation of what was true then is true now and will be true forever.

"Then I saw in the right hand of him who was seated on the throne a scroll written within and on the back, sealed with seven seals. And I saw a mighty angel proclaiming with a loud voice, 'Who is worthy to open the scroll and break its seals?' And no one in heaven or on earth or under the earth was able to open the scroll or to look into it, and I began to weep loudly because no one was found worthy to open the scroll or to look into it. And one of the elders said to me, 'Weep no more; behold, the Lion of the tribe of Judah, the Root of David, has conquered, so that he can open the scroll and its seven seals.' And between the throne and the four living creatures and among the elders I saw a Lamb standing, as though it had been slain, with seven horns and with seven eyes, which are the seven spirits of God sent out into all the earth. And he went and took the scroll from the right hand of him who was seated on the throne. And when he had taken the scroll, the four living creatures and the twenty-four elders fell down before the Lamb, each holding a harp, and golden bowls full of incense, which are the prayers of the saints. And they sang a new song, saying, 'Worthy are you to take the scroll and to open its seals, for you were slain, and by your blood you ransomed people for God from every tribe and language and people and nation, and you have made them a kingdom and priests to our God, and they shall reign on the earth.'

"Then I looked, and I heard around the throne and the living creatures and the elders the voice of many angels, numbering myriads of myriads and thousands of thousands, saying with a loud voice, 'Worthy is the Lamb who was slain, to receive power and wealth and wisdom and might and honor and glory and blessing!' And I heard every creature in heaven and on earth and under the earth and in the sea, and all that is in them, saying, 'To him who sits on the throne and to the Lamb be blessing and honor and glory and might forever and ever!' And the four living creatures said, 'Amen!' and the elders fell down and worshiped."[16]

In the mighty, magnificent, undefeated, and matchless name of Jesus Christ.

AND GOD RESPONDS

"For while we were still weak, at the right time Christ died for the ungodly. For one will scarcely die for a righteous person—though perhaps for a good person one would dare even to die—but God shows his love for us in that while we were still sinners, Christ died for us. Since, therefore, we have now been justified by his blood, much more shall we be saved by him from the wrath of God. For if while we were enemies we were reconciled to God by the death of his Son, much more, now that we are reconciled, shall we be saved by his life. More than that, we also rejoice in God through our Lord Jesus Christ, through whom we have now received reconciliation.

"Therefore, just as sin came into the world through one man, and death through sin, and so death spread to all men because all sinned—for sin indeed was in the world before the law was given, but sin is not counted where there is no law. Yet death reigned from

Adam to Moses, even over those whose sinning was not like the transgression of Adam, who was a type of the one who was to come.

"But the free gift is not like the trespass. For if many died through one man's trespass, much more have the grace of God and the free gift by the grace of that one man Jesus Christ abounded for many. And the free gift is not like the result of that one man's sin. For the judgment following one trespass brought condemnation, but the free gift following many trespasses brought justification. For if, because of one man's trespass, death reigned through that one man, much more will those who receive the abundance of grace and the free gift of righteousness reign in life through the one man Jesus Christ.

"Therefore, as one trespass led to condemnation for all men, so one act of righteousness leads to justification and life for all men. For as by the one man's disobedience the many were made sinners, so by the one man's obedience the many will be made righteous. Now the law came in to increase the trespass, but where sin increased, grace abounded all the more, so that, as sin reigned in death, grace also might reign through righteousness leading to eternal life through Jesus Christ our Lord."[17]

DAY 5

". . . that the love with which you have
loved me may be in them . . ."

JOHN 17:25–26

"O righteous Father, even though the world does not know you, I
know you, and these know that you have sent me. I made known
to them your name, and I will continue to make it known, that the
love with which you have loved me may be in them, and I in them."[1]

Jesus is hours from the Cross, and yet, He kneels in the garden
and prays these words. Allowing us insight into an intimate conversation with His Father. A glimpse into some of the most precious
words in all of Scripture, for they reveal the reason for Jesus. To
restore what was lost. The love of the Father. For us.

But when was it lost?

"Therefore the Lord God sent him out from the garden of Eden
to work the ground from which he was taken. He drove out the
man."[2]

In God's kingdom, in His world, sin must be accounted for. Paid
for. Atoned for. There's no getting around it, and He's not sweeping
it under the rug. I've heard people ask, "Yeah, but why?"

If you or your loved one—your child—was attacked or murdered,

37

wouldn't you want the murderer brought to justice? Okay, why? Why not just let it go? "No big deal. He just made a bad choice." Wrong. It's a really big deal. That thing in us that wants justice came from God, and that emotion and that need start with Him. The point is this—from that garden moment in the history of mankind, God in His justice requires payment for sin, yet in His mercy He also makes the payment. Which explains the dead animal and the skins. And remember, the sinless animal gave its life to "cover" theirs. This is why Paul called God both "just and the justifier of the one who has faith in Jesus."[3]

You and I were intended for perfect relationship with the Father. Perfect union. If there is something in you that looks around this world, scratches your head, and thinks, *Something isn't right. Something's broken*, you're right. It is. We weren't designed for this fallen world. We were designed for that perfect Eden. And the residue of a desire for Eden flows in our veins. It's just been twisted, leaving us with a longing and gut-level knowingness that something isn't what it's supposed to be and we were meant for something and someplace else.

Adam and Eve ate dinner with God. At the table. They looked into His eyes. Laughed. He tucked them in at night. Told them stories. Tickled them. Scratched their backs as they faded off to sleep. Paul told the Colossians, "For in him [Jesus] the fullness of God was pleased to dwell."[4] Meaning, what we see in Jesus we can translate to the Father. God was then and is now a hugger. A jungle gym for kids. Touchy-feely. All up in their business. And as a result, they sat in His lap. Bounced on His knee. Danced. Tickled Him back. They knew the smell of God, the sound of His belly laugh. And what it felt like when He put them in the tub, soaped up their hair, and washed their feet.

We've trivialized the garden of Eden as a bedtime story, but

Adam and Eve were real people with real lives, real funny bones and real tears. Think about that long, silent walk out of the garden. Heads hanging, eyes darting to the ground, as the angel escorts them to the gate. They cross the threshold, turn, take one last look around. Emotions they've never known flood their minds and hearts. What did Adam and Eve lose in that moment? What changed? They had been "perfectly one," now no longer. Maybe the better question is, What didn't change? Look closely and ask, What did they know at one time that they will never know again this side of the grave? And what had they not known that they will now know for the rest of their lives?

Tears. Guilt. Regret. Shame. Pride. Arrogance. Control. Manipulation. Confusion.

Fear. They will know fear. They are walking from perfect to not. From provision to uncertainty. Limitless wealth to abject poverty. Mansion to homeless. Acceptance to rejection. Qualified to disqualified. Blessing to curse. Perfect health to disease. Abundance to need. Carefree to burdened. Humble to prideful. Weightless to heavy-laden. Effortless to impossible. Gentleness to hatred. Intimacy to alienation. Certain to uncertain. Joy to sorrow. Tenderness to torment. Praise to depression. Presence to absence. Perfection to imperfection. Grace to legalism. Righteous to unrighteous. Clean to unclean. Freedom to slavery. Heir to vagabond. Peace to a war they cannot win. Limitless to limited. From the absence of pain and the memory of pain to a lifetime of it. Power to utterly powerless. Order to chaos. Truth to lies, accusation, and falsehood—and not being able to tell the difference. From inerrant Word to blasphemy. Creator to creature. Dominion to dominated. Light to dark. Life to death. From the kingdom of heaven to the kingdom of darkness. From Immortal, Holy, and blameless to dead sinner.

Is it really this drastic? Really this bad?

Paul told the Corinthians, "So is it with the resurrection of the dead. What is sown is perishable; what is raised is imperishable. It is sown in dishonor; it is raised in glory. It is sown in weakness; it is raised in power. It is sown a natural body; it is raised a spiritual body. If there is a natural body, there is also a spiritual body. Thus it is written, 'The first man Adam became a living being'; the last Adam became a life-giving spirit."[5]

Jesus is the resurrection and the life. When He returns He will raise us up with Him, transferring us from our present condition to another. From the condition in which He finds us to the condition He intended all along. From perishable to imperishable. Dishonor to glory. Weakness to power. Natural to spiritual. Death to life. Mortal to immortal.

This is the rescue and redemption that is in Christ Jesus.

With their first step outside the gate, sin is crouching at their door, and its desire is to have them. And that word "desire" means to dominate. To own. And sin will. This is why it's called "the fall." Things are going to hell in a handbasket.

Where they could once see perfectly, now they will see through a glass darkly. Cataracts. Both physical and spiritual. Their teeth will rot and fall out of their mouths. Their ears will ring, and their hearing will fail. From this moment, they will want shiny things that do not satisfy. Adam will lust after other women.

And they will begin making idols.

And where they had known peace, they will now know war. They will be tormented, attacked, enticed, and hounded by demons who have a measure of power and authority given them by God. Inside the garden, Adam needed neither faith nor hope because both were realized—he walked with God. Why would he need either? But outside, he will need both if he's to make it.

Adam and Eve have no concept of what life holds outside the garden; they just know it'll never be as good. As the gate closes and the lock slams shut, I imagine their deepest emotion is "What have we done?" and their singular question is, "How do we get back there?"

And so the longing begins. Longing for Eden.

But they are powerless to open the gate. And they are separated from God with no mediator.

Though God drove Adam and Eve out of the garden, He never deleted their desire to be there. He left that in. On purpose. Which they passed to us. It's wrapped around our DNA. Paul told the Romans, "The wages of sin is death," and with their first steps outside the gate, they know its sting.[6] I can't prove it, but I tend to think they took about three steps and vomited from their toes until only the dry heaves remained.

Not only did they lose their perfect relationship with the Father; think through what they lost with each other. The changes they will experience from this moment. Argument. Blame. Hurt. Doubt. Mistrust. Suspicion. Sorrow. Anger. Frustration.

They are walking into a world of condemnation. False accusation. Addiction. Sore muscles. Broken bones. Arthritis. Bad vision. Maggots. Rotting food. Rotting teeth. Drought. Ringing ears. Cancer. Hopelessness. Jealousy. Rage. Curse words aimed at each other. Dissatisfaction. Depression. Anxiety. Loneliness. Failure.

Adam will come to know the sin of pride. He will stand outside the gate, pound his chest, and think, *I got this.* He might even say it. But nothing could be further from the truth. They will carve a headstone and bury a son amid a shoulder-shaking sob, unable to catch their breath. And before it's over, one of them will bury the other.

They now will live in a world where graves dot the hillside.

Something that didn't exist inside the gate. But as bad as that is, that's not the worst of it. All of that is simply the result of living in a fallen world where sin has entered. There is a bigger problem. An insurmountable problem. A problem for which they have no solution but must be dealt with if they are ever to meet God face-to-face again.

The wrath of God.

And with every moment that passes, it is storing up more and more. Ten minutes outside the garden and its sum is more than they can pay in this lifetime.

From this moment, they will suffer God's wrath and be separated from Him—they will not see His face again this side of death. Why else does God tell Moses to bless His people this way: "The Lord bless you and keep you; the Lord make his face to shine upon you and be gracious to you; the Lord lift up his countenance upon you and give you peace."[7] Because it speaks to a deep longing birthed in Eden. To see His face. From the moment they cross the threshold, the wrath of God is stored up. And it continues to be stored with every sin of every human for all time. And God is not just mildly perturbed at the sight of our sin. He is furious. He hates it. His wrath is a tsunami the likes of which the world has never seen.[1]

Not only will they bear the burden of their own sin; they will suffer the pain of the consequences of being unable to make payment or atonement. Of being unable to do anything about their plight. They will yearn for what Job desired: "For he is not a man, as I am, that I might answer him, that we should come to trial together. There is no arbiter [mediator] between us, who might lay his hand on us both. Let him take his rod away from me, and let not dread

---

1. He hates our sin. Not us.

of him terrify me. Then I would speak without fear of him, for I am not so in myself."[8]

Adam and Eve died with no mediator. No one to plead their case before the Judge.

WALK WITH ME BACK TO THE CROSS

Are we too far from the garden of Eden to really know the totality of what we're missing? I tend to think so, but the longing remains. Adam and Eve knew what Jesus wants you and me to know. Perfect love. Being perfectly one. That's why on the night before He was crucified, He prayed "that the love with which you have loved me may be in them, and I in them."[9] This love is the reason for Jesus—in His own words.

If we really knew the love of God, what would we fear? Name one thing. While the relationship was fractured, the love of the Father was not. He never stopped perfectly loving them—or us. His perfect love has never changed. Never wavered. But sin severed our ability to know and receive it, so God in His mercy and love decided to deal with our sin.

Because He knows we cannot.

PRAY WITH ME

God Most High, I have a limited ability to understand You. I'm finite. You're infinite. Even that blows my mind. There is no intellectual path to You. I can't reason with You. Can't wrap my head around You. You will never make perfect sense to me until we meet face-to-face and You reveal Yourself to me. Between now and then, please grant me a revelation of You that I can handle. Let me see You as You want to be seen by Me. Give me a right revelation of You. And while I'm at it, Lord, I realize I'm not better than Adam and Eve. I, too, have rebelled against You. Not done what You told me. Disobeyed You. Gone my own way. Astray. Ten thousand times over. I'm so sorry. Please forgive me. I know my sin has driven me from You, and I've hidden in shame and fear and blamed everyone but me; yet every time, You've brought me back to Yourself. You're bringing me still. I am so grateful that my return to You rests on Your shoulders and not mine. If it did, I'd be toast. But because it doesn't, I can turn the corner in my footy pajamas and launch myself into Your arms, and You, because You love me with a love I can't fathom, catch me and wrap Your arms around me even when I'm covered in the filth of the sewer in which I've been sleeping. King David said "these things are too high, I cannot comprehend them." He's right. Me too. Please know I am so thankful. Thank You for coming for me. For relentlessly pursuing me. For making a way back. For giving me a spirit of sonship through which I cry, "Abba." In Jesus' name.

And God Responds

"There is no fear in love, but perfect love casts out fear. For fear has to do with punishment, and whoever fears has not been perfected in love."[10]

"For by a single offering he has perfected for all time those who are sanctified."[11]

Vital note: The words "perfect love" and "perfected in love" and "perfected for all time" all share the same root (*telios*) as *tetelestai*.

DAY 6

———◆●◆———

"Shall I not drink the cup?"

MATTHEW 26:36–39; JOHN 18:11

"And going a little farther he fell on his face and prayed, saying, 'My Father, if it be possible, let this cup pass from me; nevertheless, not as I will, but as you will.'"[1] Luke, the physician, then recorded, "And his sweat became like great drops of blood falling down to the ground."[2] In this moment, God the Father is making good on His Genesis 3:15 promise. He has begun crushing the Son. Moments later, when Jesus is arrested, Peter draws his sword and cuts off the ear of the servant to the high priest, and yet Jesus is laser-focused, having set His face like a flint toward the Cross. Jesus says to Peter, "Put your sword into its sheath; shall I not drink the cup that the Father has given me?"[3]

Jesus is staring at the cup of God's wrath for our sin. If He drains it, we get the possibility of heaven, of a return to the Father. If He refuses, we get hell.

But why is God's wrath stored up in a cup, and when did He start storing it?

"Then the Lord God said, 'Behold, the man has become like one of us in knowing good and evil. Now, lest he reach out his hand and take also of the tree of life and eat, and live forever—' therefore the Lord God sent him out from the garden of Eden to work the ground from which he was taken. He drove out the man, and at the east of the garden of Eden he placed the cherubim and a flaming sword that turned every way to guard the way to the tree of life."[4]

What happened in the garden was not a misunderstanding. Eve didn't taste the fruit, then step back, cover her mouth, and turn to God, "Whoops. I didn't mean that. Can I have a do-over?" We have trivialized Adam and Eve's actions as simply taking a bite out of the wrong fruit, but they knew full well what they were doing. God didn't stutter. He had made it clear. In eating of the tree of the knowledge of good and evil, Adam and Eve didn't just disobey God; they defied Him. Openly. And in so doing, they chose a rival kingdom and its king.

God has several options: One, He can hold Adam and Eve against their will, housed in His garden, keeping them from what they've chosen and what they want. Making Him a tyrant who knows best, but a dictator nonetheless. Two, He can let them walk out the door and live out the consequences of their choice. Or three, He can zap them with a lightning bolt.

Which one will show them His love for them?

In His love for them, God gave them their choice, walking them out of His garden and into the kingdom of their choosing. Which is key. The story of redemption is the story of two kingdoms and two kings, and the choosing is up to us. Please know I am not suggesting the kings are equal in power and dominion. They're not. I'm simply stating the choices.

And right about here, we bump into this thing called "predestination" and whether or not we actually have the ability to choose God. Theologians far smarter than I have written libraries on this.

And I can't answer or settle the debate here. I will say this—the more I study Scripture, the more I see the initiation back to life and relationship lies totally with God. Paul said God acted "when we were dead in our trespasses."[5] That said, He does give us a measure of free will. Put another way, He chooses us, and yet if we don't choose Him, we end up in hell.

This is one of those things I have to take on faith. It's just bigger than I am. I figure He'll explain when we get there. Until then, I think He allows us not to choose Him until He tires of us not choosing Him. Then He does a thing in us, and we choose Him. Look closely at what Paul told the Corinthians: "And because of him you are in Christ Jesus."[6] How do we get "in Christ Jesus"? Look closely at the two phrases "because of him" and "you are in." He is the active agent. We are passive. The NASB says it this way: "But it is due to Him." The NKJV says, "But of Him you are in Christ Jesus." The Living Bible says, "For it is from God alone that you have your life through Christ Jesus." The NET says, "He is the reason you have a relationship with Christ Jesus." And lastly, while it is not a translation but an interpretation, Peterson's interpretation, the MSG says it this way: "Everything that we have—right thinking and right living, a clean slate and a fresh start—comes from God by way of Jesus Christ." Peter summed it up this way: "He has caused us to be born again."[7]

Look at the pronouns. Look at what He did and what we did. We are but dust, and what can the dust do? We can lie there until He breathes into us. I've listened to folks argue and get axle-wrapped as to who's predestined. Who's chosen and who's not. Again, I can't answer, but Scripture says this: "The Lord is not slow to fulfill his promise as some count slowness, but is patient toward you, not wishing that any should perish, but that all should reach repentance."[8]

When I look up that word "all" in Greek, it still means *all*. The NIV translates it this way: "Not wanting anyone to perish, but everyone to come to repentance." "Not wanting anyone" and "everyone" means all of us.

The motivating factor for God is His love for us. For He *is* love. And He wants us to know and receive that love. So God in all His mercy, justice, and love allowed Adam and Eve the consequences of their choice. He gave them what they chose—the kingdom of darkness—and who they chose—an evil, counterfeit king—and escorted them out. You think that broke His heart? Knowing that mankind was walking from His perfect will and freedom into slavery to the kingdom of darkness? More like shattered His heart.

So where does that leave us? God later tells Moses to tell the nation of Israel these words: "You yourselves have seen what I did to the Egyptians, and how I bore you on eagles' wings and brought you to myself."[9] When I read that, my eye is drawn to "I bore you" and "brought you to myself." If God bore us and brought us to Himself, then logically our starting point was somewhere other than with Him.

When we open our eyes for the first time on planet Earth, we do so as slaves. Understanding our true condition is vital. It's a matter of life and death. Because it counters the current argument that we're all just children of God. No, we're not. And while He has given us the right to *become* His children, we don't start there.[10] We start as mutinous, traitorous rebels giving the "I got this" finger to a loving God, and it's only after we're born again that we become heirs and coheirs with Christ.[11]

How can we be sure this is our starting point? Where and how does Scripture say this? This is Jesus. And notice it is His description of us: "I will not leave you as orphans; I will come to you."[12] Now look at these words of Paul to the Corinthians: "Or do you not know that the unrighteous will not inherit the kingdom of God?"[13] **And again to the church in Ephesus:** "Among whom we all once lived in the passions of our flesh, carrying out the desires of the body and the mind, and were by nature children of wrath, like the rest of mankind."[14] **And finally to the Colossians:** "He has delivered us from the domain of darkness and transferred us to the kingdom of his beloved Son, in whom we have redemption, the forgiveness of sins."[15] **To sum it up, we begin this life as orphaned, unrighteous children of wrath, slaves in the kingdom of darkness. And our only hope is Jesus.**

And if He doesn't drink the cup, all hope is lost.

Notice the words "delivered us from" and "transferred us to." Again, our starting point is a kingdom He doesn't want us in and, ultimately, we don't want to be in. This gives me a whole new understanding of Jesus' words: "For the Son of Man came to seek and to save the lost."[16]

Lastly, this is Paul to the Romans: "There is therefore now no condemnation for those who are in Christ Jesus."[17] **Which means we are born condemned. All of us. Our condition is that of a rebellious sinner hell-bent on mutiny. Remember how we started. Isaiah 53 says,** "All we like sheep have gone astray; we have turned—every one—to his own way; and the Lord has laid on him the iniquity of us all."[18] **Likewise,** "We have all become like one who is unclean, and all our righteous deeds are like a polluted garment."[19] **The NKJ uses the words "filthy rags." By this, Isaiah meant that, apart from God's redeeming work on the Cross, the best we can offer God, our best attempts at making ourselves righteous, are nothing but used menstrual products dumped at His feet.**

In drinking the cup, Jesus stomachs the wrath of God. He is the

Suffering Servant Isaiah prophesied about: "But he was pierced for our transgressions; he was crushed for our iniquities; upon him was the chastisement that brought us peace, and with his wounds we are healed. All we like sheep have gone astray; we have turned—every one—to his own way; and the Lord has laid on him the iniquity of us all."[20] Pay special attention to that word "iniquity." Isaiah ended with this: "Out of the anguish of his soul he shall see and be satisfied; by his knowledge shall the righteous one, my servant, make many to be accounted righteous, and he shall bear their iniquities."[21] Then six chapters later, he said, "But your iniquities have made a separation between you and your God, and your sins have hidden his face from you so that he does not hear."[22]

The word Isaiah used in verse 6 for "iniquity" is *avon*. It comes from a word that means to bow down or make crooked. To pervert. To do wickedly. *Avon* means perversity, depravity, and guilt. But it also includes the consequences for the guilt. I'm hammering this point because not only did Jesus bear our guilt, He also accepted the consequences due to us.

The punishment that brought us peace occurred when Jesus drained the last drop. Swallowing all of hell. Which He did on the Cross.

WALK WITH ME BACK TO THE CROSS

Jesus said, "Everyone who practices sin is a slave to sin."[23] That's all of us. How do we gain our freedom? We must be bought. Which Jesus does. "You are not your own, for you were bought with a price."[24] What price? Every last drop of His blood. For this reason, He was born. "You shall call his name Jesus, for he will save his people from their sins."[25] **How do you know the Cross worked? How do you know you're free?** "If the Son sets you free, you will be free indeed."[26] And none of this is possible if Jesus doesn't willingly drink the Father's cup.

No wonder when the mother of the sons of Zebedee asks Jesus if her sons could sit at His side in His kingdom He replies, "'You do not know what you are asking. Are you able to drink the cup that I am to drink?' They said to him, 'We are able.'"[27] **No. They're not.** Jesus responds with, "You will drink my cup, but to sit at my right hand and at my left is not mine to grant, but it is for those for whom it has been prepared by my Father."[28]

Held within the Father's cup is an inescapable guilty verdict. Eternal condemnation. Death. All the consequences of all our sin for all time. And because He willingly drank the Father's cup of death, He alone extends to us His cup of forgiveness poured out. Everlasting life.

PRAY WITH ME

Jesus, we're only a week into this walk up to Your Cross, and I don't know that I can look up any longer. It hurts too much. I'm so sorry. I can't fathom what You endured to purchase me. An inconceivable exchange of which I am not worthy, couldn't earn in ten thousand lifetimes, and don't deserve. But for the fathomless love of God, it makes zero sense. I know that when You prayed in John 17:26 before being arrested, You told Your Father, "That the love with which you have loved me may be in them." *I know that's Your reason because You said so, but I live in a world where the word "love" is battered around and abused, and I don't think it means here how You mean* it. *Please help me understand this love. The love You share with Your Father. Please pour this love into me. When I think about You in the garden, staring at the Father's cup, I cringe. My sin and all the consequences due to me for that sin are contained within. You took what was mine. And in return, in exchange, You hold out to me Your cup of love. Of forgiveness. Of unmerited grace. Nowhere does this make sense except in the enormity of Your love for us. And even then I can't wrap my head around it. All I know to do is say thank You and I'm Yours. It seems so little a response for so great a sacrifice, but it's what I have, so take me as Your own. I am more grateful than I can say. In Jesus' name.*

AND GOD RESPONDS

"So Jesus said to them, 'Truly, truly, I say to you, unless you eat the flesh of the Son of Man and drink his blood, you have no life in you. Whoever feeds on my flesh and drinks my blood has eternal life, and I will raise him up on the last day. For my flesh is true food, and my blood is true drink. Whoever feeds on my flesh and drinks my blood abides in me, and I in him. As the living Father sent me, and I live because of the Father, so whoever feeds on me, he also will live because of me.'"[29]

"In the same way also he took the cup, after supper, saying, 'This cup is the new covenant in my blood. Do this, as often as you drink it, in remembrance of me.' For as often as you eat this bread and drink the cup, you proclaim the Lord's death until he comes."[30]

DAY 7

"In the beginning was the Word."

JOHN 1:1–5

"In the beginning was the Word, and the Word was with God, and the Word was God. He was in the beginning with God. All things were made through him, and without him was not any thing made that was made. In him was life, and the life was the light of men. The light shines in the darkness, and the darkness has not overcome it."[1]

Throughout written history, writers have attempted to describe the preexistent, preeminent, omniscient, omnipresent, all-powerful, outside-of-time God. The One who made the heavens. Who made the sun and moon and strung the sky with ten trillion stars—each of which He calls by name. Who fashioned the earth and the sea, the hippopotamus, the hummingbird, and you and me. Describing Him has never been easy. We are finite. He's infinite. One of these things is not like the other.

That said, writers have tried with the tools we have. Words. This is the apostle John, writing from the island of Patmos:

"After this I looked, and behold, a door standing open in heaven! . . . At once I was in the Spirit, and behold, a throne stood in heaven, with one seated on the throne. And he who sat there had the appearance of jasper and carnelian, and around the throne was a rainbow that had the appearance of an emerald. Around the throne were twenty-four thrones, and seated on the thrones were twenty-four elders, clothed in white garments, with golden crowns on their heads. From the throne came flashes of lightning, and rumblings and peals of thunder. . . . Around the throne . . . are four living creatures. . . . And day and night they never cease to say, 'Holy, holy, holy is the Lord God Almighty, who was and is and is to come!' And whenever the living creatures give glory and honor and thanks to him who is seated on the throne, who lives forever and ever, the twenty-four elders fall down before him who is seated on the throne and worship him who lives forever and ever. They cast their crowns before the throne, saying, 'Worthy are you, our Lord and God, to receive glory and honor and power, for you created all things, and by your will they existed and were created.'"[2]

John's glimpse into the throne room suggests heaven is a nonstop, top-of-the-lungs chorus of spontaneous praise, sung by hundreds upon hundreds of millions, aimed at the One seated on the throne who, by His own will, created everything, everywhere. David said, "By the word of the Lord the heavens were made, and by the breath of his mouth all their host. He gathers the waters of the sea as a heap; he puts the deeps in storehouses. Let all the earth fear the Lord; let all the inhabitants of the world stand in awe of him! For he spoke, and it came to be; he commanded, and it stood firm."[3] And at the sight of Him, the lesser rulers seated around Him launch themselves off the thrones He gave them, press their faces to the floor, and cast their golden crowns at His feet.

And still, with all of this, He leaves the door open. Granting access to the throne. And the One seated on it.

King Nebuchadnezzar attempted to describe the same One after he was humbled: "His dominion is an everlasting dominion, and his kingdom endures from generation to generation; all the inhabitants of the earth are accounted as nothing, and he does according to his will among the host of heaven and among the inhabitants of the earth; and none can stay his hand or say to him, 'What have you done?' . . . For all his works are right and his ways are just; and those who walk in pride he is able to humble."[4]

Late in his life, having been exiled to the island of Patmos, John described Jesus this way in his revelation: "And the armies of heaven, arrayed in fine linen, white and pure, were following him on white horses. From his mouth comes a sharp sword with which to strike down the nations, and he will rule them with a rod of iron. He will tread the winepress of the fury of the wrath of God the Almighty. On his robe and on his thigh he has a name written, King of kings and Lord of lords."[5]

Consider Paul's description to the church in Colossae: "He is the image of the invisible God, the firstborn of all creation. For by him all things were created, in heaven and on earth, visible and invisible, whether thrones or dominions or rulers or authorities—all things were created through him and for him. And he is before all things, and in him all things hold together. And he is the head of the body, the church. He is the beginning, the firstborn from the dead, that in everything he might be preeminent. For in him all the fullness of God was pleased to dwell, and through him to reconcile to himself all things, whether on earth or in heaven, making peace by the blood of his cross."[6]

Go with me to John 12. Jesus' final Passover. He is telling the parable about a grain of wheat. Notice the conversation that follows. In an agrarian society, His listeners would understand the pragmatics of planting. Life from death. They get it. But do they get Jesus? He's standing before them looking like one of them—and according to Isaiah 53, He was nothing special to look at. Didn't stand out. And He certainly did not look like a King. Some of those standing around Him are studying him like He's a cool, walkabout prophet with a posse and a few cool sayings. Some of those rubbing shoulders with Him won't give Him the time of day.

Jesus tells the Father to glorify His name. The Father tells the Son, "I have and I will." Now look again at the conversation through the lens of the previous descriptions of Jesus. That One in the throne room is speaking to that One who is before all things and in Whom all things hold together—and Who made all things—and those standing about have no idea. They think He's just some dude.

But the Father knows better: "I have glorified it, and I will glorify it again."

Then without complaint, without opening His mouth, the Creator—who made all things—lets the created mock Him. Punch Him. Beat Him. Spit on Him. Strip Him. Shame Him. Then they drop a crossbar on His striped shoulders and parade Him out of the city where He climbs up on a criminal's cross and breathes His last.

But not before uttering one single word.

Try to hear this for the first time: "For God so loved the world, that he gave his only Son, that whoever believes in him should not perish but have eternal life."[7] Out of the overflow of His love, God gave His Son as payment rather than require us to pay with our lives. The glory of God was on display in the form of an executed Son, who died for sinners. Who didn't then and doesn't now deserve it.

And yet He did it.

God escorted Adam and Eve out of the garden and shut the gate. Cursed. Dead in their sins. Jesus walked outside the city and wrapped curse and death around Him like a blanket. Taking what was due to us. So that He might wrap us in His life.

WALK WITH ME BACK TO THE CROSS

All of heaven sings praise. Hands raised. Faces pressed to the floor. Crowns cast down. Piled at the feet of the One who hangs here. "Holy, Holy, Holy . . . worthy is the Lamb." How is this even possible? Why would He do this? Now study the crowd. Milling about. Arms crossed. Unimpressed. Thinking about dinner. And yet, feet away, having cloaked His divinity, the Son of God hangs. Suspended between earth and heaven. Choking on your and my sin.

Paul told the Corinthians, "We preach Christ crucified, a stumbling block to Jews and folly to Gentiles, but to those who are called, both Jews and Greeks, Christ the power of God and the wisdom of God. For the foolishness of God is wiser than men, and the weakness of God is stronger than men."[8] Then a few verses later, wanting to make sure they heard him the first time, Paul said it again: "I decided to know nothing among you except Jesus Christ and him crucified."[9] Not Him who fed the five thousand. Or Him who healed the paralytic. Or Him who raised Lazarus. But Him dead on a cross. Notice the contradiction. "For the word of the cross is folly to those who are perishing, but to us who are being saved it is the power of God."[10]

Folly or power. What say you?

PRAY WITH ME

King Jesus, Adam and Eve were not bad people. They were dead people. As are we. Dead in our sin. The reason for the Cross is not to make bad people better but to make dead people alive. This is why You told Nicodemus we must be born again. Despite this, for some reason, I routinely compare myself to others. "I'm not as bad as Hitler." Or "I'm not as bad as [name some evil person or even some other average person that I judge to be more sinful, annoying, frustrating, or unforgivable than myself]." Maybe, but what I'm reading in Your Word is that "bad" is not the plumb line. We're all bad. The question is not whether we're bad but how dead we are. Am I any more dead than anyone else? Is there a degree of dead? Can I be more dead than someone else? No. Dead is dead. Period. "When we were dead in our sins . . ."

Like Adam and Eve, from the moment we are born, we are all dead, and we need someone to do for us what we cannot do for ourselves—satisfy the righteous requirement of the law (live a sinless life), pay our debt, and bring us back to life. You did this. You alone. This is the beauty, the majesty, the wonder, and the I-just-don't-deserve-it inconceivability of the Cross. And for that, I say thank You. Please receive my gratitude and let it be a sweet aroma around Your throne today. Please let me join my voice with all of heaven and say, "You are Holy and You alone are worthy." In Jesus' name.

AND GOD RESPONDS

"For God did not send his Son into the world to condemn the world, but in order that the world might be saved through him. Whoever believes in him is not condemned, but whoever does not believe is condemned already, because he has not believed in the name of the only Son of God. And this is the judgment: the light has come into the world, and people loved the darkness rather than the light because their works were evil. For everyone who does wicked things hates the light and does not come to the light, lest his works should be exposed. But whoever does what is true comes to the light, so that it may be clearly seen that his works have been carried out in God."[11]

"For God so loved the world, that he gave his only Son, that whoever believes in him should not perish but have eternal life."[12]

DAY 8

"Young man, I say to you, arise."

LUKE 7:1–17

"After he had finished all his sayings in the hearing of the people, he entered Capernaum. Now a centurion had a servant who was sick and at the point of death, who was highly valued by him. When the centurion heard about Jesus, he sent to him elders of the Jews, asking him to come and heal his servant. And when they came to Jesus, they pleaded with him earnestly, saying, 'He is worthy to have you do this for him, for he loves our nation, and he is the one who built us our synagogue.' And Jesus went with them."[1]

When the centurion hears Jesus is on His way, he sends his friends with word to Jesus: "Lord, do not trouble yourself, for I am not worthy to have you come under my roof. Therefore I did not presume to come to you. But say the word, and let my servant be healed. For I too am a man set under authority, with soldiers under me: and I say to one, 'Go,' and he goes; and to another, 'Come,' and he comes; and to my servant, 'Do this,' and he does it."[2] When Jesus hears this, He marvels.

Twice in Scripture, Jesus marveled. Once at the faith of the centurion. And a second time at the unbelief of those in His hometown of Nazareth.

Here He says, "I tell you, not even in Israel have I found such faith."[3] The friends return to the centurion's house and find the servant healed.

Jesus ventures from Capernaum to Nain, followed by His disciples and a growing crowd. Nearing the gate, he finds pallbearers carrying the casket of a man who was the only son of his mother, a widow. The crowd following Jesus meets the crowd following the casket.

"And when the Lord saw her, he had compassion on her and said to her, 'Do not weep.' Then he came up and touched the bier [casket], and the bearers stood still. And he said, 'Young man, I say to you, arise.' And the dead man sat up and began to speak, and Jesus gave him to his mother. Fear seized them all, and they glorified God, saying, 'A great prophet has arisen among us!' and 'God has visited his people!' And this report about him spread through the whole of Judea and all the surrounding country."[4]

The word used to describe the widow's son is *monogenes*, and it means "the only one of its kind." It's also used to describe Jesus in John 3:16—the only begotten Son. I wonder if Jesus felt a special kinship or sorrow for the mother upon seeing the procession? Perhaps He knew the pain His own mother would one day feel. Jesus speaks to the woman, risks ceremonial uncleanness by touching a casket, and then speaks to the boy. Watch that in slow motion. Jesus leans over and speaks; the boys sits up, scratches his head, and asks for his mother. The crowd watching Jesus is losing their minds. A dead boy is now speaking.

Upon seeing this, fear seizes the people, and they glorify God by declaring a prophet has arisen. God has visited. But they've missed it. Jesus is not just a prophet. And He didn't just visit. He, the living God, is visiting. Standing right there. In the middle of them.

WALK WITH ME BACK TO THE CROSS

Approximately twenty years after Jesus was crucified on this cross, Paul wrote the church in Corinth saying this: "And because of him you are in Christ Jesus."[5] I talked about this in days 4 and 6, so why a third time? Why hammer such a small, seemingly inconsequential phrase? One we tend to skim over. Is it really that big a deal?

Yes. Why? Because it takes the pressure off us. And puts it on Him where it belongs. Other translations read "from Him" or "by His doing." All of which results "in Christ Jesus." Were it not true, it would be inconceivable. If we were to see it as an equation, it would read:

By His Doing = In Christ Jesus

Six years later, mired in a Roman prison, Paul wrote four letters now known as the prison epistles: Philippians, Colossians, Philemon, and Ephesians. In his letter to the church in Ephesus, he said, "But God, being rich in mercy, because of the great love with which he loved us, even when we were dead in our trespasses, made us alive together with Christ—by grace you have been saved—and raised us up with him and seated us with him in the heavenly places in Christ Jesus, so that in the coming ages he might show the immeasurable riches of his grace in kindness toward us in Christ Jesus. For by grace you have been saved through faith. And this is not your own doing; it is the gift of God."[6]

These are some of the most beautiful words ever penned. "But God . . . made us alive . . . raised us up . . . and seated us with him." How? "By His doing." What doing was that? He touches our casket and says, "Arise."

Right this second, Jesus is speaking, "Arise." To you. To me. Maybe for the first time. Maybe the ten thousandth. My question is, Will you?

PRAY WITH ME

Lord Jesus, I'm asking You to speak a word in me. The more I read Your Word, the more I realize that I am the boy in the casket. What I see in the mirror, You molded me with Your hands and then breathed life into me. My life, my existence, everything that I know, think, and believe came at Your initiation. You did a thing and I opened my eyes. Just as You gave life to the widow's son with a word, You gave me life with a word. While the world would tell me I can heal and save myself, the truth is, I cannot. That's like saying the canvas can paint itself. Or the book can write itself. It can't. It needs a Creator. A Master's hand. What can the dust do? Nothing. It's dust. That means I am totally dependent upon my Creator for everything I need. Which, if I'm being totally honest, is just fine with me. I need "By His doing," or I am forever dead. And forever lost.

During Your earthly ministry, You raised three dead people to life with a word—Jairus's daughter, Lazarus, and the son of the widow of Nain. But when I read back through the events of Your public life, I tend to think You were sending a signal. A foretelling of what was to come: You said as much in John 10: "The thief comes only to steal and kill and destroy. I came that they may have life and have it abundantly."[7] Abundant life. That's the offer. Who needs life? Dead people. Me. I do. From a certain view, Your Word reads like a math equation: By His Doing + when you were dead + He made you alive + He has caused us to be born again = in Christ Jesus.

When I rewind the tape of my life, and I look at all You've done to heal me and give me life, I am left speechless. Then when I walk back up here and look at the Cross, at Your mangled body, and hear You speak a singular word, and see the dead raised to life, I want to fall to my knees and plant my face to the earth. I am so not worthy, and yet You prove otherwise. I cannot wrap my head around the fact that You did that for me. For us. It is inconceivable that You, the King of all kings, Ruler of this universe and every other, the Bright Morning Star, the Alpha and Omega, the One who upholds all things by the word of His power, took my death and gave me Your life. Words fail me. Just please know. As much as I am able to express, I am grateful. Jesus, I'm Yours. Thank You for making me, this day and forever, "in Christ Jesus." In Jesus' name.

AND GOD RESPONDS

"For as in Adam all die, so also in Christ shall all be made alive."[8]

"Therefore, if anyone is in Christ, he is a new creation. The old has passed away; behold, the new has come."[9]

DAY 9

*"Today this Scripture has been
fulfilled in your hearing."*

LUKE 4:16–21

"And Jesus, full of the Holy Spirit, returned from the Jordan and was led by the Spirit in the wilderness for forty days, being tempted by the devil."[1]

When He had done this, Scripture records: "And Jesus returned in the power of the Spirit to Galilee, and a report about him went out through all the surrounding country. And he taught in their synagogues, being glorified by all."[2]

Then He went to His hometown. Nazareth.

"And as was his custom, he went to the synagogue on the Sabbath day, and he stood up to read. And the scroll of the prophet Isaiah was given to him. He unrolled the scroll and found the place where it was written, 'The Spirit of the Lord is upon me, because he has anointed me to proclaim good news to the poor. He has sent me to proclaim liberty to the captives and recovering of sight to the blind, to set at liberty those who are oppressed, to proclaim the year of the Lord's favor.' And he rolled up the scroll and gave it back to the attendant and sat down. And the eyes of all in the synagogue were fixed on him. And he began to say to them, 'Today this Scripture has been fulfilled in your hearing.'"[3]

But the people in Nazareth do not receive His words. "When they heard these things, all in the synagogue were filled with wrath. And they rose up and drove him out of town and brought him to the brow of a hill on which their town was built, so that they could throw him down the cliff. But passing through their midst, he went away."[4]

Why did they react this way? Because in reading Isaiah 61 and declaring "this . . . has been fulfilled in your hearing," Jesus is claiming to be the Suffering Servant. The only begotten Son of God. Not only is He claiming Isaiah 61, but He's also claiming Isaiah 53.

Jesus is standing face-to-face with and telling the people of His day: I am the Messiah.

Yeshua Hamashiach.

This is why they hate Him.

The crushing that starts in Genesis 2:7 gets specific in Isaiah 53. Seven hundred years before it happened, the prophet Isaiah described exactly what was coming: "Who has believed what he has heard from us? And to whom has the arm of the Lord been revealed? For he grew up before him like a young plant, and like a root out of dry ground; he had no form or majesty that we should look at him, and no beauty that we should desire him. He was despised and rejected by men, a man of sorrows and acquainted with grief; and as one from whom men hide their faces he was despised, and we esteemed him not. Surely he has borne our griefs and carried our sorrows; yet we esteemed him stricken, smitten by God, and afflicted. But he was pierced for our transgressions; he was crushed for our iniquities; upon him was the chastisement that brought us peace, and with his wounds we are healed. All we like sheep have gone astray; we have turned—every one—to his own way; and the

Lord has laid on him the iniquity of us all. He was oppressed, and he was afflicted, yet he opened not his mouth; like a lamb that is led to the slaughter, and like a sheep that before its shearers is silent, so he opened not his mouth. By oppression and judgment he was taken away; and as for his generation, who considered that he was cut off out of the land of the living, stricken for the transgression of my people? And they made his grave with the wicked and with a rich man in his death, although he had done no violence, and there was no deceit in his mouth. Yet it was the will of the Lord to crush him; he has put him to grief; when his soul makes an offering for guilt, he shall see his offspring; he shall prolong his days; the will of the Lord shall prosper in his hand. Out of the anguish of his soul he shall see and be satisfied; by his knowledge shall the righteous one, my servant, make many to be accounted righteous, and he shall bear their iniquities. Therefore I will divide him a portion with the many, and he shall divide the spoil with the strong, because he poured out his soul to death and was numbered with the transgressors; yet he bore the sin of many, and makes intercession for the transgressors."[5]

Here's my abbreviated list of what happens to the Suffering Servant of Isaiah 53: Root out of dry ground, no majesty, no beauty, despised, rejected, overcome with sorrow, knows grief (by experience), men hid their faces from Him when He walked through town, not esteemed, bore our griefs, carried our sorrows, stricken, smitten by God Himself, pierced for our sin, crushed for our rebellion, chastised because of us, wounded, carried all our iniquity, oppressed, afflicted, didn't complain, judged, cut off from the land of the living, murdered, sealed in a grave, innocent, never told a lie, crushed by His Father (rejected/forsaken), put to grief, suffered, an anguished soul, poured out His soul to death (paid the price for our guilt), numbered with sinners though sinless, bore the sin of all, makes intercession.

This means that at the Cross, Jesus took upon Himself all the evil that rightly belonged to us and, in exchange, gave us all the good that rightly belonged to Him. An inconceivable exchange. It makes no sense whatsoever.

It would be like walking into a bank with more debt than you could repay in a hundred lifetimes and handing the bank manager all your bills. Collection notices. Late fees. Repossessions. Bankruptcies. Foreclosures. Dropping all that on his desk, watching him size up your insurmountable mountain of debt and then reach in his drawer and hand you the keys to the bank.

Why does God do this? What possible reason could He have?

"In this the love of God was made manifest among us, that God sent his only Son into the world, so that we might live through him. In this is love, not that we have loved God but that he loved us and sent his Son to be the propitiation for our sins."[6]

And.

"But God shows his love for us in that while we were still sinners, Christ died for us."[7]

And.

"That the love with which you have loved me may be in them."[8]

And.

"For the Son of Man came to seek and to save the lost."[9]

You get the point.

WALK WITH ME BACK TO THE CROSS . . . AND LET ME ASK YOU AGAIN

What kind of King takes from us what He did not deserve and gives us what we didn't deserve and can't ever earn?

Now look up.

That King.

PRAY WITH ME

Jesus, I know that on the Cross, God the Father put on You all the sin, shame, guilt, and consequences of all mankind for all time—and You never opened Your mouth. Never complained. Never objected. You willingly accepted what You did not deserve in order to give us what we don't. What kind of crazy, inconceivable, furious, overwhelming, limitless love is this? The writer of Hebrews said, "Therefore, since we are surrounded by so great a cloud of witnesses, let us also lay aside every weight, and sin which clings so closely, and let us run with endurance the race that is set before us, looking to Jesus, the founder and perfecter of our faith, who for the joy that was set before him endured the cross, despising the shame, and is seated at the right hand of the throne of God."[10] *When he said,* "lay aside every weight, and sin which clings so closely," *where do we lay it? Where is the only place on this earth or any other that we can lay it down? Just speaking for myself, what bucket can hold everything I'm about to drop in it? Jesus, it's Your Cross. And when I do, You look at me and say,* "Who for the joy that was set before Him." *The joy? Jesus, that means that when I come to You and lay all this ugly stuff down, I am Your joy.*

Jesus, Your brother James said this: "Listen, my beloved brothers, has not God chosen those who are poor in the world to be rich in faith and heirs of the kingdom, which he has promised to those who love him?"[11] *You call us heirs. And if I'm honest, that's tough for me to wrap my head around. What kind of King takes the arrogant, prideful murderer off the street and not only gives him the keys to the* kingdom but also pulls him into the throne room, up into His lap, wraps His arms around him, covers his face in kisses, and says, "I've missed you. I'm so glad you made it. I've prepared a place for you, and I want you to live here with me forever"?

King of all kings, the Lord of Hosts, the One to whom and at whom every voice in heaven is forever offering face-to-the-floor-and-crown-to-your-feet praise, it is inconceivable to me that You would leave your throne to come and die for a rebellious, mutinous, wicked sinner like me. From the moment my eyes opened on planet Earth, all I've ever done is sin against You. More times than I can count. The amount of my sin and debt is more than I can conceive, and yet You left the right hand of God and came here to rescue me from all that. To ransom me. You took on Yourself what was rightly due to me. I don't have words for that. I just don't even know where to start. Jesus, I'm so sorry. I am so, so sorry. Please forgive me. I hate that I did that. I hate that I do that. I hate that I will do that in the future. I know me, and I'm not worthy of You; but I am reading what You said, and I'm asking You for that love. I want to know the love with which the Father loves You. You freely offer it, and I want to willingly accept it. I know my words don't really get at the totality of what You have done in and for me, what You have finished in my life, but please accept these words—I receive it and I am so thankful. So grateful. So utterly blown away. And so unworthy.

Lord Jesus, here and now, I lay it all down. All my sin. All my shame. All my guilt. All the times and places where I, like Adam and Eve, just outright defied and disobeyed You. In Your bucket at the foot of the Cross. And I receive this beautiful exchange from You. From my hand to Yours and from Your hand to mine. I give You all my horrible, ugly sin; and in exchange, I receive Your righteousness. Your unmerited grace. And, if I may, I would love to meet You and my

Father. Please take me to Him. Here's my hand. Lead me. Not only do You know the way; You are the Way. In Jesus' name.

AND GOD RESPONDS

"For our sake he made him to be sin who knew no sin, so that in him we might become the righteousness of God."[12]

DAY 10

"Did you not know that I must be in my Father's house?"

LUKE 2:41–50

"Now his parents went to Jerusalem every year at the Feast of the Passover. And when he was twelve years old, they went up according to custom. And when the feast was ended, as they were returning, the boy Jesus stayed behind in Jerusalem. His parents did not know it, but supposing him to be in the group they went a day's journey, but then they began to search for him among their relatives and acquaintances, and when they did not find him, they returned to Jerusalem, searching for him. After three days they found him in the temple, sitting among the teachers, listening to them and asking them questions. And all who heard him were amazed at his understanding and his answers."[1]

Twelve-year-old Jesus is standing toe to toe with the religious elite, astounding them. What they don't know is that He is the incarnate living God, Emmanuel—"God with us"—who first spoke the Word to Moses and the prophets some fifteen hundred years ago. That He knows it by heart is a given, as it came out of His heart.[2]

There's only one problem. His parents have no idea where He is, and after three days of looking, His mom is about to lose her mind.

"And when his parents saw him, they were astonished. And his mother said to him, 'Son, why have you treated us so? Behold, your father and I have been searching for you in great distress.'"[3]

Jesus' response is tender. Honest. And it is telling. It is also the beginning of the end.

"And he said to them, 'Why were you looking for me? Did you not know that I must be in my Father's house?'"[4]

Twenty-one years from this weekend, these same men will gather on this same mountain, and they will kill the man this boy becomes. Why?

Fast-forward to Pilate's praetorium. Jesus has been arrested and questioned. The Jewish leaders are in an uproar. Pilate says, "Take him yourselves and crucify him, for I find no guilt in him."[5] The leaders respond, "We have a law, and according to that law he ought to die because he has made himself the Son of God."[6]

What law? Leviticus 24:16: "Whoever blasphemes the name of the Lord shall surely be put to death. All the congregation shall stone him. The sojourner as well as the native, when he blasphemes the Name, shall be put to death."

Boy Jesus is changing the way these people think about God, but no one understands. Not even His parents. "And they did not understand the saying that he spoke to them."[7]

Throughout His earthly ministry, one of the single greatest revelations of Jesus is of God as Father. He used this word over 165 times in the Gospels. When healing the man at the pool of Bethesda, He used "Father" fifteen times in two paragraphs—which, to me, suggests Jesus was ministering to a deeper wound than the man's lameness. His father wound. In the Sermon on the Mount, He said "Father" seventeen times. And the high-water mark occurs between John 14 and 17 where Jesus used it fifty-one times.

While the longing for Eden resides in Adam and Eve's children to this day, look what resides in the Father. When Jesus is talking with His Father the night before He goes to the Cross, He says, "O righteous Father, even though the world does not know you, I know you, and these know that you have sent me. I made known to them your name, and I will continue to make it known, that the love with which you have loved me may be in them, and I in them."[8]

What name is that? Father. Abba.

Repeating that word 165 times is browbeating to the Pharisees. Fingernails on a chalkboard. They hate Him for it. And according to the Law, they're right. Unless of course, Jesus really is the only begotten Son of God. In Jesus' day, so intimate was the usage of *Abba* that slaves were not allowed to refer to their masters by this name. But Jesus—sinless, perfect Jesus—is fulfilling the Law we could not and, in so doing, is restoring us into right relationship with God.[9] The same God who fashioned us from the dust. And it is His desire that we call Him Father. Abba.

Paul told the Romans: "For you did not receive the spirit of slavery to fall back into fear, but you have received the Spirit of adoption as sons, by whom we cry, 'Abba! Father!'"[10] Notice, first we receive. Which means He gives. The initiation once again rests with Him. Just as in, "For God so loved the world that He gave . . .". Second, notice what's contrasted: On one hand is a spirit of slavery. On the other, adoption as sons. Sons who cry, "Abba!" Slavery versus sonship. Beggar versus heir. Likewise, Paul told the Galatians: "And because you are sons, God has sent the Spirit of his Son into our hearts, crying, 'Abba! Father!'"[11] Again, notice the sending. The action. God does it. And once the Spirit is sent, notice the resulting cry of our hearts: Abba, Father. And can any of this happen without Jesus? Not a chance.

With, by, and through Jesus, we can be and are restored to the relationship He desires with us. Only one thing is required.

"I am the way, and the truth, and the life. No one comes to the Father except through me."[12]

Adam and Eve walk out of the garden having chosen the father of lies. Once outside the gate, they will give birth to orphans born into slavery, no longer children of God but rather children of wrath (you and me) housed in the kingdom of darkness, governed by an evil king.

There is a false teaching in the church today that says we are all children of God. We're not. But we can be. Jesus promised, "I will not leave you orphans; I will come to you."[13] How? "But to all who did receive him, who believed in his name, he gave the right to become children of God."[14]

The "right to become" means we can be. But how?

Jesus came to return us to the Father. The Father has been, is, and will always be the destination. But there's only one way. Paul told the Galatians, "As many of you as were baptized into Christ have put on Christ."[15] "Put on" means He is in us. We are identified by Him in us. And if He's in us, His Spirit is in us.

Here, Paul lays the issue to rest: "You, however, are not in the flesh but in the Spirit, if in fact the Spirit of God dwells in you. Anyone who does not have the Spirit of Christ does not belong to him. But if Christ is in you, although the body is dead because of sin, the Spirit is life because of righteousness. If the Spirit of him who raised Jesus from the dead dwells in you, he who raised Christ Jesus from the dead will also give life to your mortal bodies through his Spirit who dwells in you. So then, brothers, we are debtors, not to the flesh, to live according to the flesh. For if you live according to the flesh you will die, but if by the Spirit you put to death the deeds of the body, you will live. For all who are led by the Spirit of God are sons of God. For you did not receive the spirit of slavery to fall back into fear, but you have received the Spirit of adoption as sons, by whom we cry, 'Abba! Father!' The Spirit himself bears witness with our spirit that we are children of God, and if children, then heirs— heirs of God and fellow heirs with Christ, provided we suffer with him in order that we may also be glorified with him."[16]

The Cross is God's final word. His stake in the ground. Without it, there is no "becoming," and we cannot cry, "Father." We have no right to do so.

But with the Cross, we can cry out at the top of our lungs, and not only can we cry out, but we can expect a beautiful and kind and gentle response. "Let us then with confidence draw near to the throne of grace, that we may receive mercy and find grace to help in time of need."[17]

Walk with Me Back to the Cross

One more time. Humbly and yet with confidence. To this execution stake. To this majestic and inconceivable throne of grace. To the courtroom where our Father adopts us and transfers us into His family.

And let's cry out. And become.

Pray with Me

Jesus, I don't even know what to make of this. You take me, with all my junk, all my sin; and then because of Your Cross, You drape me in a robe of righteousness I don't deserve and take me by the hand and walk me up to Your—and now my—Father. You restore me to Abba. To my Father. To sonship. From beggar to heir. It is beyond my ability to understand this. You, in Your mercy, take a wretched, black-hearted rebel like me and adopt him into Your family. To give me all the rights and privileges of sonship. You exchange my rebellion and sin and guilt for a right standing before the Father. And then when I get here, You, My Father, take me in Your arms. Such knowledge is too wonderful for me. Were it not for Jesus, it would be too good to be true. Jesus, You told Philip, "If you've seen me, you've seen the Father." I don't know how to make sense of all that, but I believe. I believe. I receive this exchange. Father, Abba, I need You. Take me in Your arms and let me hear the sound of Your voice calling me Your child. Let me smell You. Let me hear You laugh with me and sing songs of deliverance over me. Now, if I could ask one more thing. Please don't ever let me leave here. Just let me sit here with You, my Father. Abba. Abba. Abba. Forever Abba. In Jesus' name.

And God Responds

"Likewise the Spirit helps us in our weakness. For we do not know what to pray for as we ought, but the Spirit himself intercedes for us with groanings too deep for words. And he who searches hearts knows what is the mind of the Spirit, because the Spirit intercedes for the saints according to the will of God. And we know that for those who love God all things work together for good, for those who are called according to his purpose. For those whom he foreknew he also predestined to be conformed to the image of his Son, in order that he might be the firstborn among many brothers. And those whom he predestined he also called, and those whom he called he also justified, and those whom he justified he also glorified. What then shall we say to these things? If God is for us, who can be against us? He who did not spare his own Son but gave him up for us all, how will he not also with him graciously give us all things? Who shall bring any charge against God's elect? It is God who justifies. Who is to condemn? Christ Jesus is the one who died—more than that, who was raised—who is at the right hand of God, who indeed is interceding for us. Who shall separate us from the love of Christ? Shall tribulation, or distress, or persecution, or famine, or nakedness, or danger, or sword? As it is written, 'For your sake we are being killed all the day long; we are regarded as sheep to be slaughtered.' No, in all these things we are more than conquerors through him who loved us. For I am sure that neither death nor life, nor angels nor rulers, nor things present nor things to come, nor powers, nor height nor depth, nor anything else in all creation, will be able to separate us from the love of God in Christ Jesus our Lord."[18]

PART TWO

Why Blood Was
the Only Way to
Settle Our Debt

DAY 11

"Woman, believe me ..."

JOHN 4:4–26

"There was a man sent from God, whose name was John. He came as a witness, to bear witness about the light, that all might believe through him."[1]

Believe. The Gospel of John uses the word eighty-four times. This use is the first. "That all might believe through him."

John continued, "He was not the light, but came to bear witness about the light. The true light, which gives light to everyone, was coming into the world. He was in the world, and the world was made through him, yet the world did not know him. He came to his own, and his own people did not receive him. But to all who did receive him, who believed in his name, he gave the right to become children of God, who were born, not of blood nor of the will of the flesh nor of the will of man, but of God."[2]

Looking back to the garden, at what was lost, this is one of the most astounding statements in Scripture: "To all who did receive him, who believed in his name, he gave the right to become children of God." Think through the ramifications. The undoing of what was done in the garden? Can you see the progression? From orphan. To child. To heir.

Okay, but how do we do that? Sounds a bit too good to be true. According to Scripture, we receive and believe in. But what does that mean? It's one thing to believe *that* His words are true and *that* Jesus is the Son of God, and it's quite another to believe *in* Jesus as the Son of God and place our whole trust *in* Him.

In short, "believing that" is *not* "believing in." Many "believe that," but far fewer "believe in." And Jesus wants disciples who "believe in."

Let's look first for examples of what it means to "believe in." Get ready, Jesus is about to use the word *believe* twenty-two times in just the first five chapters of John. He did so to make a point. Jesus is invited to a wedding in Cana where He performs an undeniable sign, witnessed by several, in which He turns water to wine. Of this John recorded, "This, the first of his signs, Jesus did at Cana in Galilee, and manifested his glory. And his disciples believed in him."[3]

Following the miracle at Cana, Jesus goes up to Jerusalem for Passover; and first thing, He walks into the temple, makes a whip of cords, and cleans house, driving everyone out. "Take these things away; do not make my Father's house a house of trade."[4] Jesus is not angry that they are selling animals. He is angry they are selling blemished animals and profiting off fellow Jews who had traveled long distances intent on obeying the Law and offering a sacrifice, only to be charged an exorbitant price. The Jews, who can't stand the fact that Jesus has just called God His Father, want a sign to support His authority to do what He's done. Jesus then says something they can't understand: "Destroy this temple and in three days I will raise it up."[5] They think He's talking about the actual temple, which took forty-six years to build, but He's talking about His body. "When therefore he was raised from the dead, his disciples remembered that he had said this, and they believed the Scripture and the word that Jesus had spoken."[6] The very next verse goes on to say,

"When he was in Jerusalem at the Passover Feast, many believed in his name when they saw the signs that he was doing."[7]

While in Jerusalem, Jesus bumps into Nicodemus, who asks how a man can be born again. This is the first real conversation about what it means to become a child of God. Jesus answers, "You must be born again." Nicodemus scratches his head, "How can this be?" Jesus puts it in language Nicodemus can understand. "And as Moses lifted up the serpent in the wilderness, so must the Son of Man be lifted up, that whoever believes in him may have eternal life."[8]

Which brings us to the most famous verses in all of Scripture. "For God so loved the world, that he gave his only Son, that whoever believes in him should not perish but have eternal life. For God did not send his Son into the world to condemn the world, but in order that the world might be saved through him. Whoever believes in him is not condemned, but whoever does not believe is condemned already, because he has not believed in the name of the only Son of God."[9]

Jesus then walks into the Judean countryside with His disciples and begins baptizing people. (His disciples did the baptizing.) Coincidentally, John the Baptizer is also baptizing people. A local Jew notices the two camps and the possible competition for followers and begins a conversation with John the Baptist. John responds, "I am not the Christ" and then goes on to point out, "The Father loves the Son and has given all things into his hand. Whoever believes in the Son has eternal life; whoever does not obey the Son shall not see life, but the wrath of God remains on him."[10]

When Jesus realizes that the Pharisees have heard that He and John are baptizing and that Jesus is baptizing more disciples than John, Jesus departs Judea for Galilee. To do so, He passes through Samaria and a town called Sychar. Being thirsty, He stops at Jacob's well about noon when a woman from Samaria stops to draw water, and Jesus says to her, "Give me a drink."[11] This is unusual in that Jews and Samaritans have been enemies a long time. Regardless, Jesus engages her in conversation about the water, her husbands, and how He is the Messiah. In the middle of the conversation, Jesus says this: "Woman, believe me." He then goes on to talk about worship. Seconds later, the woman says, "I know that Messiah is coming (he who is called Christ). When he comes, he will tell us all things." To this, Jesus responds: "I who speak to you am he."[12]

These are mind-blowing words. *Believe me*—I am the Messiah."

Jesus leaves Samaria, where "many believed" based on the testimony of the woman—which might make her the first evangelist—and He walks by a pool at the Sheep Gate called Bethesda. The sick, blind, lame, and withered are waiting for an angel to stir the waters because the first one in after the stirring will be made well. Jesus speaks to a man who has been lying there thirty-eight years and asks him, "Do you wish to get well?"[13] The sick man responds, "Sir, I have no one to put me into the pool."[14] So Jesus, who is the fount of living waters, says "Get up! Pick up your mat and walk."[15] Which the man does.

The Pharisees are watching Jesus through skeptical eyes. Trying to trap Him. "Therefore the Jews sought all the more to kill Him, because He not only broke the Sabbath, but also said that God was His Father, making Himself equal with God."[16]

There it is. The reason they killed Him. Because He called God His Father and claimed to be the Son of God.

Which He is.

Jesus responds with this: "Truly, truly, I say to you, whoever hears my word and believes him who sent me has eternal life. He does not come into judgment, but has passed from death to life."[17]

Five chapters into John's gospel and he's now used the word

believe twenty-two times. Over the course of his gospel, John used it eighty-four times! As a writer, if I mention something twenty-two times in the first five chapters of any book I write, trust me, I'm beating you over the head. It's akin to ringing a church bell three feet from your ear. I'm wanting you to hear me. I'm telegraphing that this is probably the most important thing.

Why does Jesus do this?

After Jesus walks on water, a crowd gathers and asks Him, "What must we do, to be doing the works of God?"[18] Jesus answers it simply: "This is the work of God, that you believe in him whom he has sent."[19] Then, moments later, He says this: "For this is the will of my Father, that everyone who looks on the Son and believes in him should have eternal life, and I will raise him up on the last day."[20]

Because without "belief in," there is no life.

The word *believe* comes from the Greek word *pisteuo*, and while it means to intellectually comprehend and agree with someone or some concept, *pisteuo* is more than that. It not only means to comprehend; it means to "put your trust in." Completely.

Suppose you and I are standing on the side of a vast bridge that crosses a chasm several thousand feet deep. And as we sit there watching, people walk to the middle of the bridge, wrap a strap around their ankles, climb up on the railing, and take a swan dive out over the edge, falling thousands of feet, before the bungee snaps them back to the bridge. It's one thing for us to stand on the side and remark, "I believe *that* bungee will hold me if I were to do the same." It's another thing entirely to walk out on the bridge, strap in, and take a Peter Pan off the railing. One is believing *that* it will hold us. The other is believing *in* its ability to hold us and then trusting *in* it—entirely—to do just that.

Big difference.

We *pisteuo* in a chair or swing when we sit on it. We *pisteuo* in a bridge when we drive across it. We *pisteuo* in an elevator when the doors close and it either ascends or descends. And we *pisteuo* in the bungee when we lock it around our ankles and dive.

Belief *that* is little more than an intellectual exercise that never strays far from the safe recesses of our minds. Belief *that* is faithlessness in action. It requires nothing. No commitment. No buy-in. Just cavalier indifference on display. While belief *in* flows from our guts. The same place we feel butterflies. Fear. Courage. And gumption. Down where our love lives.

Walk with Me Back to the Cross

See the sign above His head? "KING OF THE JEWS." It was a joke. They were mocking Him. Same with the crown. They fashioned it from the branches of an acacia tree then beat the three-inch thorns into His skull with rods. See how they pierce His skull? Now walk around to the side. See that crude puncture hole between the ribs? The soldiers did that too. With a spear. And that wet spot on the ground is where the blood and water splashed out.

The writer of Hebrews said, "Fixing our eyes on Jesus, the author and perfecter of faith, who for the joy set before Him endured the cross, despising the shame, and has sat down at the right hand of the throne of God."[21] It's easy to imagine what He endured, but have you ever wondered what brought Him joy? Try looking through His eyes. Who do you see?

So, let me ask you: Do you believe *in* this man hanging here?

Do you want to?

Because there's only one way to know if the bungee will hold.

Pray with Me

Jesus, to "believe in" is to receive Your words, do them, and to unreservedly bungee jump, placing my whole trust, hope, and faith in them and in You. I believe You are the only begotten Son of God, the only way to God, that You died on the Cross for my sins, and that after three days You rose again from the dead. I believe that You and You alone bore my iniquities and drained the cup of the wrath of God and that Your death on the Cross paid the total penalty, the total payment, for my sin, allowing You to present me holy and righteous to Your and my Father. I believe that You became sin for me and that You transferred me out of the kingdom of darkness and into Your kingdom so that I might know the love with which the Father loves You.

Jesus, despite the fact that I deserve none of this, nor could I earn it in a thousand lifetimes, I receive all this from You. And, for the record, I want to proclaim across the stratosphere, I pisteuo in You. I believe in and trust in You. You alone. Jesus, into Your hands I commit my body, my mind, my soul, and my spirit. I'm Yours. Because of Your grace and unmerited mercy, You have allowed me to become what is the deepest desire of my heart—Your child. Words fail when I try to thank You, but please just know I am so thankful.

Lastly, Lord, I know that right now I'm telling You I believe in You and I believe that You will accomplish what You started and that You will continue to do what You have done and are doing. But I also know me. And I know my unbelief might creep back in. I hate it, but it might. Please forgive me when it does. Please help my unbelief. Please grant me greater faith. Please add steel to my spine. Grant me greater belief so that I believe with every ounce of me that Your Word is true and You did what the Bible says You did and that You will continue to do what You said You will do. In Jesus' name.

AND GOD RESPONDS

"Eight days later, his disciples were inside again, and Thomas was with them. Although the doors were locked, Jesus came and stood among them and said, 'Peace be with you.' Then he said to Thomas, 'Put your finger here, and see my hands; and put out your hand, and place it in my side. Do not disbelieve, but believe.' Thomas answered him, 'My Lord and my God!' Jesus said to him, 'Have you believed because you have seen me? Blessed are those who have not seen and yet have believed.' Now Jesus did many other signs in the presence of the disciples, which are not written in this book; but these are written so that you may believe that Jesus is the Christ, the Son of God, and that by believing you may have life in his name."[22]

DAY 12

"Be merciful to me, a sinner!"

LUKE 18:10–14

"Two men went up into the temple to pray, one a Pharisee and the other a tax collector. The Pharisee, standing by himself, prayed thus: 'God, I thank you that I am not like other men, extortioners, unjust, adulterers, or even like this tax collector. I fast twice a week; I give tithes of all that I get.' But the tax collector, standing far off, would not even lift up his eyes to heaven, but beat his breast, saying, 'God, be merciful to me, a sinner!' I tell you, this man went down to his house justified, rather than the other. For everyone who exalts himself will be humbled, but the one who humbles himself will be exalted."[1]

Notice where the Pharisee is looking. Out across the crowd. His vision is horizontal. Mired in the sin of comparison. Seething with arrogance. Exalting himself. Now study the tax collector. In Jesus' day, tax collectors were hated. Most were Jews who had betrayed their own countrymen, sold out to Rome, and were now employed by Rome to collect taxes from their own people. They made a living by charging a percentage above what Rome required. So they profited off their own, hated by everyone. But notice where the tax collector is looking. Or, better yet, where he's not. Of the two, the tax collector has a clear view of his own sin. And it's wrecking him. He can't even lift his eyes. Why? Look at his prayer: "Be merciful to me, a sinner!" The word "sinner" comes from a word that was adapted for use in archery. It means "to miss the mark." Which he had. Completely. Second, he uses the phrase "be merciful." But this isn't just asking God to take it easy on him because he knows he messed up. The Greek verb *hilaskomai* is used only twice in the New Testament, and it means "to conciliate" or "atone for" and can also be translated as "be propitious."

Which brings us back to Jesus and the Cross. To be propitious means to make propitiation. Or to pay my debt when I cannot. Not in ten thousand lifetimes. The only other place the verb is used in the New Testament is in Hebrews to describe Jesus' death on the Cross: "Therefore he had to be made like his brothers in every respect, so that he might become a merciful and faithful high priest in the service of God, to make propitiation for the sins of the people."[2] To "make propitiation" points to an Old Testament act by the high priest whereby he sacrificed a spotless lamb and then walked into the holy of holies and painted the mercy seat with blood, thereby making a payment that satisfied the wrath of God against our sin. The arrogant Pharisee in Luke 18 is comparing himself to others while the tax collector is ashamed, afraid to lift his eyes off the dirt, yet humbly asking God to be merciful and atone for his sin because he knows he can't. Not now. Not ever. And according to Jesus, the tax collector went home justified.

Of the two, who had a right view of God?

Posture matters. Specifically, the posture of our hearts when we approach Jesus.

What is your view of you? Do you know the depth of your own

need? Let me ask it this way: What do you bring to the Cross? What do you contribute?

Nothing. Save the sin that brings you there.

I mentioned this briefly in day 6, but it bears repeating. Isaiah said this: "We have all become like one who is unclean, and all our righteous deeds are like a polluted garment."[3] NKJV says it this way: "But we are all like an unclean thing, and all our righteousnesses are like filthy rags." "Filthy rags" means "used menstrual cloths." I'm not repeating this to gross you out. I'm trying to get your attention. And according to the inspired Word of God, the best we bring on our best day is equal to used feminine products. The tax collector saw himself clearly. The Pharisee was blind to himself. And remember, the Pharisee knew this same word. He could quote it from memory. He just didn't think it applied to him.

Which one are you?

From Moses to Isaiah to John, Thomas, and Paul, something was birthed in each of them when they encountered Jesus. Solomon described it as "the fear of the Lord." He used the word "fear" to mean "reverence," not "scary." "The fear of the Lord is the beginning of wisdom, and the knowledge of the Holy One is insight."[4] Meaning, before we can have wisdom and insight, we must first fear. Again he wrote, "The fear of the Lord leads to life, and whoever has it rests satisfied; he will not be visited by harm."[5] The NKJV translation reads "will not be visited with evil." This is one of the most astounding statements in Scripture. "Not visited with evil." Let that sink in. Now let me ask you: Do you fear God? Revere Him? Even if you don't completely understand Him? Because none of these people completely understood Him but all feared Him.

How will you approach God? As the Pharisee or the tax

collector? The thief who reviled Him or the thief who asked to be remembered? The soldiers who mocked or the centurion who believed? Are you an indifferent bystander, viewing Jesus as a cool walkabout prophet with a posse, or are you Thomas—with your fingers in the hole—"My Lord and my God!"?

The difference matters. Actually, it's life or death.

WALK WITH ME BACK TO THE CROSS

How bad is the problem? Look up. The Father's solution to your and my problem is a dead Jesus. Lifted high. Crucified. His back, neck, and sides shredded. Unrecognizable as a man. "Marred, beyond human semblance."[6]

Do we approach with fear and clear vision? With a right view of who He really is? And who we are in light of Him? Because that man hanging there is King Jesus. Who will soon slay His enemies by appearing—by just showing up.

Being honest, crucified Jesus doesn't look like any king I've ever seen. What kind of King dies such a death for His subjects? What kind of King would allow it if He had the power to prevent it? Seems like an awful waste.

In Paul's letter to the Colossians, he said, "He is the image of the invisible God, the firstborn of all creation. For by him all things were created, in heaven and on earth, visible and invisible, whether thrones or dominions or rulers or authorities—all things were created through him and for him. And he is before all things, and in him all things hold together. And he is the head of the body, the church. He is the beginning, the firstborn from the dead, that in everything he might be preeminent. For in him all the fullness of

God was pleased to dwell, and through him to reconcile to himself all things, whether on earth or in heaven, making peace by the blood of his cross. And you, who once were alienated and hostile in mind, doing evil deeds, he has now reconciled in his body of flesh by his death, in order to present you holy and blameless and above reproach before him."[7]

We'll come back to this, but notice what is finished. Who is reconciled. And how.

Knowing this about Jesus as He hangs there is the wonder, the mystery, and the majesty of the Cross.

These are the words of the chorus of one of my favorite hymns. I can't really say it any better:

> *Turn your eyes upon Jesus,*
> *Look full in His wonderful face,*
> *And the things of earth will grow strangely dim,*
> *In the light of His glory and grace.*[8]

How would we change if we just do that? If we turn our eyes upon Jesus and cry out for Him to have mercy? To be propitious. On us. Sinners.

PRAY WITH ME

Lord, I want to see You clearly. Please help. Please give me a right revelation of You. Take off the scales. Forgive my arrogance. Allow me to see You as You want to be seen by me. And if I don't have it already, please put in me a right fear of the Lord. Allow me to walk in the fear of You. Please have mercy on me, a sinner. In Jesus' name.

AND GOD RESPONDS

"For if we go on sinning deliberately after receiving the knowledge of the truth, there no longer remains a sacrifice for sins, but a fearful expectation of judgment, and a fury of fire that will consume the adversaries. Anyone who has set aside the law of Moses dies without mercy on the evidence of two or three witnesses. How much worse punishment, do you think, will be deserved by the one who has trampled underfoot the Son of God, and has profaned the blood of the covenant by which he was sanctified, and has outraged the Spirit of grace? For we know him who said, 'Vengeance is mine; I will repay.' And again, 'The Lord will judge his people.' It is a fearful thing to fall into the hands of the living God."[9]

DAY 13

"Whoever believes in him is not condemned."

JOHN 3:16–18

"Now there was a man of the Pharisees named Nicodemus, a ruler of the Jews. This man came to Jesus by night and said to him, 'Rabbi, we know that you are a teacher come from God, for no one can do these signs that you do unless God is with him.' Jesus answered him, 'Truly, truly, I say to you, unless one is born again he cannot see the kingdom of God.'"[1]

Nicodemus, whom Jesus will later call "the teacher of Israel," knows he cannot escape the law. No one can. It's an unbearable, crushing yoke that has condemned everyone to die in their sins. The only way to a right standing before God is to live a sinless life, which Nicodemus knows he has not done and cannot do. Jesus jumps to the point and tells him he must be born again. But what does this mean? Nicodemus is left scratching his head. For he knows the law, and the sentence of the law is death. "Indeed, under the law almost everything is purified with blood, and without the shedding of blood there is no forgiveness of sins."[2]

But what is the specific law and how did this come to be?

God commanded Moses that once a year, on the Day of Atonement, the high priest would enter the holy of holies and sprinkle the ark of God with the blood of a lamb to make atonement for the people. To cover the sins of the people for one year. "And he shall take some of the blood of the bull and sprinkle it with his finger on the front of the mercy seat on the east side, and in front of the mercy seat he shall sprinkle some of the blood with his finger seven times."[3] (Notice the number; this will become relevant when we walk back to the Cross.)

"Then he shall kill the goat of the sin offering that is for the people and bring its blood inside the veil and do with its blood as he did with the blood of the bull, sprinkling it over the mercy seat and in front of the mercy seat. . . . And he shall sprinkle some of the blood on it with his finger seven times, and cleanse it and consecrate it from the uncleannesses of the people of Israel. . . . For on this day shall atonement be made for you to cleanse you. You shall be clean before the LORD from all your sins."[4]

The Hebrew word for "mercy seat" is *hilasterion*. It means "place of propitiation, place of expiation, place of conciliation." The mercy seat is the physical place where the presence of God meets with man *and* accepts payment that expiates or conciliates the wrath of God. And God only accepts payment in blood from a spotless lamb. Why did God choose blood? "For the life of the flesh is in the blood, and I have given it for you on the altar to make atonement for your souls, for it is the blood that makes atonement by the life."[5]

Only the blood makes atonement. And that blood was sprinkled seven times.

But how is payment made, and what does this have to do with Jesus? And what about that number seven?

Jump back to the other side of the Cross. The writer of Hebrews said: "Therefore he [Jesus] had to be made like his brothers in every respect, so that he might become a merciful and faithful high priest in the service of God, to make propitiation for the sins of the people."[6] **John said,** "He is the propitiation for our sins, and not for ours only but also for the sins of the whole world."[7] **Two chapters later, he added,** "In this is love, not that we have loved God but that he loved us and sent his Son to be the propitiation for our sins."[8]

But specifically, how did Jesus make propitiation? How did He sprinkle the mercy seat seven times? The Gospels go into great detail to make sure we understand that Jesus made payment seven times with His very own blood—and in doing so, fulfilled the law and the prophets.

1. Luke 22:41–44

    "And he withdrew from them about a stone's throw, and knelt down and prayed, saying, 'Father, if you are willing, remove this cup from me. Nevertheless, not my will, but yours, be done.' And there appeared to him an angel from heaven, strengthening him. And being in agony he prayed more earnestly; and his sweat became like great drops of blood falling down to the ground."

2. Matthew 26:65–68

    "Then the high priest tore his robes and said, 'He has uttered blasphemy. What further witnesses do we need? You have now heard his blasphemy. What is your judgment?' They answered, 'He deserves death.' Then they spit in his face and struck him. And some slapped him, saying, 'Prophesy to us, you Christ! Who is it that struck you?'"

3. Matthew 27:24–26

    "So when Pilate saw that he was gaining nothing, but rather that a riot was beginning, he took water and washed his hands before the crowd, saying, 'I am innocent of this man's blood; see to it yourselves.' And all the people answered, 'His blood be on us and on our children!' Then he released for them Barabbas, and having scourged Jesus, delivered him to be crucified."

4. Matthew 27:27–31

"Then the soldiers of the governor took Jesus into the governor's headquarters, and they gathered the whole battalion before him. And they stripped him and put a scarlet robe on him, and twisting together a crown of thorns, they put it on his head and put a reed in his right hand. And kneeling before him, they mocked him, saying, 'Hail, King of the Jews!' And they spit on him and took the reed and struck him on the head. And when they had mocked him, they stripped him of the robe and put his own clothes on him and led him away to crucify him."

5 & 6. John 19:17–18

"And he went out, bearing his own cross, to the place called The Place of a Skull, which in Aramaic is called Golgotha. There they crucified him, and with him two others, one on either side, and Jesus between them."[9]

7. John 19:33–37

"But when they came to Jesus and saw that he was already dead, they did not break his legs. But one of the soldiers pierced his side with a spear, and at once there came out blood and water. He who saw it has borne witness—his testimony is true, and he knows that he is telling the truth—that you also may believe. For these things took place that the Scripture might be fulfilled: 'Not one of his bones will be broken.' And again another Scripture says, 'They will look on him whom they have pierced.'"

Here they are in brief:

1. Jesus' blood vessels burst, and He sweated blood.
2. They struck Him in the face and plucked out His beard.
3. They scourged Him with a Roman cat-o'-nine-tails, rendering Him beyond human recognition.
4. They beat a crown of thorns on His head with sticks.
5. They drove nails through His hands.
6. And through His feet.
7. They pierced His side with a spear.

This is the sevenfold bleeding of Jesus, our High Priest, sprinkling the mercy seat, making payment with His very own blood. Seven times. This is, as John said, the Lamb of God taking away the sins of the world.

I know we've all heard this a lot, but try to hear it through Nicodemus's ears, who was the first person to ever hear this as he was staring up at Jesus, just as Moses lifted up the serpent in the wilderness. "For God so loved the world, that he gave his only Son, that whoever believes in him should not perish but have eternal life. For God did not send his Son into the world to condemn the world, but in order that the world might be saved through him. Whoever believes in him is not condemned, but whoever does not believe is condemned already, because he has not believed in the name of the only Son of God."[10]

Whoever believes is not condemned. There it is. The answer Nicodemus has been looking for his entire life. How do I become reborn? How do I get back to God when I am powerless to get me there? Which, I think, is the very same question Adam and Eve asked as the angel locked them out of the garden.

WALK WITH ME BACK TO THE CROSS

I don't know for sure if Nicodemus attended the crucifixion of Jesus. I tend to think he did. Had he, he would have heard Jesus utter the word *tetelestai* and seen the spear enter Jesus' chest cavity, and when it did, he would have seen the blood and water flow out. Which is also what happens at a birth. And he would have known Psalm 22:14, "My heart is like wax; it is melted within my breast"—which points to the Messiah. I think that's the moment Nicodemus would have known, "*That's* how I'm born again." I can imagine him putting the pieces together in amazement: "He told me, 'Whoever believes in him should not perish but have eternal life.' That means He died in my place. His shed blood made propitiation for my sins. His death satisfied the wrath of God. He is *the* Lamb of God. He paid my sin debt. It is finished! And when I believe in Him—that He is the Son of God who has come to take away the sin of the whole world—I get credit for what He has done. God the Father imputes Jesus' righteousness to me. Which means His death counts for me!"

When I think of Nicodemus, I see him kneeling at the cross. Face to the dirt. Tears. Snot. Hands held high. No, I can't prove it. But how could he not? Scripture records that Joseph of Arimathea and Nicodemus took down the body of Jesus. Which means that one of them reached up and closed Jesus' eyes.

Paul summed up being born again this way: "For through the law I died to the law, so that I might live to God. I have been crucified with Christ. It is no longer I who live, but Christ who lives in me. And the life I now live in the flesh I live by faith in the Son of God, who loved me and gave himself for me."[11]

My pastor, Joby Martin, says that when we surrender our lives to the lordship of Jesus, we are overtaken by an alien righteousness. I can't say it any better.

PRAY WITH ME

Jesus, I'm undone. I don't have the words. I can't fathom what You endured on my behalf. I just know You did. And with all that I am and as much as I am able, I say thank You. I am so grateful. You are my propitiation. Through Your shed blood, You made the payment on my behalf that satisfied the wrath of God. You have cleansed me. Washed me white as snow. Peter, who watched You die, said, when You were reviled, You did not revile in return; when You suffered, You did not threaten but continued entrusting Yourself to Him who judges justly. You Yourself bore my sins in Your body on the tree, that I might die to sin and live to righteousness. By Your wounds I have been healed. Have been delivered. For I was straying like sheep but have now returned to the Shepherd and Overseer of my soul.[12]

And Paul said, though You were in the form of God, You did not count equality with God a thing to be grasped, but emptied Yourself, by taking the form of a servant, being born in the likeness of men. And being found in human form, You humbled Yourself by becoming obedient to the point of death, even death on a cross.[13] This is inconceivable to me, but I believe it's true. I believe that for the joy set before You, You endured the Cross and despised the shame and that I am that joy. Or at least, one part of it. Jesus, I'm Yours. All that I have, all that I hope, dream, and believe, I lay down at Your feet. For You alone are Lord, God, King, and Savior of the world. In Jesus' name.

AND GOD RESPONDS

"But now the righteousness of God has been manifested apart from the law, although the Law and the Prophets bear witness to it—the righteousness of God through faith in Jesus Christ for all who believe. For there is no distinction: for all have sinned and fall short of the glory of God, and are justified by his grace as a gift, through the redemption that is in Christ Jesus, whom God put forward as a propitiation by his blood, to be received by faith. This was to show God's righteousness, because in his divine forbearance he had passed over former sins. It was to show his righteousness at the present time, so that he might be just and the justifier of the one who has faith in Jesus."[14]

DAY 14

⸻ ◆ • ◆ ⸻

"Why are you afraid?"

MATTHEW 8:24–27

"And behold, there arose a great storm on the sea, so that the boat was being swamped by the waves; but he was asleep. And they went and woke him, saying, 'Save us, Lord; we are perishing.'

"And he said to them, 'Why are you afraid, O you of little faith?'

"Then he rose and rebuked the winds and the sea, and there was a great calm. And the men marveled, saying, 'What sort of man is this, that even winds and sea obey him?'"[1]

Seasoned fishermen, who grew up on boats on the Sea of Galilee, cower in fear. As the waves roll over the gunnels, they voice the universal fear of every one of us: "I am going to die, and You [God] don't care."

And there's Jesus, taking a nap.

In John 11, Mary and Martha send word to Jesus, "Lord, he whom you love is ill."[2] John then recorded that Jesus loved Mary and Martha and Lazarus, "So, when he heard that Lazarus was ill, he stayed two days longer in the place where he was."[3]

Two days. During which, Lazarus died. Seems like a strange way to show your love for someone. Why does Jesus do this? "For the glory of God, so that the Son of God may be glorified through it."[4] The disciples think Lazarus has only fallen asleep, but Jesus corrects them. "Lazarus has died, and for your sake I am glad that I was not there, so that you may believe."[5]

Jesus let Lazarus die so that you may believe.

Jesus then walks into Bethany after Lazarus has been in the tomb four days. Stone-cold dead. Martha runs out to meet him and says, "Lord, if you had been here, my brother would not have died."[6]

These are the same words His disciples uttered in the boat when the storm threatened: "We are going to die and You don't care," although Martha has added one more implication: "We sent word. Why didn't You come when we called You?" This also gets at the root fear of all of us: *I tried Jesus, and He didn't help when I needed Him. He hung me out to dry.* And feeding our fear is satan, whispering, "Did God really say He would help you? See, He doesn't care."

It's an age-old lie. The same one he spoke in the garden—the "Did God say" lie.

"Jesus said to her, 'I am the resurrection and the life. Whoever believes in me, though he die, yet shall he live, and everyone who lives and believes in me shall never die. Do you believe this?' She said to him, 'Yes, Lord; I believe that you are the Christ, the Son of God, who is coming into the world.'"[7]

So that you and I may believe.

This problem of facing a ship-swamping storm is not new.

When Moses dies, Joshua is tasked with walking the nation of Israel, some three million Hebrews, into the promised land. The ten spies return with a report that is not good: "The place is everything we've dreamed of, but there's just one problem. It's populated by giants." It's true, it is, but God has given them the land and told them to go. All that is required is obedience to step foot onto the land and believe that He will do what He promises to do—despite what their eyes tell them.

Standing in the shadow of Goliath, how does God respond to Joshua?

"No man shall be able to stand before you all the days of your life. Just as I was with Moses, so I will be with you. I will not leave you or forsake you. Be strong and courageous, for you shall cause this people to inherit the land that I swore to their fathers to give them. Only be strong and very courageous, being careful to do according to all the law that Moses my servant commanded you. Do not turn from it to the right hand or to the left, that you may have good success wherever you go. This Book of the Law shall not depart from your mouth, but you shall meditate on it day and night, so that you may be careful to do according to all that is written in it. For then you will make your way prosperous, and then you will have good success. Have I not commanded you? Be strong and courageous. Do not be frightened, and do not be dismayed, for the LORD your God is with you wherever you go."[8]

On the one hand are the spies; on the other is God. Joshua stands in the middle. I think the reason the Lord tells him to be strong and courageous so many times is because he felt weak and afraid.

Throughout Scripture, God says "do not fear" 365 times. He also says, "Let not your hearts be troubled."[9] And, "Do not be anxious about your life."[10] In fact, Paul said, "Do not be anxious about anything."[11]

How different would your life be if you were not afraid?

John said, "Whoever makes a practice of sinning is of the devil, for the devil has been sinning from the beginning. The reason the Son of God appeared was to destroy the works of the devil."[12]

Destroy the works of the devil. This is either true, or it isn't.

The writer of Hebrews said, "Since the children share in flesh and blood, He Himself likewise also partook of the same, that through death He might render powerless him who had the power of death, that is, the devil."[13]

I'm not suggesting satan doesn't have a measure of power and authority here on earth; he does. God gave it to him for a time. But ultimately, he's defeated and is powerless over your eventual outcome—where you spend eternity and who you spend it with. This, too, is either true or it isn't.

The opposite of faith is not faithlessness. It's fear. Meaning, if faith does not drive you, then fear does. And most of us, if we're honest, are driven and make daily decisions based not in faith but out of our fear. We are afraid of giants. And we are afraid of storms. Which makes us a lot like the disciples. And like them, we face a choice: focus on the waves, or lift our eyes to the One who stills them with a word.

Jesus has just fed the five thousand, and the disciples climb in a boat and begin rowing to Capernaum. It is dark, Jesus is not with them, and once again the sea becomes rough, and a strong wind blows. When they have only rowed three or four miles, they see Jesus. Walking on the water. "And they were frightened."[14]

What does Jesus do? He says, "It is I; do not be afraid."[15]

Jesus hasn't changed. He still walks on water.

What is your single greatest driving fear? Or top three? Write them down. Be gut-level honest. And let's take them to Jesus. Because He is either asleep and doesn't care, or even the wind and waves obey. Because either the giants are going to eat you for breakfast, or He is going to keep His promises and never leave you or forsake you.

Again, the writer of Hebrews said, "Since therefore the children share in flesh and blood, he himself likewise partook of the same things, that through death he might destroy the one who has the power of death, that is, the devil, and deliver all those who through fear of death were subject to lifelong slavery."[16] When Jesus spoke the word *tetelestai*, He delivered us—past tense—from lifelong slavery imposed on us by the fear of death. He also speaks the word in the perfect present tense, which means He continues to deliver and He is delivering still. Even now. And forever. Throughout all eternity. Jesus is the author and perfecter of our faith. I'm not so naive as to suggest you and I will never again be afraid, but when we are, when we do, where will we go?

WALK WITH ME BACK TO THE CROSS

From a certain perspective, the Cross is a stake driven into the ground. A declaration. What is God declaring? In essence, He is saying the same thing He said when He completed creation: "It [is] very good."[17] Here on the Cross, Jesus completes the work of redemption and declares, "It is finished"—or "It is complete." "It is perfect." And by and through that finishing, completing, perfect work, Jesus defeated fear. Forever. So, this Cross, this mercy seat, this place of expiation, this bloody spot on the earth, is the place where we choose to either stare at the waves and the giants and cave in to the whispers, or fix our eyes on Jesus and believe Him when He says, "It is I; do not be afraid." And herein lies the crux of the matter: What do you believe? Do you believe the wind and the waves, the stench wafting from the tomb, or the One who turns the sea to glass and raises the dead with a single word?

PRAY WITH ME

Jesus, King of angels, King of glory, the Beginning and the End, the One who conquered death and the grave, I confess, fear is wrecking my life. Despite the fact that I say I believe in You, I make decisions more often than not out of my fear and not my faith. When pressed, I'm more afraid of the raging storm—the wind and the waves—than I believe in Your ability and willingness to still them. I confess my knee-jerk reaction is to assume the worst—that You don't care or, at best, You're indifferent, asleep in the boat, and it's up to me to figure a way out. Which just puts me, rather than You, on the throne of my heart.

Jesus, I'm so sorry. I want a faith that stares at the storm and does not fear. No matter the height of the waves, the crack of the lightning, or the clap of the thunder. I want a faith that believes despite my fears. I want a faith that while what I'm facing might make me afraid, I turn to You and believe that You love me, You will not abandon me, that You will never leave me nor forsake me, that You even care about the little things, and that I can trust You in all things and with all things.

Having said that, I want to be honest—here are my three biggest fears:

_____

_____

_____

These are the things that keep me up at night. That paralyze me. These are the things I listen to rather than You. Jesus, I know You gave me the emotion of fear, but the enemy twists it and even sends a spirit of fear to torment and entice me. To hold my head under the water. In the name of Jesus, by and through and because of the blood of Jesus, I rebuke, bind, and cast out of my life the spirit of fear and all its helpers. Get out. Go now. I'm a blood-bought, blood-washed, and blood-redeemed child of God. You may not have my mind, my *emotions, my thoughts, or any part of me. You must flee me now because greater is He who is in me than he who is in the world. And on the Cross, Jesus defeated you, fear. Permanently. Your defeat is irrevocable. There's nothing you can do about it. I am in Christ, and you have been overcome and rendered powerless in my life.*

King Jesus, today, I give You all my fear. I'm leaving it right here at the foot of Your Cross. And tomorrow, when I find that overnight I took it back and stuffed it in my backpack, I'm coming back here to Your throne of grace to receive mercy and find grace and dump it again because I know when I do, You receive me without shame and with open arms.

Last, Lord, faith is also a gift; so today, I receive it. From You. Please fill me up. I don't want to be someone of little faith; I want to have storm-stilling, wind-and-wave-obeying, raising-Lazarus-from-the-dead faith, and I want to believe You with every cell in my body when You say, "It is I; do not be afraid." In Jesus' name.

AND GOD RESPONDS

"What then shall we say to these things? If God is for us, who can be against us? He who did not spare his own Son but gave him up for us all, how will he not also with him graciously give us all things? Who shall bring any charge against God's elect? It is God who justifies. Who is to condemn? Christ Jesus is the one who died—more than that, who was raised—who is at the right hand of God, who indeed is interceding for us. Who shall separate us from the love of Christ? Shall tribulation, or distress, or persecution, or famine, or nakedness, or danger, or sword? As it is written, 'For your sake we are being killed all the day long; we are regarded as sheep to be slaughtered.'

No, in all these things we are more than conquerors through him who loved us. For I am sure that neither death nor life, nor angels nor rulers, nor things present nor things to come, nor powers, nor height nor depth, nor anything else in all creation, will be able to separate us from the love of God in Christ Jesus our Lord."[18]

DAY 15

"The truth will set you free."

JOHN 8:1–36

"Jesus went to the Mount of Olives. Early in the morning he came again to the temple. All the people came to him, and he sat down and taught them. The scribes and the Pharisees brought a woman who had been caught in adultery, and placing her in the midst they said to him, 'Teacher, this woman has been caught in the act of adultery. Now in the Law, Moses commanded us to stone such women. So what do you say?' This they said to test him, that they might have some charge to bring against him. Jesus bent down and wrote with his finger on the ground."[1]

We know very little about the woman; we know even less about the man. Scripture does not say if she was dressed. Given the Pharisees' tone, I tend to doubt it. Hefting stones like a pitcher with a baseball, they toss her into the temple, shaming her, and attempt to trap Jesus. There's a lot here. Too much for one day. Given that, I'll circle back here on day 33. "And as they continued to ask him, he stood up and said to them, 'Let him who is without sin among you be the first to throw a stone at her.' And once more he bent down and wrote on the ground."[2] As a writer, I'd love to know what He

111

wrote. Without paying them too much attention, Jesus says, "Let him who is without sin among you be the first to throw a stone at her."

This was not what they expected. It's as if Jesus stands up, brushes off His hands, and steps aside. "Alright, boys, have at her. First sinless one of you can start us off."

And notice, too, how Jesus so seamlessly draws everyone's attention away from the naked woman. We don't know what Jesus wrote, but I'd like to offer a guess. For starters, Jesus is God. The same God that met Moses on the mountain and gave the Law—writing it with His very own finger in tablets of stone: "Then Moses turned and went down from the mountain with the two tablets of the testimony in his hand, tablets that were written on both sides; on the front and on the back they were written. The tablets were the work of God, and the writing was the writing of God, engraved on the tablets."[3] Every indignant, self-righteous, puffed-up man staring at Jesus can quote these words by heart. And when He stoops to doodle, I believe they do. Roll the tape. Also, how'd they know where to find her? In the act? Makes me wonder if one or more had been with her.

Dropping their stones, they leave the woman with Jesus. I find this interaction both oddly comical and incredibly tender. Alone with the woman, Jesus said, "'Woman, where are they? Has no one condemned you?' She said, 'No one, Lord.' And Jesus said, 'Neither do I condemn you; go, and from now on sin no more.'"[4]

Look carefully at His words. Jesus doesn't sugarcoat. Doesn't compromise. Doesn't tell her that her sin is not sin. It is. He just doesn't beat her over the head with it. Doesn't shame her. And He certainly doesn't condemn her. I said it in day 3, and I'll say it again before we finish because we are a stubborn, stiff-necked people who forget: there is more mercy in Jesus than sin in us. Your sin, no matter how great, does not compare to the love of God poured out through the shed blood of His Son on the Cross of Calvary.

Let me pause. We're two weeks into this pilgrimage, and some of you need to hear this. To be reminded. This is John, describing Jesus: "And the Word became flesh and dwelt among us, and we have seen his glory, glory as of the only Son from the Father, full of grace and truth. . . . For from his fullness we have all received, grace upon grace. For the law was given through Moses; grace and truth came through Jesus Christ."[5] The Gospels of Matthew and Mark don't use the word "grace." Luke used it once. John four times. But after his fourth use, John then used the word "truth" some fifty-five times. Why? Because God bathes His truth in grace upon grace. It's the delivery system. Which Jesus offers this woman. Grace is not only the railroad track; it is the train, and only when it runs you over—grace upon grace—can you hear the truth of the Conductor. Think of it this way: when we fall, we fall on His grace; and when we stand, we stand upon the grace on which we once fell. So whether we fall or stand, we do so on His grace. How many times have I shown up at His throne of grace, fresh from some sin in thought, word, or deed, and He meets me with unmerited grace followed by sweet conviction that leads me to repentance?

I cannot count.

Back to the temple—after their trap fails, Jesus looks at the men and throws down the gauntlet regarding His identity. "Again Jesus spoke to them, saying, 'I am the light of the world. Whoever follows me will not walk in darkness, but will have the light of life.'"[6] Jesus is seconds from shining a light on their sin, and yet in their discomfort, the Pharisees miss the point entirely and raise a finger to object to Jesus testifying about Himself. "You are bearing witness about yourself; your testimony is not true."[7] Jesus shakes His head.

"I judge no one. Yet even if I do judge, my judgment is true, for it is not I alone who judge, but I and the Father who sent me."[8]A second time, they miss the point. "They said to him therefore, 'Where is your Father?' Jesus answered, 'You know neither me nor my Father. If you knew me, you would know my Father also.'"[9]

Jesus follows that zinger with this one: "So he said to them again, 'I am going away, and you will seek me, and you will die in your sin. Where I am going, you cannot come.'"[10]

This phrase "die in your sin" does not sit well. Uncomfortable with the knowledge of their own sin, the guilt they carry, and the consequences they know they deserve, the Pharisees try to flip the spotlight and ask sarcastically, "Will he kill himself, since he says, 'Where I am going, you cannot come'?"[11]

Jesus is not fazed. "He said to them, 'You are from below; I am from above. You are of this world; I am not of this world. I told you that you would die in your sins, for unless you believe that I am he you will die in your sins.'"[12]

That's three times: you are from below, and you will die in your sins. These words pierce to the depth of joint and marrow. Soul and spirit.

The Pharisees then ask Jesus, "Who are you?" but they're not asking because they want the answer. They're asking in another attempt to deflect and trap Jesus. "So Jesus said to them, 'When you have lifted up the Son of Man, then you will know that I am he, and that I do nothing on my own authority, but speak just as the Father taught me. And he who sent me is with me. He has not left me alone, for I always do the things that are pleasing to him.'"[13]

"When you have lifted up the Son of Man" is a chest-poking reference to Moses and the serpent—an event with which all of them are familiar and a further acknowledgment and indictment of their sin. But notice what happens. Not all are angered by Jesus: "As he was saying these things, many believed in him."[14]

"Many believed in."

Jesus pulls aside those who believe and speaks to their heart's cry: "If you abide in my word, you are truly my disciples, and you will know the truth, and the truth will set you free."[15]

The word "abide" means "to remain under, willingly, to stand firm," and when they do, the offer is freedom from the eternal consequences of their sin. Which they all want—and need. The Pharisees answer him, "We are offspring of Abraham and have never been enslaved to anyone. How is it that you say, 'You will become free'?"

Jesus knows otherwise. "Truly, truly, I say to you, everyone who practices sin is a slave to sin. The slave does not remain in the house forever; the son remains forever. So if the Son sets you free, you will be free indeed."[16]

There it is again, both the diagnosis and the remedy: you are all slaves of sin, captive in the kingdom of darkness, and I alone offer you freedom.

Blinded by their arrogance, they sidestep the issue and joust once more: "'Abraham is our father.' Jesus said to them, 'If you were Abraham's children, you would be doing the works Abraham did.'"[17]

What works did Abraham do? Everyone listening to the sound of Jesus' voice knows the reference. They can recite the verse from memory: "And he [Abraham] believed the Lord, and he [the Lord] counted it to him [Abraham] as righteousness."[18]

Jesus' statement exposes their problem: unbelief. He continues: "But now you seek to kill me, a man who has told you the truth that I heard from God. This is not what Abraham did. You are doing the works your father did."[19]

About here Jesus takes off the gloves and punches them in the nose: your father is not Abraham.

"They said to him, 'We were not born of sexual immorality. We have one Father—even God.' Jesus said to them, 'If God were your Father, you would love me, for I came from God and I am here. I came not of my own accord, but he sent me. Why do you not understand what I say? It is because you cannot bear to hear my word. You are of your father the devil, and your will is to do your father's desires. He was a murderer from the beginning, and does not stand in the truth, because there is no truth in him. When he lies, he speaks out of his own character, for he is a liar and the father of lies. But because I tell the truth, you do not believe me. Which one of you convicts me of sin? If I tell the truth, why do you not believe me? Whoever is of God hears the words of God. The reason why you do not hear them is that you are not of God.'"[20]

Jesus is telling the people who claim to be the most holy in Israel—you are of your father the devil and your will is to do his desire. He was a murderer. As are you. He doesn't stand in the truth. Neither do you. When he opens his mouth, he is lying. As are you. Whoever is of God, hears God; but you are not, so you don't.

Cut to the heart, these are the most soul-piercing words these people have ever heard. Feigning offense, they banter among themselves and laugh uncomfortably. *Who does this man think He is?* Having emptied their intellectual arsenal, they accuse Jesus of having a demon.

Jesus responds by telling them they're all liars, followed by: "Your father Abraham rejoiced that he would see my day. He saw it and was glad."[21]

This interaction has not gone the way they planned. In a last attempt to joust with Jesus, they say, "You are not yet fifty years old, and have you seen Abraham?"

Finally, Jesus says this: "Truly, truly, I say to you, before Abraham was, I am."[22]

The English language doesn't carry the weight of this statement as Hebrew does or would, but when spoken by Jesus, this would be the most outrageous and blasphemous word any of them had ever heard.

Unless it was true.

Having heard His claim to be God, "they picked up stones to throw at him, but Jesus hid himself and went out of the temple."[23]

WALK WITH ME BACK TO THE CROSS

Hold out your hands. Uncurl your fingers. What's that you're holding? Stones? Let them fall. Sin? Lay it down. Secrets? Confess them. Now look at His hands. See the holes? Here's the truth of you and me—our enemy likes to whisper that we are identified by our past sin. Our scars. Both in our skin and on our hearts. Our King, the One hanging here, wants you to know that from this moment in human history, you are now identified by His scars. Here's the truth of us—we are all the woman caught in adultery. We are all the self-righteous men who dragged her in. We are them, and they are us. Sinners all. And yet, despite our sin and our heart's wicked intention, Jesus meets us with grace upon grace, speaks the truth, and offers freedom. Which begs the question: Will you accept the offer?

PRAY WITH ME

King Jesus, as the truth of me becomes clearer with each day, it's getting tougher and tougher to pray. More often than not, when You shine a light inside me and convict me of my sin, my knee-jerk is to deflect or engage You in mental jousting. To give You all the reasons that can't be true, which makes me a really good Pharisee. The truth is, I'm arrogant and unwilling to look in the mirror. Unwilling to admit my pride. I'm a slave to my sin, and I'd much rather walk around in darkness than turn on a light and be forced to wrestle with the truth of me. But that's just it. I'm a slave, and until I admit the truth of me and my sin, I'm held captive.

There is only one thing on planet Earth that will set me free. It's the truth—spoken by You. Jesus, I want to abide in Your Word, so please sear it onto my soul. Write it on my heart. I read this back-and-forth with the Pharisees, and I'm seeing a lot of me in them. I'm not better. Truth is, I'm worse. And yet, it's "for freedom Christ has set us free; stand firm therefore, and do not submit again to a yoke of slavery."[24]

Lord Jesus, I want to give You my yoke of slavery. Here it is. Take it. I don't want it anymore. I am and have been a slave to that sin, and I'm done with it. Please help me stand firm in Your Word. On Your Word. Please let me walk with You—in the light. Most of the time, for much of my life, when I open my mouth, lies come out. I'm a liar. It's just the truth. I hedge and craft and deceive because I want to control both response and outcome. Which puts me on the throne of my heart and makes me god. I don't want to be that person any longer. The devil has been my father, and I hate that. I'm done with his kingdom. I'm done doing his bidding and his work. I want out. Right now. I want to do the work of My Father, which is to believe in

You. Come, please, Lord Jesus. Break this yoke off me. Free me from this other kingdom. Take me. I'm Yours. Forgive me for a lifetime of lying. Please purify my heart and my mouth, and let the truth bubble up and pour out of me.

I believe. I believe. I believe. You are who You say You are. You did what Scripture says You did. And You are doing it still. I believe there is more mercy and grace and forgiveness in You than sin in me— which, were it not true, would be inconceivable. And lastly, when You said, "Tetelestai," You weren't kidding—for which I grow more and more grateful every day. In Jesus' name.

AND GOD RESPONDS

"For I am not ashamed of the gospel, for it is the power of God for salvation to everyone who believes, to the Jew first and also to the Greek. For in it the righteousness of God is revealed from faith for faith, as it is written, 'The righteous shall live by faith.' For the wrath of God is revealed from heaven against all ungodliness and unrighteousness of men, who by their unrighteousness suppress the truth. For what can be known about God is plain to them, because God has shown it to them. For his invisible attributes, namely, his eternal power and divine nature, have been clearly perceived, ever since the creation of the world, in the things that have been made. So they are without excuse. For although they knew God, they did not honor him as God or give thanks to him, but they became futile in their thinking, and their foolish hearts were darkened. Claiming to be wise, they became fools, and exchanged the glory of the immortal God for images resembling mortal man and birds and animals and creeping things. Therefore God gave them up in the lusts of their hearts to impurity, to the dishonoring of their bodies among themselves, because they exchanged the truth about God for a lie and worshiped and served the creature rather than the Creator, who is blessed forever! Amen."[25]

DAY 16

————◆◆◆————

"Whoever finds his life will lose it."

MATTHEW 10:23–39

"As they were going away, behold, a demon-oppressed man who was mute was brought to him. And when the demon had been cast out, the mute man spoke. And the crowds marveled, saying, 'Never was anything like this seen in Israel.' But the Pharisees said, 'He casts out demons by the prince of demons.'"[1]

Prior to the arrival of Jesus, prophets healed the sick and raised the dead. Miracles occurred by the hand of God. But casting out demons is new. And the Pharisees don't like it. What occurs next is a clash of kingdoms.

"And Jesus went throughout all the cities and villages, teaching in their synagogues and proclaiming the gospel of the kingdom and healing every disease and every affliction. When he saw the crowds, he had compassion for them, because they were harassed and helpless, like sheep without a shepherd."[2]

Jesus gathers his twelve disciples and gives them authority to do as He is doing—to cast out unclean spirits and to heal every disease and sickness. Until now, they have followed and watched. After this, they will be sent to do.

Then He sends them to the lost sheep of Israel, telling them, "And proclaim as you go, saying, 'The kingdom of heaven is at hand.' Heal the sick, raise the dead, cleanse lepers, cast out demons. You received without paying; give without pay."[3]

Given the confused looks on their faces, Jesus explains: "Behold, I am sending you out as sheep in the midst of wolves, so be wise as serpents and innocent as doves."[4]

When the confusion doesn't clear, Jesus explains:

"Beware of men, for they will deliver you over to courts and flog you in their synagogues, and you will be dragged before governors and kings for my sake, to bear witness before them and the Gentiles. When they deliver you over, do not be anxious how you are to speak or what you are to say, for what you are to say will be given to you in that hour. For it is not you who speak, but the Spirit of your Father speaking through you. Brother will deliver brother over to death, and the father his child, and children will rise against parents and have them put to death, and you will be hated by all for my name's sake. But the one who endures to the end will be saved."[5]

It's a hard word. Especially the word "endure." It means "to remain under, to sustain a load of miseries."

But a harder word is coming: "When they persecute you in one town, flee to the next, for truly, I say to you, you will not have gone through all the towns of Israel before the Son of Man comes. A disciple is not above his teacher, nor a servant above his master. It is enough for the disciple to be like his teacher, and the servant like his master. If they have called the master of the house Beelzebul, how much more will they malign those of his household."[6]

Jesus then addresses the emotion they will experience as they preach, heal, raise, cleanse, and cast out:

"So have no fear of them, for nothing is covered that will not be revealed, or hidden that will not be known. What I tell you in the dark, say in the light, and what you hear whispered, proclaim on the housetops. And do not fear those who kill the body but cannot kill the soul. Rather fear him who can destroy both soul and body in hell.

"Are not two sparrows sold for a penny? And not one of them will fall to the ground apart from your Father. But even the hairs of your head are all numbered. Fear not, therefore; you are of more value than many sparrows."[7]

And right about here is where the true followers of Jesus are to be separated from those who are merely entertained by Him:

"So everyone who acknowledges me before men, I also will acknowledge before my Father who is in heaven, but whoever denies me before men, I also will deny before my Father who is in heaven."[8] The NASB says, "Everyone who confesses Me before people, I will also confess him before My Father."

Now look at the effect of Jesus' words when preached:

"Do not think that I have come to bring peace to the earth. I have not come to bring peace, but a sword. For I have come to set a man against his father, and a daughter against her mother, and a daughter-in-law against her mother-in-law. And a person's enemies will be those of his own household. Whoever loves father or mother more than me is not worthy of me, and whoever loves son or daughter more than me is not worthy of me."[9]

Some who hear will choose to believe. Some won't. Thereby dividing families.

WALK WITH ME BACK TO THE CROSS

Jesus often said hard things, which He seldom explained. Eat My flesh. Drink My blood. Confess Me and I'll acknowledge you before My Father. Don't, and I won't. And these: "And whoever does not take his cross and follow me is not worthy of me. Whoever finds his life will lose it, and whoever loses his life for my sake will find it."[10] *Worthy. Find. Lose.* Many have tried to lessen or water down the words of Jesus to make them more palatable. Easier to digest. So they don't cut as deeply and require as much. I won't. The gospel of Jesus Christ is a hard gospel. It's why people walk away. But here we are, and the blood has yet to dry. Gone is the luxury of cavalier indifference. Do you confess Him as King, or are you here to be entertained?

PRAY WITH ME

Jesus, first, I want to confess my fear of man, of what others think if I follow You and do what You command. I don't know why I fear them. You promise to be with me, and yet for some reason, I really care what others think about me, and I'm afraid they'll make fun of me or criticize me. I'm sorry. Please bolster my will. My faith.

Second, I want to confess You and Your Father before men. However that looks. In whatever way You want me to. From my knees to the rooftops, I want to declare and confess You as Lord, God, King, Savior, and only begotten Son of God. Please give me eyes to see what is demonic that needs casting out. Then give me the words to do so. I want to be faithful to do that. Please give me the eyes to see who is sick and needs healing. Then please give me the words to do so.

Last, please show me what in me needs to be nailed to the Cross. I don't want to hold on to any part of me that You want to crucify. My desire is to be obedient. To simply follow You. That's what I want to do. If You want to preach, I'll preach. You want to cleanse, I'll cleanse. You want to cast out, I'll cast out. You want to heal, I'll heal. You want to raise the dead, I'll raise the dead. Do I know what that looks like or exactly how that all pans out? No, but I'm available. I'll do what You say. I don't have to have everything figured out, because You do. The crux is, I believe You are still doing today what You did when You walked this earth because when I read the book of Acts, Your followers did what You did. And I want to follow You. All the way to the Cross, and beyond. In Jesus' name.

And God Responds

"Truly, truly, I say to you, whoever believes in me will also do the works that I do; and greater works than these will he do, because I am going to the Father. Whatever you ask in my name, this I will do, that the Father may be glorified in the Son. If you ask me anything in my name, I will do it."[11]

"I have been crucified with Christ. It is no longer I who live, but Christ who lives in me. And the life I now live in the flesh I live by faith in the Son of God, who loved me and gave himself for me."[12]

DAY 17

—◆◆◆—

"Blessed are . . ."

MATTHEW 5:1–11

"Seeing the crowds, he went up on the mountain, and when he sat down, his disciples came to him. And he opened his mouth and taught them, saying: 'Blessed are the poor in spirit, for theirs is the kingdom of heaven.'"[1]

Following His baptism, His temptation in the desert, and moving to Capernaum, Jesus calls His first disciples—Peter, Andrew, and the two sons of Zebedee, James and John—saying, "Follow me, and I will make you fishers of men,"[2] and begins His public ministry along the banks of the Sea of Galilee preaching a simple gospel: "Repent, for the kingdom of heaven is at hand."[3] As He does, the crowds grow, and Jesus begins healing every disease and affliction and casting out demons. Then He preaches the Sermon on the Mount.

But why choose these words? Why start with "blessed are"?

In the most famous sermon ever, of all the things He could have said, why gather the crowd on the side of a mountain and start with nine blessings?

Because He is talking with a cursed people, who—through generational sin passed down from their ancestors, coupled with their own sin—know they are living under the curse of the law with no remedy. No way out. While Jesus is speaking, the words of Isaiah ring in their ears: "Therefore a curse devours the earth, and its inhabitants suffer for their guilt."[4] And yet they are completely unable to remove the guilt or lift or break the curse. Each of them has been born into a world in which they are powerless against the curse of the law.

Let me clarify one thing: there is a difference between living under a curse (either from the generational sin of your ancestors or your own sin) and being condemned to hell for all eternity. The former involves the here and how. The latter the hereafter. A curse in this life does *not* equal condemnation in the next. Under the old covenant, a curse was (in a grossly oversimplified description) the unavoidable consequences of failure to obey God's law.

Condemnation (or spending eternity in hell apart from God) resulted from failure to put one's faith in God. That meant, in the old covenant, it was entirely possible for someone to live their entire life under a curse while also living in the hope and promise that they would spend eternity in the kingdom of heaven with God because they had put their faith in the Messiah to come. "These all died in faith, not having received the things promised, but having seen them and greeted them from afar, and having acknowledged that they were strangers and exiles on the earth."[5] Why was this seeming dichotomy possible? How could they live cursed on this side of the grave but saved beyond it?

Because one did not determine the other. Obedience determined blessing or curse. Faith determined salvation or condemnation. This meant the people listening to Jesus, who may have had great faith, still lived cursed lives under the curse of the law. They had no remedy.

But we do, and I'll get to that. (It was also possible to live cursed and condemned, but that seems self-explanatory.)

Also, the law is not cursed. There's no problem with the law. It's perfect.[6] It's us who are imperfect. "Cursed" is the biblical description of us who disobey the law. The question for us on this side of the Cross is, How do we obey the law?

What might a curse have looked like in their lives? According to Deuteronomy, a curse could look like addiction. Hereditary sickness. Mental illness. Infertility. Being accident-prone. Never reaching your full potential despite overqualification. Poverty. Chronic frustration and defeat in multiple areas of your life. There were many more.[7] But a simple answer might be, if it runs in the family, it could be caused by a curse.[1]

Jesus scans the crowd and knows they are wearing the yoke of the law that neither they nor their fathers have been able to bear.[8] He, on the other hand, can and will. He will obey all of the law in its entirety. Changing everything forever for everyone who believes in Him. You starting to see the connection? In starting with "blessed are," Jesus is answering one of the deepest cries of their individual and collective hearts: We are cursed with no hope of becoming uncursed. How do we get back to blessing?

Which is not all that different from Adam and Eve walking out of the garden asking, "How do we get back there?"

The problem these people have is that they know the Word of God. They know the law of Moses. And because of this, every person sitting at the feet of Jesus can't believe what they're hearing. They know that the last few chapters of Deuteronomy lay out God's

---

1. Note: just because something "runs in the family" does not mean it is caused by a curse. But it might be.

blessings resulting from obedience to the law and God's curses resulting from disobedience. They also know that throughout the entirety of the law and prophets, God promises four times, including His covenantal name in Exodus 34,[9] to pass down the sin of the fathers to the children to the third and fourth generation.[10] And ten generations for sexual sin. This means there's no escaping it. Every single person staring at Jesus is living under the inescapable consequences that generational curses have passed down to them before they even opened their eyes on planet Earth.

Simply put, follow the law perfectly, every day, for the rest of your life, and you will live a blessed life on this earth. Don't obey, and curse follows. Your choice. Ready? Break.

But since not one single human ever (save Jesus) can last more than about five minutes without sinning, curse followed everyone. The specifics of the curses are outlined in Deuteronomy, but in short, when we disobey the law we are cursed to die apart from God. Cursed in our bodies. Cursed in our homes. Cursed in our careers. Cursed in our relationships. Cursed in our hopes and dreams. We are cursed in every conceivable way, with no hope of stepping out from under that curse. Ever.[11]

How do we know?

Here's Paul describing this condition: "For all who rely on works of the law are under a curse; for it is written, 'Cursed be everyone who does not abide by all things written in the Book of the Law, and do them.'"[12]

The people sitting at the feet of Jesus know—beyond any doubt—that they are cursed because they do not and have not, nor have their ancestors, abided by the book of the law. This makes the words of Jesus strangely hopeful and oddly impossible.

These people have suffered, do suffer, and will continue to suffer the consequences of ancestral sin. Not only that, they also know that God, through the prophet Malachi, commands His people to remember the law of Moses. The statutes and the rules. All of them. Further, through Malachi, God promises to send one like Elijah to return the hearts of the fathers to the children and the hearts of the children to the fathers, and if the people don't return and are not restored, and if they don't obey His law, He will smite the earth with a curse that will "overtake" and devour them.[13] And all of this is promised under God's stated eternal nature, which is: "For I the Lord do not change."[14]

God's last word, before He closes out the age of the law and prophets, is to promise a curse for disobedience. This means every single person born under the law is cursed—devoured, defiled, and desolate.[15] There's no getting around this. Not for anyone.

Then Jesus stands on the side of a mount, a small, ordinary hill, and promises blessing.

"Blessed are the poor in spirit, for theirs is the kingdom of heaven.

"Blessed are those who mourn, for they shall be comforted.

"Blessed are the meek, for they shall inherit the earth.

"Blessed are those who hunger and thirst for righteousness, for they shall be satisfied.

"Blessed are the merciful, for they shall receive mercy.

"Blessed are the pure in heart, for they shall see God.

"Blessed are the peacemakers, for they shall be called sons of God.

"Blessed are those who are persecuted for righteousness' sake, for theirs is the kingdom of heaven.

"Blessed are you when others revile you and persecute you and utter all kinds of evil against you falsely on my account. Rejoice and be glad, for your reward is great in heaven, for so they persecuted the prophets who were before you."[16]

This is mind-blowing. How is this possible?

The men, women, and children sitting at the feet of Jesus are scratching their heads wondering, *What?! Who is this guy? Doesn't He know the law?* Some even laugh; it seems too good to be true. Living under the curse of the law was like swimming with weights. No one escaped it.

Until now.

Jesus finishes His sermon and then walks down the mountain, where He cleanses a leper, heals the centurion's paralyzed servant, heals Peter's mother-in-law who is sick with a fever; and by evening, word of signs and wonders has spread, and the place is packed with the infirm. They "brought to him many who were oppressed by demons, and he cast out the spirits with a word and healed all who were sick."[17] He then climbs into a boat, calms a storm, and delivers the demon-possessed man coming out of the tombs in the Gadarenes, sending the demons into a herd of pigs. Then, climbing back into the boat, He crosses back over the Sea of Galilee and returns to Capernaum where He heals the paralytic lowered down through the roof by saying, "Take heart, my son; your sins are forgiven."[18]

The man is paralyzed. So why does Jesus forgive the man's sin? Why not just heal him? Because He knows sin is the cause of his paralysis, and the reason for it lies in Deuteronomy chapter 28. The disciples know this too. This is why in John 9, as they pass by the man born blind at birth, the disciples ask, "Rabbi, who sinned, this man or his parents?"[19] To those listening to Jesus on the mount, it was a given that physical infirmity and sickness were the cursed result of sin.

As they follow Jesus, the disciples' heads are on a swivel. The miraculous is coming at them faster than they can process. They have no box for this. The kingdom of heaven has come, and they are staring at Him. And as they do, every single one of them is wondering if He has the power and the authority to do something about the curse of the law. The curse under which they live. Because they don't. Never have.

Back to that mount: "Blessed are . . ." And the moment He says this, hope sparks in every heart. What if there's a way out? A remedy? What if I don't have to live the rest of my life on this earth cursed? What if this is the Christ who can redeem me from the curse and lift this yoke off my shoulders? What if I can pass from curse to blessing?

Contrary to popular teaching, Jesus did not come to abolish the law but fulfill it. This means that His death doesn't nullify the law in our lives and that the righteous requirement of the law still stands. In other words, we are still responsible for obeying the law. All of it. Earlier, I asked how we, on this side of the Cross, obey the law. The answer is almost inconceivable were it not true.

God in His mercy sent Jesus to die on our behalf so that when He declares "it is finished," He has actually changed—forever—the way we relate to the law and how we obey it. Now we obey the law *through His obedience.* When we believe that Jesus is the only begotten Son of God who died in our place and His death counts on our behalf, satisfying the wrath of God, we get credit for His obedience. His righteousness. This means His sinless life is credited to our account, and we can live blessed lives here in this life. Don't miss this: when we *pisteuo* in Jesus, we obey the entirety of the law through the sinless life of Jesus—who obeyed for us when we could not and can't. Because of this, we can pass from curse to blessing. Right here. Right now. How? The same way we pass from death to life. Repentance. Both for our and our ancestors' sins.

Walk with Me Back to the Cross

Why does He look so mangled? So unrecognizable as a man?[20] So tormented and disfigured? Why do all His bones look out of joint? Because He who had never sinned is now cursed, bearing the curse of all mankind. For all time. So that you and I are not and don't have to be. On this Cross, "Christ redeemed us from the curse of the law by becoming a curse for us—for it is written, 'Cursed is everyone who is hanged on a tree.'"[21] And "For our sake he made him to be sin who knew no sin, so that in him we might become the righteousness of God."[22] Here on this tree, Jesus took on Himself every curse due to us, and in exchange, He gave us every blessing due to Him. As He pushes up on His nail-pierced feet and gravity tears the flesh at the holes in His wrists, He is the curse-breaking Messiah, pouring out blessing.

Pray with Me

Jesus, there's just more going on here than I ever thought possible. On the Cross, You took on Yourself every curse of mankind brought about through generational or individual sin. And from the Cross, You offer blessing in exchange. But while it is God's desire that none should perish, there's a condition. Repentance. Where there is repentance, there is forgiveness—and the breaking of the curse. Where there is no repentance, there is no forgiveness, and the curse remains.[2]

Lord Jesus, I want to repent for all of my sins—every thought, word, or deed, known and unknown—and I repent for all my ancestors'

---

2. There is a difference between the curse of the law and the curse of the fall. We will not escape the curse of death until Jesus returns. But fear not. We will. When He does return.

sins—known and unknown. Especially any sin in which any ancestor of mine bowed down to any god other than You. I'm so sorry, and I humbly repent. Please forgive us. I thank You that on the Cross You took every curse due to me and gave me every blessing due to You. Please show me, by the power of Your Holy Spirit, any place in my life where I am subject to a generational curse that might require specific repentance. I am willing. Please show me. Until then, please accept my blanket repentance for all of it.

Now, Lord, having confessed, I receive Your forgiveness. I hear You saying, "Your sins are forgiven you." And I receive it. And in the name of Jesus, and with, by, and through the blood of Jesus, I break every generational curse that has had or might have had influence or attachment in my and/or my family's life. Because of Your blood, I break every curse over my life, my husband's/wife's life, our children's lives, and our children's children's lives and their children. Forever. I plead the warm, red, living blood of Jesus over us, which cleanses us from all sin.[23] And I accept from You every blessing You offer in exchange.

When I sit back, this is difficult for me to fathom. What kind of King does this? What kind of mercy is this? What kind of grace poured out? Having now been convicted by the level and depth of my own sin, it is inconceivable to me that You would make such an offer, but You did, and because of that, I receive it with deep gratitude. Jesus, You told us that by our words we will be justified,[24] so I speak in agreement with Your Word, and I declare: I am dead to sin,[25] that sin shall not have dominion over me, for I am not under law but under grace,[26] that I have become dead to the law through the body of Christ,[27] that I have been delivered from the law having died to what we were held by,[28] that the law of the Spirit of life in Christ Jesus has made me free from the law of sin and death,[29] and that Christ is the end of the law for righteousness to everyone who believes. In Jesus' name.

AND GOD RESPONDS

"There is therefore now no condemnation for those who are in Christ Jesus. For the law of the Spirit of life has set you free in Christ Jesus from the law of sin and death. For God has done what the law, weakened by the flesh, could not do. By sending his own Son in the likeness of sinful flesh and for sin, he condemned sin in the flesh, in order that the righteous requirement of the law might be fulfilled in us, who walk not according to the flesh but according to the Spirit."[30]

DAY 18

"She is a sinner."

LUKE 7:36–50

"One of the Pharisees asked him to eat with him, and he went into the Pharisee's house and reclined at table. And behold, a woman of the city, who was a sinner, when she learned that he was reclining at table in the Pharisee's house, brought an alabaster flask of ointment, and standing behind him at his feet, weeping, she began to wet his feet with her tears and wiped them with the hair of her head and kissed his feet and anointed them with the ointment."[1]

As Jesus eats dinner with the religious elite, a prostitute enters, stands behind Him, then breaks open an expensive bottle of perfume and bathes Jesus' feet with both tears and ointment, wiping them with her hair and kissing His feet. Given her occupation, the

---

1. Luke 7:36–38. It has been suggested that this unnamed woman in Luke 7 is Mary Magdalene mentioned in Matthew 26, Mark 14, and John 12. I don't think so. I believe they are two different women. The first difference is that Luke 7 occurs in Galilee, while the other three take place in Bethany, which is near Jerusalem. Also, in Luke, Jesus speaks of her forgiveness. In the other three, Jesus speaks of how she has anointed Him for His burial and she will be remembered wherever the gospel is proclaimed. In sum, Luke 7 occurs at a different time, in a different place, with a different woman, whose critics say differing things, and which brings about a different response from Jesus.

ointment may well have been used as a necessity of her trade, to disguise the previous customer from the next. Meaning, the smell would have identified her.

"Now when the Pharisee who had invited him saw this, he said to himself, 'If this man were a prophet, he would have known who and what sort of woman this is who is touching him, for she is a sinner.'"[1]

The word "sinner" in Greek is *hamartolos*. To help us understand it, English translators used a twelfth-century archery term meaning "to miss the mark." By default, it also means "to not win the prize." The Pharisees' statement, "if this man were a prophet," suggests that Jesus must not be a true prophet since He let the woman touch His feet.

Jesus knows this.

"And Jesus answering said to him, 'Simon, I have something to say to you.' And he answered, 'Say it, Teacher.' 'A certain moneylender had two debtors. One owed five hundred denarii, and the other fifty. When they could not pay, he cancelled the debt of both. Now which of them will love him more?' Simon answered, 'The one, I suppose, for whom he cancelled the larger debt.' And he said to him, 'You have judged rightly.'"[2]

As He speaks to Simon, the woman is still weeping, kissing His feet and wiping them with her hair.

"Then turning toward the woman he said to Simon, 'Do you see this woman? I entered your house; you gave me no water for my feet, but she has wet my feet with her tears and wiped them with her hair. You gave me no kiss, but from the time I came in she has not ceased to kiss my feet. You did not anoint my head with oil, but she has anointed my feet with ointment.'"[3]

All three actions by the woman were first-century signs of hospitality not afforded Jesus by Simon. And in the Old Testament, incense or ointment that emitted a beautiful fragrance represented worship.

"Therefore I tell you, her sins, which are many, are forgiven—for she loved much."

"For she loved much" describes the result of her forgiveness. It's the present condition of her heart being poured out at the feet of Jesus. It does not describe the many sexual sins that caused her to be publicly labeled a sinner.

"'But he who is forgiven little, loves little.' And he said to her, 'Your sins are forgiven.'"[4]

By including this, Luke established the fact that Jesus—as the Son of God—has the right and power to forgive sins. He is also answering the question before it is asked by the doubters at the table, "Who is this man?"

"Then those who were at table with him began to say among themselves, 'Who is this, who even forgives sins?'"

And once again the Pharisees hate Him for claiming—by His actions—to be the Son of God. Which He is.

"And he said to the woman, 'Your faith has saved you; go in peace.'"[5]

Four things: First, the woman's sin was great. She probably had many partners and had been used by many over a long period of time. She was covered in shame. It's why she entered and stood behind Jesus. She couldn't look Him in the face. Therefore, to her, forgiveness and salvation seemed impossible. It is probable, given her tearful expression to Jesus on her knees, that she had long wondered, *Who could forgive so great a sin?*

Second, her faith. Jesus recognized her faith in the same way He does the centurion's and the thief's on the Cross. Faith that declares either by word or deed that Jesus is who He says He is: the Son of God, the Savior of the world.

Third, the fragrance filled the room. Wafted outside. This, along with her posture of kneeling at the feet of Jesus, exemplified worship. A stark contrast to those around her as she was the only one in the room to do so.

Fourth, Jesus answered not only the first cry of her heart, which was her need for forgiveness, but also the second cry—peace—which she'd not known in a long time. Her tears and the fact that she used her hair suggest torment and a feeling of total and complete unworthiness. It's probable she had long used her hair to attract customers. Here she used it to wash dirt and manure off the sandaled feet of Jesus.

Walk with Me Back to the Cross

Maybe you thought we covered this yesterday. In my experience with sexual sin, it's rarely one and done. The shame is too deep. So let me poke the wound. Have you committed sexual sin? Had many partners? Do you carry the shame of that sin? Secrets? Skeletons in the basement? A child you've never admitted? An abortion? Two? A raging porn addiction? When you think back, do you shudder and want to close your eyes? Wish you could forget? Is the shame crushing? Let me encourage you—no, let me entreat you. We're all in this together. *All* have strayed. *All* gone our own way. *All* are dead in our sin. When the billions of us on planet Earth approach this Cross of grace, the only thing we bring is our sin. Not some good work, not some worthiness that allows us to jockey for position. Right here we are all equal. Equally dead. The only thing we bring to this exchange is the sin that causes us to need this Cross. So hold it up. Offer it. "Jesus, this is what I'm ashamed and afraid to show You. This is the truth of me I don't want You or anyone else to know." Now lay it down. And leave it. Today, right this very second, shame dies. Crucified. Nailed to this undefeated tree.

One more thing—before you leave, just sit and listen. Let the fragrance fill the room. He's whispering now. What is He saying? "Your faith has saved you; go in peace. I am making all things new."

Pray with Me

Lord Jesus, here. Take it. I don't want this anymore. My sin is crushing me. The memories are tormenting me. I'm a sinner. I've not only missed the mark; I've missed the entire target. You know the enormity of my sin. All of it. None of it is hidden from You. You know all the details. Every last one. I'm so sorry I've used what You meant for purity and joy with my spouse for something else. You know how I've not treated my body or my mind as the temple of the Holy Spirit. I repent of all my sexual sin. In all its ugliness, I give it to You.

I come to You now like this magnificent woman. I bring my shame and all my sin and all my unworthiness, and I bow before You. Laid bare. I pour out my worship upon You. I take what I once used to attract and disguise lust of all kinds, and I offer it up as worship to You. Paul said we are the fragrance of Christ. Please let me be that. Now. Here. Let my worship rise to Your throne—a sweet aroma. Wash me thoroughly from my sin. Your Word promises that Your blood cleanses us from all sin, so please cleanse me. Completely.

And I pray You bless those with whom I've sinned, whether with my body or with my mind, and I ask that You and they would forgive me. Please return the parts of their souls to them that I took. And please return to me the parts of my soul that they took. Please make us whole as You intended. Please cut me free now from all tethers to anyone outside of the covenant of my marriage (whether present or future).

Also, Lord, I pray for my husband/wife. That You would heal and restore our relationship where it has been hurt by my sin. Please return to us the joy You intended. Jesus, in obedience with Your Word, I bring to You all this ugly stuff and unload it at Your feet, and in exchange, I receive forgiveness, purity, Your righteousness, and Your acceptance before the Father. Your Word promises me that You will appear at the end of the ages to put away sin by the sacrifice of Yourself.⁶ And when You had offered for all time a single sacrifice for sins, You sat down at the right hand of God, waiting from that time until Your enemies should be made a footstool for Your feet. For by a single offering You have perfected for all time those who are being sanctified.⁷ Jesus, I thank You that You have put away my sin and that by, and through, Your shed blood, I have been perfected and am being sanctified. In Jesus' name.

And God Responds

"Your sins are forgiven. Go in peace."

"Therefore, if anyone is in Christ, he is a new creation. The old has passed away; behold, the new has come. All this is from God, who through Christ reconciled us to himself and gave us the ministry of reconciliation; that is, in Christ God was reconciling the world to himself, not counting their trespasses against them, and entrusting to us the message of reconciliation. Therefore, we are ambassadors for Christ, God making his appeal through us. We implore you on behalf of Christ, be reconciled to God. For our sake he made him to be sin who knew no sin, so that in him we might become the righteousness of God."[8]

"But now in Christ Jesus you who once were far off have been brought near by the blood of Christ. For he himself is our peace, who has made us both one and has broken down in his flesh the dividing wall of hostility by abolishing the law of commandments expressed in ordinances, that he might create in himself one new man in place of the two, so making peace, and might reconcile us both to God in one body through the cross, thereby killing the hostility."[9]

DAY 19

―――――◆‧◆‧◆―――――

"I will . . ."

MATTHEW 8:1–4

"When he came down from the mountain, great crowds followed him. And behold, a leper came to him and knelt before him, saying, 'Lord, if you will, you can make me clean.' And Jesus stretched out his hand and touched him, saying, 'I will; be clean.' And immediately his leprosy was cleansed. And Jesus said to him, 'See that you say nothing to anyone, but go, show yourself to the priest and offer the gift that Moses commanded, for a proof to them.'"[1]

Lepers were not allowed near other people. Not allowed inside the temple. They had no communication with the priest and, hence, no access to God. No mediator. He or she was an outcast. Disqualified. Forbidden to touch another human. Save other lepers. Leprosy was an agonizing existence and a social death sentence. Lepers were the walking dead. In Leviticus, the law of Moses, two entire chapters are devoted to leprosy and the requirements placed on those afflicted with it. Lepers were publicly and permanently declared "unclean," and anyone who touched them or touched anything they touched was unclean for seven days. Given this, people kept their distance.

The leper here in Matthew 8 is at the end of himself. But he's heard the stories. So he picks his way through the crowd, risks being shunned further, and kneels. First he makes a proclamation, "Lord." Then he utters a cry of desperation. "You can make me clean." Jesus is his last hope.

Jesus doesn't recoil at his condition. Doesn't turn up His nose. Doesn't keep His distance. In fact, He crosses the distance and does the unimaginable. He stretches out His hand and touches the man. "I will; be clean."

And the man is made clean. Forever.

Walk with Me Back to the Cross

When Jesus said, "'I will,'" He was speaking in the present tense. He was willing in that moment to make the man clean. He was also speaking in the future tense. His will here and now on this Cross. Jesus was declaring that, then and throughout all eternity, He was and is taking that man's leprosy and all the leprosy of all mankind, and in exchange He grants inescapable, undeniable, unerasable purity to those who would receive it.

And the offer still stands.

So hold out your hands. What about you feels unclean? Dirty? Ingrained into your soul? What about you has kept you on the outside? Disqualified? Now, let's take that dirty bird's nest of a memory and offer it up. Scars, sounds, feelings. All of it. And let's give it to the King on the throne who humbled Himself to take your and my place on this Cross. It's okay. He's willing. He's not ashamed of you, and you're not a burden. You can be clean. And you can come back tomorrow.

No matter your condition, Jesus looks at you, and His response is "I will."

Pray with Me

King Jesus, I'm back. It's me. I want to speak Your Word back to You. It's my foundation. "When evening came, they brought to Him many who were demon-possessed; and He cast out the spirits with a word, and healed all who were ill. This happened so that what was spoken through Isaiah the prophet would be fulfilled: 'He Himself took our illnesses and carried away our diseases.'"[2] *Jesus, You did it then; You are doing it now. And when You said, "Tetelestai," You weren't kidding. My sin is finished. No matter how I feel. Nailed to this Cross and I'm leaving all this ugly stuff right here. In and by and through Your mercy, You hang there and offer to take from me the worst I have produced. And when I give it to You, You in Your unimaginable mercy give me Your purity. You wash me white as snow. You cleanse me. Such knowledge is too wonderful for me, but nevertheless, I receive it. The psalmist said,* "Be gracious to me, O Lord! See my affliction from those who hate me, O you who lift me up from the gates of death."[3] *For You have not despised or abhorred the affliction of the afflicted, and You have not hidden Your face from me but have heard when I cried to You.*[4] "Consider my affliction and my trouble, and forgive all my sins."[5] "I will rejoice and be glad in your steadfast love, because you have seen my affliction; you have known the distress of my soul."[6] "Many are the afflictions of the righteous, but the Lord delivers him out of them all."[7] *In Jesus' name.*

AND GOD RESPONDS

"Already you are clean because of the word that I have spoken to you."[8]

"For in him all the fullness of God was pleased to dwell, and through him to reconcile to himself all things, whether on earth or in heaven, making peace by the blood of his cross. And you, who once were alienated and hostile in mind, doing evil deeds, he has now reconciled in his body of flesh by his death, in order to present you holy and blameless and above reproach before him."[9]

DAY 20

"What shall I do to inherit eternal life?"

LUKE 10:25

"And behold, a lawyer stood up to put him to the test, saying, 'Teacher, what shall I do to inherit eternal life?'"

Notice the pronoun: *I.*

Jesus said to him, "'What is written in the Law? How do you read it?' And he answered, 'You shall love the Lord your God with all your heart and with all your soul and with all your strength and with all your mind, and your neighbor as yourself.' And he said to him, 'You have answered correctly; do this, and you will live.'"[1]

While this is our nature, it is impossible.

"But he, desiring to justify himself, said to Jesus, 'And who is my neighbor?' Jesus replied, 'A man was going down from Jerusalem to Jericho, and he fell among robbers, who stripped him and beat him and departed, leaving him half dead. Now by chance a priest was going down that road, and when he saw him he passed by on the other side. So likewise a Levite, when he came to the place and saw him, passed by on the other side. But a Samaritan, as he journeyed, came to where he was, and when he saw him, he had compassion. He went to him and bound up his wounds, pouring on oil and wine.

Then he set him on his own animal and brought him to an inn and took care of him. And the next day he took out two denarii and gave them to the innkeeper, saying, "Take care of him, and whatever more you spend, I will repay you when I come back." Which of these three, do you think, proved to be a neighbor to the man who fell among the robbers?' He said, 'The one who showed him mercy.' And Jesus said to him, 'You go, and do likewise.'"[2]

Now jump forward to Luke 18:

"And a ruler asked him, 'Good Teacher, what must I do to inherit eternal life?'"[3]

Again, notice the pronoun—*I*. Also notice, like the first ruler, he doesn't ask, "What must I do to be saved?" Or "What must I do to follow you?" He wants eternal life on his terms.

"And Jesus said to him, 'Why do you call me good? No one is good except God alone. You know the commandments: "Do not commit adultery, Do not murder, Do not steal, Do not bear false witness, Honor your father and mother.'"

"And he said, 'All these I have kept from my youth.'"

Again, notice the pronoun—*I*. Also notice the assumption: "I have justified me."

"When Jesus heard this, he said to him, 'One thing you still lack. Sell all that you have and distribute to the poor, and you will have treasure in heaven; and come, follow me.' But when he heard these things, he became very sad, for he was extremely rich."[4]

The rich man's reaction shows he lied. He loved his riches more than God, proving he kept neither the first nor the tenth commandment. And he wasn't interested in following Jesus. He was asking how to live forever on terms he manages and controls, suggesting the basis of his question was fear coupled with arrogance wallowing in the soup of self-justification.

"Jesus, seeing that he had become sad, said, 'How difficult it is for those who have wealth to enter the kingdom of God! For it is easier for a camel to go through the eye of a needle than for a rich person to enter the kingdom of God.'"[5]

The problem was not the man's wealth but his attachment to it and his belief that his works, like his wealth, justified him and granted him right of access to eternal life. His response suggests he believed he was entitled to it.

"Those who heard it said, 'Then who can be saved?' But he said, 'What is impossible with man is possible with God.'"[6]

Jesus' response is akin to: "You can't. It's on Me."

We should write that down.

Years later, another rich young ruler named Saul comes along. He wrote, "If anyone else thinks he has reason for confidence in the flesh, I have more: circumcised on the eighth day, of the people of Israel, of the tribe of Benjamin, a Hebrew of Hebrews; as to the law, a Pharisee; as to zeal, a persecutor of the church; as to righteousness under the law, blameless."[7]

And then he encounters Jesus.

And when he sees Jesus rightly, for who He is, high and lifted up as resurrected King of all kings, Saul's posture changes. He sees himself in relation to Jesus, and the difference is heartbreaking. Arrogance erased, he can't stand before Jesus. And Saul, who becomes Paul, asks the right question: "Wretched man that I am! Who will deliver me from this body of death?"[8]

Paul then declares: "But whatever gain I had, I counted as loss for the sake of Christ. Indeed, I count everything as loss because of the surpassing worth of knowing Christ Jesus my Lord. For his sake I have suffered the loss of all things and count them as rubbish, in order that I may gain Christ."[9]

There's a popular lie today that we, as people, are good—or have some level of goodness. That some of us are better than others. We're not. None of us are good. All we like sheep have gone astray. All of us are dead in our sins. Some of us may act out of that condition less often, but to make that point is simply to argue our level or percentage of deadness—that I'm somehow less dead than you.

The autopsy shows we're all dead.

WALK WITH ME BACK TO THE CROSS

You and I come to Jesus like the two rulers just discussed. Morally and spiritually bankrupt. We bring nothing to this Cross other than our deep-rooted arrogance and our entitled notions. Filled with "I." The truth of the gospel of Jesus Christ is this: It is impossible for man to save himself. For us to justify us. If we could, there'd be no reason for the Cross. And God sacrificed His only Son in vain. You and I can't do one single thing to earn or inherit eternal life. So how are we justified? Look again. Go on. Look closely. We are blood-bought, blood-washed, and blood-redeemed. And what is impossible for us was and is made possible right here.

PRAY WITH ME

King Jesus, I know that, too often, I come to You like these young rulers. Arrogant, entitled, and proud of my self-justifying works. This picture of me is just gross, and I'm so sorry. I humbly repent. To be justified before You means to stand before You just-as-if-I'd-never-sinned. And the only way that happens is for You, Jesus, to stand in my place. My justification, my right of access to Your very presence, is a blood-bought grace-gift from God. I bring nothing to the table other than a heart surrendered to You. And You in Your mercy gave me that heart in the first place.

Jesus, I know I'm spiritually bankrupt. Every time I look up at You, I'm more and more convinced. By the time these forty days are over, I won't even be able to lift my head. But here and now, looking at You and Your Word, I know that You and You alone justified me. You stood in my place, and in so doing, washed me white as snow so that when You bring me to Your and my Father, I will stand there as if I had never sinned. I'm justified. Not because of anything I've done but because of what You did on that dark Friday afternoon.

I know that when You died, the veil in the temple, the thick curtain that separated the very presence of God from man, was torn in two. From top to bottom. That's because You tore it. To get to us. You did it. Not us. You came to us on a rescue mission and did what we could not do and never would do. I know gratitude is not gratitude until it's expressed. So, Lord Jesus, please know that all I have are these words. Please accept them. I am so grateful. Thank You for doing what I could not do and for standing in my place. For justifying me. Thank You for the blood-bought grace-gift of Your mercy. When I was the traveler on the road, wounded, bleeding out, unable to care for myself, You stopped, picked me up, and carried me. Jesus, I thank You that You alone made the impossible possible. In Jesus' name.

AND GOD RESPONDS

"For by grace you have been saved through faith. And this is not your own doing; it is the gift of God, not a result of works, so that no one may boast. For we are his workmanship, created in Christ Jesus for good works, which God prepared beforehand, that we should walk in them."[10]

PART THREE

But Why
Jesus'
Blood?

DAY 21

"If you believed Moses, you would believe me."

JOHN 5:46

"This was why the Jews were seeking all the more to kill him, because not only was he breaking the Sabbath, but he was even calling God his own Father, making himself equal with God."[1]

Until now, the self-righteous religious elite have been persecuting Jesus because He healed on the Sabbath. But that changes at a feast in Jerusalem. In John 5, Jesus turns a corner in His message. And in so doing, He throws down the gauntlet. Draws a line in the sand. He uses the term "Father" when talking to or about God Most High. And He doesn't just say it once; He says it over 165 times in the Gospels. And over 100 times in John alone. To the religious elite, this is browbeating. Fingernails on the chalkboard. And they hate Him for it.

Calling God "Father" is the signature of the Son and sets Jesus apart from every prophet or want-to-be Messiah. It is the strongest of claims, and I doubt there is anything Jesus could say that would irritate and inflame them more.

But Jesus is not worried about their threats. He's trying to get their attention. His repetitive use of the word "Father" is akin to a man standing on a rooftop and shouting at the top of his lungs.

"So Jesus said to them, 'Truly, truly, I say to you, the Son can do nothing of his own accord, but only what he sees the Father doing. For whatever the Father does, that the Son does likewise. For the Father loves the Son and shows him all that he himself is doing.'"

He's saying, "Not only am I His Son, but we talk. We are in constant communication because we are One." We talked about this at greater length in day 15.

"And greater works than these will he show him, so that you may marvel. For as the Father raises the dead and gives them life, so also the Son gives life to whom he will."[2]

Salvation starts with the Father and continues with and through the Son. It's the reason for the rescue mission. Jesus will say this again in John 10:10: "I came that they may have life and have it abundantly."

He continues in John 5, "For the Father judges no one, but has given all judgment to the Son, that all may honor the Son, just as they honor the Father. Whoever does not honor the Son does not honor the Father who sent him. Truly, truly, I say to you, whoever hears my word and believes him who sent me has eternal life. He does not come into judgment, but has passed from death to life."[3]

This is the key: hear and believe.

And it has always been the key. When Moses first spoke to the nation of Israel in Egypt, "they did not listen to Moses, because of their broken spirit and harsh slavery."[4] During the deliverance from Egypt, God commanded, "If you will diligently listen to the voice of the LORD your God, and do that which is right in his eyes, and give ear to his commandments and keep all his statutes . . ."[5] But they didn't. And after the exodus, "it shall come about, if you listen obediently to my commandments which I am commanding you today, to love the Lord your God and to serve Him with all your heart and all your soul."[6] But they didn't.

Then in Deuteronomy 18, Moses says this: "The LORD your God will raise up for you a prophet like me from among you, from your brothers—it is to him you shall listen."[7] Jesus is that One, and He is currently speaking to the descendants of those very people. Moses continues, "And whoever will not listen to my words that he shall speak in my name, I myself will require it of him."[8] The religious elite listening to Jesus know well these words of Moses. Most can recite them from memory. They also know that throughout their history, the commandment from God has been to listen and to do. To listen and obey. And they also know neither they nor their forefathers have done this. They would also have known the words of Moses' successor, Joshua: "The men of war who came out of Egypt, perished, because they did not obey the voice of the LORD."[9] Incidentally, Jesus' Hebrew name is Yeshua, which is actually closer to Joshua.

Jesus continues, "Truly, truly, I say to you, an hour is coming, and is now here, when the dead will hear the voice of the Son of God, and those who hear will live. For as the Father has life in himself, so he has granted the Son also to have life in himself. And he has given him authority to execute judgment, because he is the Son of Man."[10]

The hour is here. Jesus is saying, "I am God's Son, and I will judge you. If you hear and believe, you pass from death to life. But you, like your ancestors, are not hearing Me. Hence, you're all dead in your sin."

Then Jesus contrasts them to Himself: "I can do nothing on my own. As I hear, I judge, and my judgment is just, because I seek not my own will but the will of him who sent me."[11]

Jesus is saying, "Unlike you, I listen to my Father, and based on what He says, I judge and I judge justly. You, on the other hand, seek your own agendas and judge unjustly. As you've judged me." He then goes on to list how John the Baptist and even God Himself—whose voice rolled back the clouds and echoed from heaven—testified as to His authenticity, and yet the people still won't listen.

Then Jesus pierces them with this: "And you do not have his word abiding in you, for you do not believe the one whom he has sent. You search the Scriptures because you think that in them you have eternal life; and it is they that bear witness about me, yet you refuse to come to me that you may have life. I do not receive glory from people. But I know that you do not have the love of God within you."[12]

This is a scathing indictment. "You do not have his word." "You refuse to come." "You do not have the love of God within you." He is speaking to men who literally have small Torah scrolls rolled up in tiny boxes tied around their foreheads.

"I have come in my Father's name, and you do not receive me. If another comes in his own name, you will receive him. How can you believe, when you receive glory from one another and do not seek the glory that comes from the only God?"[13]

You're arrogant and blind, puffing one another up. You are missing the forest for the trees. But of all His words, these might pierce the most: "Do not think that I will accuse you to the Father. There is one who accuses you: Moses, on whom you have set your hope. For if you believed Moses, you would believe me; for he wrote of me. But if you do not believe his writings, how will you believe my words?"[14]

The One greater than Moses is standing before them. "If you believed Moses, you would believe me," is akin to telling them they're hypocrites. But watch what Jesus does: He goes to the other side of the Sea of Galilee, and a large crowd follows because of the signs He has performed with the sick. Remember, these people are slaves to sin. No different from the Israelites who exited Egypt, having witnessed so great a deliverance through signs and wonders, and were hungry in the desert. So Jesus accepts a boy's five barley loaves and two fish and feeds over five thousand men and their families. Maybe twenty-five thousand people. Then His disciples gather up twelve baskets of leftovers. Sitting on the mountain, their bellies full, the people make the connection. Just as Moses fed the people in the wilderness with manna, the greater Moses is here. "This is indeed the Prophet who is to come into the world!"[15] Where the religious elite missed it and Him, the common people did not.

WALK WITH ME BACK TO THE CROSS

If we're honest, their problem is our problem. In our arrogance, our stubbornness, in our "I got this" mentality, we don't listen and obey. Truth is, we don't got this. Never have. After the exodus, Moses gathered the people and commanded: "Hear, O Israel: The Lord our God, the Lord is one. You shall love the Lord your God with all your heart and with all your soul and with all your might. And these words that I command you today shall be on your heart."[16] It's called the Shema, it's the greatest commandment, and it starts with the word "hear." It can also be translated "listen, listening." Or, listen with both your ears and your heart—and then obey. What would it look like for you, today, right here, not to be offended by the words of Jesus but to listen with both your ears and your heart? And then do what He says?

PRAY WITH ME

Jesus, this is my problem: I am no different from the slaves who walked out of Egypt or the Pharisees who disregarded Jesus' direct words. I don't listen. Not really. Most of the time, I give lip service. I want what You offer, I want You to fill my belly; I just don't really want to obey You beyond that. Standing here at Your Cross, listening to the echo of Your words—"Deny yourself, pick up your cross daily, and follow Me"—this is the hard part. Doing what You say. Crucifying my flesh. I read this story of these uppity religious people who were putting on a great show, but inwardly they were empty. Just shells. Jesus, I don't like when I see that in me, and I don't want to be that way. And I'm sorry. I repent. Please forgive me. I know I don't listen and obey, but I want to.

I feel like Paul in Romans 7. I do the thing I don't want to do, and I don't do the thing I want to do. O wretched human that I am. Who will deliver me from this? Jesus, I need You more than ever. You're the only One who can deliver me. This listen-and-do thing, this obedience thing, has always been my problem. It's my problem today. And it's going to be my problem tomorrow. But here's what I know that I know. I know that You are who You say You are and the death You died counted for me. You took my place. And You did it knowing full well that this is my problem. You've always known. My disobedience is rooted in my rebellion and the fact that I put me before You. Constantly. I know this is gross sin, but I'm confessing it, and I also know I'm not telling You anything You don't already know. You know it full well.

And yet, somehow, You love me. You love me even when I'm not listening and obeying. Jesus, please forgive me, and please know that I am so grateful that even when I was dead in my sin, You died for me. Yours is an inconceivable kind of love. Were it not true, were it not on display for all the world to see, it would be unimaginable. But I can imagine it. Because of the Cross. Jesus, for the record, and one more time, I believe You are the Son of God. The Son of Man. The Lamb who takes away my sin. You came on a rescue mission to ransom a sinner like me. Such knowledge is more than I can wrap my head around. It's too wonderful. Jesus, I'm Yours. I worship You and You alone, for You are God. In Jesus' name.

AND GOD RESPONDS

"Jesus then said to them, 'Truly, truly, I say to you, it was not Moses who gave you the bread from heaven, but my Father gives you the true bread from heaven. For the bread of God is he who comes down from heaven and gives life to the world.' They said to him, 'Sir, give us this bread always.' Jesus said to them, 'I am the bread of life; whoever comes to me shall not hunger, and whoever believes in me shall never thirst. But I said to you that you have seen me and yet do not believe. All that the Father gives me will come to me, and whoever comes to me I will never cast out.'"[17]

DAY 22

"This is the work of God."

JOHN 6:29

"On the next day the crowd that remained on the other side of the sea saw that there had been only one boat there, and that Jesus had not entered the boat with his disciples, but that his disciples had gone away alone. Other boats from Tiberias came near the place where they had eaten the bread after the Lord had given thanks. So when the crowd saw that Jesus was not there, nor his disciples, they themselves got into the boats and went to Capernaum, seeking Jesus. When they found him on the other side of the sea, they said to him, 'Rabbi, when did you come here?'"[1]

Jesus has been busy. After preaching, healing, and casting out demons, He fed the five thousand and walked on water. And while busy, He's not unaware of the motivation of the crowd: "Perceiving then that they were about to come and take him by force to make him king, Jesus withdrew again to the mountain by himself."[2]

Jesus answered them, "Truly, truly, I say to you, you are seeking me, not because you saw signs, but because you ate your fill of the loaves. Do not work for the food that perishes, but for the food that endures to eternal life, which the Son of Man will give to you. For on him God the Father has set his seal."[3]

The "Son of Man" is a messianic claim in the strongest of terms. Jesus is claiming to be the Messiah seen in Daniel's vision: "I saw in the night visions, and behold, with the clouds of heaven there came one like a son of man, and he came to the Ancient of Days and was presented before him. And to him was given dominion and glory and a kingdom, that all peoples, nations, and languages should serve him; his dominion is an everlasting dominion, which shall not pass away, and his kingdom one that shall not be destroyed."[4]

But the people aren't interested in food that endures to eternal life. The people are looking for entertainment. A circus show. They want to fill their bellies, while Jesus wants to save them from the wrath to come. Temporal satisfaction versus eternal salvation. The Son of God is standing before them, revealing Himself. By claiming to have the seal of the Father, He's doubling down. It's shouting through a microphone. A shot across the bow. Not only has He made Himself equal with God, but He has been given the Father's authority. His kingdom. He and the Father are One. This is the most outrageous claim He can make.

"Then they said to him, 'What must we do, to be doing the works of God?'"[5]

Again, notice the pronoun. Remember the young ruler. At root, their question betrays their idea that they can do something, anything, to get right with God—what must *we* do?

"Jesus answered them, 'This is the work of God, that you believe in him whom he has sent.'"[6]

Of the 224 uses of the word "believe" in the New Testament, 84 occur in John, more than twice that of any other book. The next closest is Acts at 38, then Romans at 19. This repetition is like banging a gong. Jesus is hammering home a point. "This is the work of God." But still, they're not listening.

Why? Because to believe in the One whom He has sent requires something on their part. Something at a gut-check level. Or heart level. Think back fifteen hundred years before Jesus. To the exodus. The desert. The Israelites became impatient and spoke against God and Moses. "We loathe this worthless food."[7] The Lord sends fiery serpents, many Israelites are snakebit, and many die. Realizing their guilt, the people come to Moses, "We have sinned."[8] So Moses prays for the people. In His mercy, God hears and instructs Moses to fashion a bronze serpent on a pole. Then lift it up for all to see. "Everyone who is bitten, when he sees it, shall live."[9] Can you see the parallel?

In the desert God required the admission of sin and confession of guilt, then humility to look up. And at the root of that upturned face was the belief that He alone can save. Jesus is speaking to their direct descendants, and His message hasn't changed: the work of God is to believe, which means they must rely totally on Him for everything. To truly believe is to admit I can't, and completely and totally surrender to the One who can.

This is a radical paradigm shift.

"So they said to him, 'Then what sign do you do, that we may see and believe you? What work do you perform? Our fathers ate the manna in the wilderness; as it is written, "He gave them bread from heaven to eat."'"[10]

They're being cynical. "Yeah, You fed us loaves from baskets. But Moses actually made bread fall out of the sky. Can You do that?" They're trying to bait Jesus into a competition with Moses.

Note: the Son of God is standing three feet away.

"Jesus then said to them, 'Truly, truly, I say to you, it was not

Moses who gave you the bread from heaven, but my Father gives you the true bread from heaven. For the bread of God is he who comes down from heaven and gives life to the world.' They said to him, 'Sir, give us this bread always.'"[11]

Moses gave. Past tense. God gives and is giving. The contrast could not be more striking.

"Jesus said to them, 'I am the bread of life; whoever comes to me shall not hunger, and whoever believes in me shall never thirst. But I said to you that you have seen me and yet do not believe. All that the Father gives me will come to me, and whoever comes to me I will never cast out. For I have come down from heaven, not to do my own will but the will of him who sent me. And this is the will of him who sent me, that I should lose nothing of all that he has given me, but raise it up on the last day. For this is the will of my Father, that everyone who looks on the Son and believes in him should have eternal life, and I will raise him up on the last day.'"[12]

WALK WITH ME BACK TO THE CROSS

I've heard people ask, "Can you lose your salvation?" I think that's the wrong question. The right question is "Can Jesus lose you?" And according to Jesus, He can't, won't, never has, and never will. This is Jesus: "While I was with them, I kept them in your name, which you have given me. I have guarded them, and not one of them has been lost except the son of destruction, that the Scripture might be fulfilled."[13] **And,** "My sheep hear my voice, and I know them, and they follow me. I give them eternal life, and they will never perish, and no one will snatch them out of my hand. My Father, who has given them to me, is greater than all, and no one is able to snatch them out of the Father's hand. I and the Father are one."[14] **When I read these,** my eye focuses on "not one of them has been lost" and "no one will snatch them out of my hand." Think about that. The Savior of the world, the God of this universe and every other, who spoke us into existence and fashioned us from the dust, who defeated death, hell, and the grave, is talking about you and me.

Maybe you're standing here, reading my words, staring at this splintery beam and you believe, you really do; yet in the back of your mind are the whispers about the stuff in your past. The stuff you can't talk about. The stuff you buried. Maybe you think you're disqualified, and every time the memory flashes, the whispers of the enemy condemn you and tell you that you're irredeemable. That no matter how much you believe, there's no way possible for you to work your way back.

Well, that's partly true. You can't. Which is the point. That's the reason for this Cross. Let this sink in: "And you, who were dead in your trespasses and the uncircumcision of your flesh, God made alive together with him, having forgiven us all our trespasses, by canceling the record of debt that stood against us with its legal demands. This he set aside, nailing it to the cross. He disarmed the rulers and authorities and put them to open shame, by triumphing over them in him."[15]

He canceled the debt. Nailed it to His cross. My question for you is this: Will you leave it there and let it stand as your proclamation of His eternal, irrevocable, irreversible triumph? Or will you take it down in disbelief?

Which is it going to be?

Over these past twenty-two days, I have hammered this idea of "believe in." Why? Because Jesus did and still does. He never lets up. The work of God is to believe in the redeeming, sanctifying, justifying, snatching-us-back-out-of-the-hand-of-the-devil work of Jesus that *He* did on this Cross. No work we do earns us a place here. And no work we do disqualifies our place here. This is the place where *He*, Jesus, tells you and me that no gone is too far gone. This is the place where the Savior says, "Come hungry and believe." This is the place where we hit our knees, admit our unworthiness and our total inability, and surrender to the One whose perfect work has returned us—spotless—to the Father. This is where we believe—or not.

Pray with Me

Jesus, I know I sound like a broken record, but more often than not, I come to You wanting You to meet my temporal need, which You so mercifully do, and then when my belly is full, I go away and forget You. Then I get hungry and return, and the cycle starts all over. I'm just like these people wanting to see the circus in town. Jesus, I know You alone are the Bread of Life and You alone can satisfy me. And yet I treat You more like a vending machine than the Savior of the world. You were seated at the right hand of God Most High, in perfect relationship; but when the time came, You humbled Yourself, took a swan dive out of heaven, and came on a rescue mission. You left Your throne for this Cross.

I know I have spent much of my life wanting You to prove Yourself to me, over and over and over. What I'm really wanting is constant proof that You are who You say You are. That You're not indifferent to me. That You care. And yet, here we are. At this Cross. Is there anything on earth that could possibly declare Your love for me more than this splintery, bloody thing? Forgive me when I take this perfect work for granted. When I take Your perfect sacrifice for granted. When I sacrifice my belief at the altar of circus tricks and a full belly. I know I have taken You lightly, and I'm so sorry. I also know that when I've doubted You and thought there's no way back to You, that I'm too far gone, You've still reached across time and space and rescued me. When the enemy convinces me that my scarlet sins disqualify me, You wash me white as snow.[16] There's no place on planet Earth where the blood of Jesus can't rescue me. I'm not beyond Your love. You can't, won't, never have, and never will lose me. I'm Yours. And I can rest in Your ability and power and willingness and love of me to keep me in You. Jesus, I know my work is to believe in You. Please help my unbelief. When I look at the sum of You, here, all I know to do is fall on my face and say thank You. In Jesus' name.

AND GOD RESPONDS

"But we see him who for a little while was made lower than the angels, namely Jesus, crowned with glory and honor because of the suffering of death, so that by the grace of God he might taste death for everyone. For it was fitting that he, for whom and by whom all things exist, in bringing many sons to glory, should make the founder of their salvation perfect through suffering. For he who sanctifies and those who are sanctified all have one source. That is why he is not ashamed to call them brothers, saying, 'I will tell of your name to my brothers; in the midst of the congregation I will sing your praise.' And again, 'I will put my trust in him.' And again, 'Behold, I and the children God has given me.' Since therefore the children share in flesh and blood, he himself likewise partook of the same things, that through death he might destroy the one who has the power of death, that is, the devil, and deliver all those who through fear of death were subject to lifelong slavery. For surely it is not angels that he helps, but he helps the offspring of Abraham. Therefore he had to be made like his brothers in every respect, so that he might become a merciful and faithful high priest in the service of God, to make propitiation for the sins of the people. For because he himself has suffered when tempted, he is able to help those who are being tempted."[17]

DAY 23

---◆◆◆---

"For this is the will of my Father . . ."

JOHN 6:38–54

"For I have come down from heaven, not to do my own will but the will of him who sent me. And this is the will of him who sent me, that I should lose nothing of all that he has given me, but raise it up on the last day. For this is the will of my Father, that everyone who looks on the Son and believes in him should have eternal life, and I will raise him up on the last day."[1]

John's gospel can be broken down into two halves. Jesus' three years in public ministry: chapters 1–11. And Jesus' last week, followed by His crucifixion and resurrection: chapters 12–21. The first chapters are filled with recognition, signs and wonders, and the exaltation of the Father; but by the time we get to chapter 5, Jesus draws a hard line in the sand. He calls God "My Father" and claims to be the Son of Man. The only begotten Son of God. The Messiah. The Anointed One. This is problematic for the people on several levels.

The crowds are not sure what to do with Him. They like His circus act and the fact that the blind see and the lame walk, but His words are troubling. Maybe none more so than the latter half of chapter 6. Up until this point, Jesus has turned water to wine, healed an official's son who was at the point of death, healed a man who had been lying thirty-eight years at the pool of Bethesda, fed the five thousand, delivered people from demons, and walked on water. A lot has happened. But no one is ready for what's to come or what He's about to say.

There's a lot here.

Focus on one phrase: "on the last day." Jesus says it twice in the previous passage. He says it again in verse 44: "No one can come to me unless the Father who sent me draws him. And I will raise him up on the last day." And again in verse 54: "Whoever feeds on my flesh and drinks my blood has eternal life, and I will raise him up on the last day."

"On the last day" centers on a bodily resurrection—a hot topic of debate in Jesus' day. The Pharisees believed in a bodily resurrection; the Sadducees did not. Both knew "the last day" refers to Daniel's vision—the same vision in which he identifies the Son of Man:

"At that time shall arise Michael, the great prince who has charge of your people. And there shall be a time of trouble, such as never has been since there was a nation till that time. But at that time your people shall be delivered, everyone whose name shall be found written in the book. And many of those who sleep in the dust of the earth shall awake, some to everlasting life, and some to shame and everlasting contempt. And those who are wise shall shine like the brightness of the sky above; and those who turn many to righteousness, like the stars forever and ever. But you, Daniel, shut up the words and seal the book, until the time of the end. Many shall run to and fro, and knowledge shall increase."[2]

It's arguable that most everyone within the sound of Jesus' voice knew this scripture. They're basing their hope on it and in it. If nothing else, they understood the idea of time coming to an end and ending in judgment. A judgment in which a sovereign Judge will send some to everlasting life and some to everlasting condemnation. And no one escapes this. No one is exempt. Also, no one is overlooked. "I should lose nothing of all that he has given me." Everyone in the crowd listening understood one simple, logical fact: according to Jesus, there will be a last day.

But Jesus doesn't stop there. He takes it one step further. Making an extraordinary claim. A claim for which many want to kill Him—not only will there be a last day, but He will do the sending. Jesus is the Judge.

Paul said this: "At the name of Jesus every knee should bow, in heaven and on earth and under the earth, and every tongue confess that Jesus Christ is Lord, to the glory of God the Father."[3] And, "For we all must appear before the judgment seat of Christ, so that each one may receive what is due for what he has done in the body, whether good or evil."[4] Jesus alone will either raise us up with Him—or not. No one else does the raising.

Fast-forward to John chapter 11. Jesus arrives on the scene after Lazarus has been dead four days. The house is packed with mourners. Hearing Jesus has arrived, Martha runs out to meet Him. She says, "'Lord if you had been here, my brother would not have died. But even now I know that whatever you ask from God, God will give you.' Jesus said to her, 'Your brother will rise again.' Martha said to him, 'I know that he will rise again in the resurrection on the last day.'"[5]

Martha got it mostly right. She understood and believed there was going to be a last day. And that Jesus would be the Judge. She just didn't understand He was about to exercise that power and dominion in the next moment.

By the time we get to John 12, the unbelief of the people is a real problem:

"'While you have the light, believe in the light, that you may become sons of light.' When Jesus had said these things, he departed and hid himself from them. Though he had done so many signs before them, they still did not believe in him, so that the word spoken by the prophet Isaiah might be fulfilled: 'Lord, who has believed what he heard from us, and to whom has the arm of the Lord been revealed?' Therefore they could not believe. For again Isaiah said, 'He has blinded their eyes and hardened their heart, lest they see with their eyes, and understand with their heart, and turn, and I would heal them.' Isaiah said these things because he saw his glory and spoke of him. Nevertheless, many even of the authorities believed in him, but for fear of the Pharisees they did not confess it, so that they would not be put out of the synagogue; for they loved the glory that comes from man more than the glory that comes from God."[6]

Now look at Jesus' response: "And Jesus cried out."[7]

Don't miss the obvious: Jesus is crying out. Screaming at the top of His lungs. Spittle spraying from His lips. Sweat cascading down His temples. Which begs the question: Why?

He is performing signs before their eyes. Signs that prove He alone is the Son of God. And yet, they still don't believe. Jesus looks at this unbelieving people and cries out: "Whoever believes in me, believes not in me but in him who sent me. And whoever sees me sees him who sent me. I have come into the world as light, so that whoever believes in me may not remain in darkness."[8]

There it is. Eternity hangs in the balance. Darkness versus light. A choice of kingdoms, offered by *the* King. Who is standing before them, crying out, "If anyone hears my words and does not keep them, I do not judge him; for I did not come to judge the world but to save the world. The one who rejects me and does not receive my words has a judge; the word that I have spoken will judge him on the last day."[9]

The Charles Martin paraphrase reads like this: "Choose. Choose right now. Don't delay. You've heard enough. You don't need any more information. You decide—either I am who I say I am and I did what Scripture records Me as having done, or I'm not and I didn't. But know this, what you decide right here, right now, will determine your eternity. And in which kingdom you spend it. So choose wisely. It's life and death."

Walk with Me Back to the Cross

Please let me lock arm in arm and walk shoulder to shoulder and ask you, Do you hear? Are you listening?

Because the stakes could not be higher or simpler: on the last day, we either join the saints and inherit the kingdom of heaven or join the unbelievers and inherit the kingdom of darkness. Eternal life with the Father. Or the father of lies. And the determining factor? What we choose now. Before our last day.

What you are facing in this moment is the very same choice Adam and Eve faced in the garden. They chose poorly—they chose the wrong king and the wrong kingdom—and all of history has been a train wreck as a result. Conversely, all of history is a record of the Father relentlessly pursuing us. To return us to Him. To bring us to Himself. To bring you and me to this moment.

This moment.

But while He has done everything to make a way, including the selfless sacrifice of His only Son, He leaves one thing to you.

And while you're deciding, remember these words of Jesus: "And this is the will of him who sent me, that I should lose nothing of all that he has given me, but raise it up on the last day. For this is the will of my Father, that everyone who looks on the Son and believes in him should have eternal life, and I will raise him up on the last day."[10]

Of the several billion people on planet Earth, the absolute will of God the Father is directed at you. And that will is that none are lost. That everyone who looks on the Son and believes has eternal life. And today, two thousand years on this side of the Cross, "none" and "everyone" still mean none and everyone.

Imagine for a moment if Jesus were to speak to you from this Cross. What would He say? I think He'd be crying out. Top of His lungs. Red-faced. The veins on His neck bulging like rose vines. Spit spewing from His lips. Why? Because He knows the hell that awaits you if you don't choose Him. And for the record, partial surrender or half-hearted belief equals no surrender and ultimately disbelief. Just ask Judas.

Some of you are sitting on the bleachers. Not convinced. Indifferent. Watching the game while shoveling popcorn in your mouth. And yet, "an hour is coming when all who are in the tombs will hear his voice and come out, those who have done good to the resurrection of life, and those who have done evil to the resurrection of judgment."[11]

The choice before you is all or nothing. So what say you? How will you choose? You may decide now at a time of your choosing, or you can put it off, which is also a choice. Just know that while God is outside of time, we are not. The clock is ticking. And my sense is that time is running short.

PRAY WITH ME

King Jesus, in fear and trembling, on this day, I surrender. Completely. I declare and decree, either for the first time or the hundredth or the ten thousandth, You are the only begotten Son of God. The Son of Man. The Anointed One. The Messiah. God With Us. And You and You alone made propitiation on my behalf. You cleared my debt ledger. Through Your sinless life and Your shed blood, which still flows fresh from the Cross on Calvary, You paid a debt I could not pay in this life or any other. I believe You are who You say You are. And that after three days, You rose again. God the Father, through the Spirit, raised You to life again, and You are, even now, seated at the right hand of God Most High where You are interceding for me. Even in this very moment.

Your Word says it is You who work in me, both to will and to work for Your good pleasure. Please work in me. It is true, I live in a crooked and twisted generation, and I want to shine as a light in this world, to this world. By reflecting You. I pray that You will help me to hold fast to Your words. Your word of life. For you alone have the words of life. So that on the last day, You will raise me to life with You and the Father where I can live eternally in Your kingdom. In Jesus' name.

AND GOD RESPONDS

"I tell you this, brothers: flesh and blood cannot inherit the kingdom of God, nor does the perishable inherit the imperishable.

Behold! I tell you a mystery. We shall not all sleep, but we shall all be changed, in a moment, in the twinkling of an eye, at the last trumpet. For the trumpet will sound, and the dead will be raised imperishable, and we shall be changed. For this perishable body must put on the imperishable, and this mortal body must put on immortality. When the perishable puts on the imperishable, and the mortal puts on immortality, then shall come to pass the saying that is written: 'Death is swallowed up in victory.' 'O death, where is your victory? O death, where is your sting?' The sting of death is sin, and the power of sin is the law. But thanks be to God, who gives us the victory through our Lord Jesus Christ."[12]

"Therefore, my beloved, as you have always obeyed, so now, not only as in my presence but much more in my absence, work out your own salvation with fear and trembling, for it is God who works in you, both to will and to work for his good pleasure. . . . That you may be blameless and innocent, children of God without blemish in the midst of a crooked and twisted generation, among whom you shine as lights in the world, holding fast to the word of life, so that in the day of Christ I may be proud that I did not run in vain or labor in vain."[13]

DAY 24

"Do you want to go away as well?"

JOHN 6:41–69

"So the Jews grumbled about him, because he said, 'I am the bread that came down from heaven.' They said, 'Is not this Jesus, the son of Joseph, whose father and mother we know? How does he now say, "I have come down from heaven"?'"[1]

To those within earshot, this is a scandalous claim. They have no box for this.

"Jesus answered them, 'Do not grumble among yourselves. No one can come to me unless the Father who sent me draws him. And I will raise him up on the last day. It is written in the Prophets, "And they will all be taught by God."'"[2]

They have no box for this either. Because the man standing before them is claiming to be the God who teaches them.

"Everyone who has heard and learned from the Father comes to me—not that anyone has seen the Father except he who is from God; he has seen the Father. Truly, truly, I say to you, whoever believes has eternal life."[3]

Problem box number three: "I have seen the Father." These people's heads are spinning. But then Jesus says this: "I am the bread of life. Your fathers ate the manna in the wilderness, and they died. This is the bread that comes down from heaven, so that one may eat of it and not die. I am the living bread that came down from heaven. If anyone eats of this bread, he will live forever. And the bread that I will give for the life of the world is my flesh."[4]

Jesus is doing something no prophet has ever done. Or dared do. He's comparing Himself to Moses. Actually, it's not even a comparison. With all due respect to Moses, it's a mic drop. No contest. He's saying, "I'm the greater Moses." And to do so, He is counting on their knowledge of Moses' own words when he said, "The LORD your God will raise up for you a prophet like me."[5]

Jesus' words are a declaration: "I'm that prophet. I'm that priest. I'm that King."

On this side of the Cross, the comparison is clearer: both gave the law of God from the top of a mountain.[6] Both faced a murderous, wicked king as a child. Both led an exodus out of slavery. Both started their exodus at Passover. Both pleaded mercy for God's people. Both fasted forty days. Both spent time in the desert. Moses led people through water; Jesus baptizes in water and Spirit. Moses delivered the people from Pharaoh; Jesus delivers us from satan. Moses was born a slave and adopted into royalty. King Jesus humbled Himself, cloaked His divinity, and stepped off His throne, becoming a slave, to save His people. Moses turned water into blood, which no man could drink, while Jesus turned water into the best wine ever on planet Earth. Mosaic laws of purification cleansed the outer man; belief in Jesus cleanses the inner. Moses reflected the glory of God. Jesus is that glory. Moses wrote on tablets of stone. Jesus wrote in the dirt and now on our hearts. Moses lifted up the bronze serpent. Jesus was lifted up to draw all men to Himself. Moses commanded obedience. Jesus obeyed on our behalf. Moses' sin excluded him from entering the promised land. Jesus took on our sin to return us to the Father so that we might know His love. Moses ascended a mountain and returned with the law; Jesus ascended to heaven and sent the Spirit. Moses' covenant ultimately ends in death. Jesus' new covenant gives eternal life.

The writer of Hebrews summarized it this way:

"Therefore, holy brothers, you who share in a heavenly calling, consider Jesus, the apostle and high priest of our confession, who was faithful to him who appointed him, just as Moses also was faithful in all God's house. For Jesus has been counted worthy of more glory than Moses—as much more glory as the builder of a house has more honor than the house itself. (For every house is built by someone, but the builder of all things is God.) Now Moses was faithful in all God's house as a servant, to testify to the things that were to be spoken later, but Christ is faithful over God's house as a son. And we are his house, if indeed we hold fast our confidence and our boasting in our hope."[7]

But here in John 6, Jesus says something that forces the people to choose whether or not He is the One of whom Moses speaks: "I am the bread of life." Basically, Your fathers ate that bread and died. I am here to give you Myself. I am your bread. So eat My flesh and never die.

But again, they miss the forest for the trees. "The Jews then disputed among themselves, saying, 'How can this man give us his flesh to eat?'"[8]

In my mind, Jesus is shaking His head.

"So Jesus said to them, 'Truly, truly, I say to you, unless you eat the flesh of the Son of Man and drink his blood, you have no life in you. Whoever feeds on my flesh and drinks my blood has eternal life, and I will raise him up on the last day. For my flesh is true food, and my blood is true drink. Whoever feeds on my flesh and drinks my blood abides in me, and I in him. As the living Father sent me, and I live because of the Father, so whoever feeds on me, he also will live because of me. This is the bread that came down from heaven, not like the bread the fathers ate, and died. Whoever feeds on this bread will live forever.'"[9]

Those listening still can't fathom what He's talking about. True food and true drink. Whoever feeds on His flesh and drinks His blood abides in Him.

"Jesus said these things in the synagogue, as he taught at Capernaum."[10]

Now look at the reaction of those who heard it: "When many of his disciples heard it, they said, 'This is a hard saying; who can listen to it?' But Jesus, knowing in himself that his disciples were grumbling about this, said to them, 'Do you take offense at this? Then what if you were to see the Son of Man ascending to where he was before?'"[11]

"Where he was before." Many of the people listening to Jesus are fully convinced that Joseph's Son has completely lost His mind. His claims don't even make sense. They're beyond outrageous.

Unless they're true.

Jesus continues: "'It is the Spirit who gives life; the flesh is no help at all. The words that I have spoken to you are spirit and life. But there are some of you who do not believe.' (For Jesus knew from the beginning who those were who did not believe, and who it was who would betray him.) And he said, 'This is why I told you that no one can come to me unless it is granted him by the Father.'"[12]

Look at the crowd staring at Jesus. They are entertained by the miracles, but it's these words they're having trouble with. What follows are some of the saddest and most tragic words in all of

Scripture: "After this many of his disciples turned back and no longer walked with him."[13] Can you see it? They're standing three feet from the Son of God. They can feel His breath on their face. See the color of His eyes. And when He says something they don't like, they pivot and tell Him to talk to the hand.

Let me turn the mirror: What is your knee-jerk to every single word of Jesus? Total buy-in? Or cavalier indifference? Open skepticism? Half-hearted belief? Or worse, half-hearted unbelief? Before we judge them for how quickly they turned on Jesus for His outrageous words, let's be honest. They are us. And we are them. We follow when He says what we like. When He does what we want. When He fills our stomachs. Heals our infirmities. Tells someone else they've sinned against us. But the moment He says something we don't understand or have trouble with, even something aimed at us, we turn our backs. Walk away.

Jesus did not come to make bad people good. He came to raise dead people to life. And the people looking at and listening to Jesus are dead and don't know it. They are listening to the words of Jesus, asking themselves how those words make them feel, weighing the pros and cons, assessing the advantages of following versus not, when eternity hangs in the balance. How they respond to Him in the next thirty seconds will literally determine their forever, and yet, these folks are rearranging deck chairs on the *Titanic*. Jesus knows this. It's why He's "crying out." He is laser-focused on rescue. On ransoming mankind. Making final payment. Satisfying forever the wrath of God.

And mankind is arguing His word choice. Talk to the hand.

As the people walk away, turning their backs on the only begotten Son of God, Jesus looks to the Twelve, "Do you want to go away as well?"[14]

Hard stop.

This is *the* question. Eight words that get at the truth of us. That separate the believers from everyone else. When Jesus says, "The gate is narrow and the way is hard that leads to life, and those who find it are few," this is exactly what He's talking about.[15] These words are the hard, narrow gate. As the crowd dwindles, Jesus is looking at His closest friends and asking, "You heard Me. I didn't stutter. Do My words make you uncomfortable? Do you want to follow someone else?" You and I have a tendency to read this and separate ourselves from it. Place it in time. Spoken two thousand years ago. That was then. But was it? These words of Jesus have, somehow, echoed through eternity, circumnavigated the globe, survived multiple translations, and just now landed on this page. To be filtered by your retinas (or your ear drums) and translated to your brain. Read by you. Was this by accident, or did He know you'd be here? However you answer, the question stands: "Do you want to go away as well?"

Simon Peter answers him, "Lord, to whom shall we go? You have the words of eternal life, and we have believed, and have come to know, that you are the Holy One of God."[16]

Jesus could have explained Himself in sixty seconds but didn't. He could have easily said, "Hey, listen, I'm not talking about cannibalizing My body. In the years ahead, all of you will gather round and 'take, eat,' and call this 'Communion.' This is how you will remember My death." But He doesn't do that.

Look at Peter's description of their own process: "You spoke words. We heard You. We believed. We made a decision. We have come to know. We are starting to understand."

Now look at the chronology: Jesus spoke. They heard. They believed. They came to some understanding. And even though they didn't understand everything, they still followed. My point is this: belief came before understanding. They chose to believe before they completely understood. We often demand it the other way around. We want to understand, gather all the facts, weigh the possibilities, and then maybe we'll believe if we can come to the right understanding. If we can wrap our heads around it. If it benefits us. Not Peter. Peter has seen Jesus, heard His words, then walked out onto the bridge, strapped that little contraption around his ankles, and taken a swan dive off the railing without really understanding the physics behind the bungee's physical ability to keep him from implanting his face into granite three thousand feet below.

Peter and the other disciples may not understand everything, and if he were CEO of marketing for Jesus, Inc., he might talk to his influencer and rebrand the message, maybe launch a corrective social media campaign, but he doesn't. He doesn't argue. Doesn't correct. Doesn't acquiesce. Doesn't weasel, compromise, or attempt to lessen. He jumps to the issue at hand. "Where would we go? You have the words of eternal life." No, Peter doesn't understand everything. He's far from it. Has a thousand questions. But he understands enough to know that as wonky as these words of Jesus might sound at the moment, he knows that he knows that he knows they are still better off with Jesus than without.

Which is the point.

Standing in a crowd, Jesus knows the hearts of those following Him, so He begins separating the crowd into two groups: those looking for a free meal, entertained by the miracle-maker and His circus, and those who have found Messiah and surrendered to the Son of God. To do so, He drops this bomb: "Unless you eat the flesh of the Son of Man and drink his blood, you have no life in you."[17] Place yourself in the mix. Hear it for the first time.

You and I have the context of history. We have some understanding of what He's talking about. They have no idea. Knowing what they're thinking, He follows it with this: "Do you take offense at this? Then what if you were to see the Son of Man ascending to where he was before?"[18]

The Charles Martin translation is this: "If eating My flesh and drinking My blood gives you pause, how will you respond when the clouds part, the trumpet sounds, and you see Me sitting on a throne next to the Ancient of Days? The God of Angel Armies. Surrounded by several hundred million angels praising Me at the top of their lungs?"

I think this dilemma is the reason C. S. Lewis wrote these words:

"I am trying here to prevent anyone saying the really foolish thing that people often say about Him: I'm ready to accept Jesus as a great moral teacher, but I don't accept his claim to be God. That is the one thing we must not say. A man who was merely a man and said the sort of things Jesus said would not be a great moral teacher. He would either be a lunatic—on the level with the man who says he is a poached egg—or else he would be the Devil of Hell. You must make your choice. Either this man was, and is, the Son of God, or else a madman or something worse. You can shut him up for a fool, you can spit at him and kill him as a demon or you can fall at his feet and call him Lord and God, but let us not come with any patronizing nonsense about his being a great human teacher. He has not left that open to us. He did not intend to."[19]

Therein lies the rub and the question for you and me: Who has the words of eternal life?

WALK WITH ME BACK TO THE CROSS

Look around. Where are you in this crowd? Have you turned your back while He hangs here, bleeding into the earth? Or have you hit your knees, raised your hands, and cried out, "Lord, where else would we go?" Chances are good we won't understand everything Jesus says. But He's not asking us to. He's asking us to believe even when we don't understand.

On the day of His crucifixion, not a single follower understood the Cross. Not even His mother. Jesus didn't stop to explain.

The words of Jesus are either the words of eternal life, or they're lies from the pit of hell. There's no in-between. No Switzerland. You choose.

Do you want to go away as well?

PRAY WITH ME

Lord Jesus, here and now I decree and declare that You and You alone are the Bread of Life and all life. That You are the greater Moses. That You alone have the words of life, and I don't want to go anywhere but to You. I know that out of the abundance of the heart the mouth speaks, so fill my heart with Your words, and let me shout and write and speak and proclaim You, Your Word, and Your praise. For You alone have the words of eternal life. Where else would I go? God forbid I go anywhere but to You.

Please forgive me when I have and when I do. When my fear entices me to listen to some other voice. Jesus, I'm so sorry. Open my ears and give me ears to hear You. Jesus, I'm just being honest, I'm looking at the coming days, and I know we are headed to Your crucifixion, and I don't want to see it. I don't want to look at what my sin did to You. I don't know if my heart can take it, so please take me by the hand and lead me back again to Your Cross. Where You shed Your blood for a demon-oppressed, deaf-and-dumb sinner like me. For the record, I know I've said this, but today is a new day, so I want to say again, You are who You say You are. The Son of God. The Lamb. Who takes away the sin of the world. With Your very own blood that Your Father has given to us upon the altar—which is Your Cross—to make atonement for our souls. Because the life of the flesh is in the blood. That's why we eat Your flesh and drink Your blood. Because in You, there's life. Jesus, I receive Your life today. Come, Lord Jesus. Fill me, please. Forgive my careless words. And put Your words on my tongue. And, Jesus, please don't ever let me walk away from You when You say something I don't like. Something I don't understand. Something You don't explain. Jesus, here and now, I choose to believe even when I don't understand. I know You've never lost one of us, but I'm just raising my hand. I'm Yours. Hold me, please, in the hollow of Your hand. In Jesus' matchless, magnificent, and undefeated name.

AND GOD RESPONDS

"The mystery hidden for ages and generations but now revealed to his saints. To them God chose to make known how great among the Gentiles are the riches of the glory of this mystery, which is Christ in you, the hope of glory."[20]

"For I want you to know how great a struggle I have for you and for those at Laodicea and for all who have not seen me face to face, that their hearts may be encouraged, being knit together in love, to reach all the riches of full assurance of understanding and the knowledge of God's mystery, which is Christ, in whom are hidden all the treasures of wisdom and knowledge."[21]

"For in him the whole fullness of deity dwells bodily, and you have been filled in him, who is the head of all rule and authority. In him also you were circumcised with a circumcision made without hands, by putting off the body of the flesh, by the circumcision of Christ, having been buried with him in baptism, in which you were also raised with him through faith in the powerful working of God, who raised him from the dead. And you, who were dead in your trespasses and the uncircumcision of your flesh, God made alive together with him, having forgiven us all our trespasses, by canceling the record of debt that stood against us with its legal demands. This he set aside, nailing it to the cross. He disarmed the rulers and authorities and put them to open shame, by triumphing over them in him."[22]

DAY 25

"Everyone who acknowledges me before men . . ."

LUKE 12:8–12

"In the meantime, when so many thousands of the people had gathered together that they were trampling one another, he began to say to his disciples first, 'Beware of the leaven of the Pharisees, which is hypocrisy. Nothing is covered up that will not be revealed, or hidden that will not be known. Therefore whatever you have said in the dark shall be heard in the light, and what you have whispered in private rooms shall be proclaimed on the housetops.'"[1]

Leaven here represents sin. Unrepented sin. Which insidiously spreads and affects everything it touches. Paul defined it this way: "Your boasting is not good. Do you not know that a little leaven leavens the whole lump? Cleanse out the old leaven that you may be a new lump, as you really are unleavened. For Christ, our Passover lamb, has been sacrificed. Let us therefore celebrate the festival, not with the old leaven, the leaven of malice and evil, but with the unleavened bread of sincerity and truth."[2]

Jesus is calling the Pharisees hypocrites—straight up—to their faces. While the Pharisees have been arguing the proper way to ceremonially wash prior to eating (which is found nowhere in the law of Moses but arose out of the traditions of men—see Mark 7), Jesus has been casting out demons, healing the sick, and teaching His disciples to pray starting with the word "Father." As a result, the crowds are growing larger—trampling one another—while the Pharisees are growing nervous. They also don't like the idea of their secrets being revealed.

"And when the demon had been cast out, the mute man spoke. And the crowds marveled, saying, 'Never was anything like this seen in Israel.' But the Pharisees said, 'He casts out demons by the prince of demons.'"[3]

Jesus has a power they've never seen and with which they cannot compete, so they use the only weapon they have: lies. Jesus responds by doing something no king has ever done: He gives away His power and sends out seventy-two disciples to do what He's been doing. When they return "with joy," they say: "'Lord, even the demons are subject to us in your name!' And he says to them, 'I saw Satan fall like lightning from heaven. Behold, I have given you authority to tread on serpents and scorpions, and over all the power of the enemy, and nothing shall hurt you. Nevertheless, do not rejoice in this, that the spirits are subject to you, but rejoice that your names are written in heaven.'"[4]

Jesus is saying as much between the lines as through them. His implication is at least threefold. All of which the Pharisees hate. First, Jesus is saying: "I was in heaven with the Father when He cast out the serpent of old satan. I saw it happen firsthand." Second, "The Father has entrusted Me with that same power, which I exercise and give to whom I will." Everyone listening would clue in to the phrase "tread on serpents," as only the Serpent Crusher—the Messiah— can do that. They would have known the *Protoevangelium*[5] by heart, even if not by that name (remember, we unpacked this on day 3). And third, "Despite your (Pharisees) best attempts at self-righteousness, your names are not written in heaven."

This is not just mental jousting. It's a seething indictment for which they have no rebuttal. Their only option is to silence Him. And there's only one way to do that.

Then Jesus says something amazing. He speaks to and with the Father (in the same way He does in John 17), and we get to listen in. The Holy Spirit actually gives us a transcription of the conversation between the Ancient of Days, God Most High, and His only begotten Son: "In that same hour he rejoiced in the Holy Spirit and said, 'I thank you, Father, Lord of heaven and earth, that you have hidden these things from the wise and understanding and revealed them to little children; yes, Father, for such was your gracious will. All things have been handed over to me by my Father, and no one knows who the Son is except the Father, or who the Father is except the Son and anyone to whom the Son chooses to reveal him.'"[6]

The Pharisees hear Jesus describe them as those who claim to be wise and understanding and yet they are not. The implication is that they are fools. While the less educated, who are trampling one another following Jesus, have received a revelation into the Son of Man.

Jesus responds with: "But if it is by the finger of God that I cast out demons, then the kingdom of God has come upon you. When a strong man, fully armed, guards his own palace, his goods are safe; but when one stronger than he attacks him and overcomes him, he takes away his armor in which he trusted and divides his spoil. Whoever is not with me is against me, and whoever does not gather with me scatters."[7]

Jesus cannot be more blunt: The kingdom of God is here, staring you in the face; and you, Pharisees, are scattering. This does not end well for you.

The Pharisees are indignant. Who does this man think He is?

Jesus returns His attention to the crowd because He knows the thoughts of the Pharisees, and while He addresses the crowd, His words pierce the religious elite: "I tell you, my friends, do not fear those who kill the body, and after that have nothing more that they can do. But I will warn you whom to fear: fear him who, after he has killed, has authority to cast into hell. Yes, I tell you, fear him!"[8]

The Pharisees have been pointed out. Called on the carpet. Revealed as the pretenders they are. "Don't fear these men. All they can do is kill this body. Instead, fear the Father. For He can either cast you into hell or return you to Himself. You choose."

Jesus then silences the critics with this: "And I tell you, everyone who acknowledges me before men, the Son of Man also will acknowledge before the angels of God, but the one who denies me before men will be denied before the angels of God. And everyone who speaks a word against the Son of Man will be forgiven, but the one who blasphemes against the Holy Spirit will not be forgiven."[9]

Someone in the crowd then asks Jesus, "Tell my brother to divide the inheritance with me,"[10] proving that he has missed the point entirely. Jesus is talking about eternity and the one condition required to spend it with the Father, and the rich fool is talking about now and what's his. Focused on the temporary, he is blind to the eternal.

After teaching a few parables, Jesus ends with this: "I have a baptism to be baptized with, and how great is my distress until it is accomplished!"[11]

On the Cross, Jesus is going to be baptized with suffering and death, which will pour over Him like a flood: "Your wrath lies heavy upon me, and you overwhelm with all your waves."[12] And that phrase "until it is accomplished" can also be translated "until it is finished."

WALK WITH ME BACK TO THE CROSS

I used to read these words "the one who denies . . . will be denied" as a finger-poking-me-in-the-chest warning. As if Jesus were saying, "Better not deny Me." But I don't think that's His intention. And I'm pretty sure it's not His heart for us who believe. Let's come at it from the other side. Jesus' words are not a "don't do"; they are a "get to." Without this Cross, there is no confession. No acknowledgment. Jesus is just another dead man. But by and because and through the blood shed here on this hill by this Son of Man, Jesus, we *get to* acknowledge, confess, and shout, "This man was and is the Son of God! This man is the long-awaited Messiah. The Savior of the world. This is the Lamb of God who has taken away our sin. This is *Yeshua Hamashiach*." Paul said to the Romans, "For if we have been united with him in a death like his, we shall certainly be united with him in a resurrection like his."[13]

If Jesus were sitting here, looking up at His cross with you, how would He see you? A Pharisee spreading leaven?

Or one of the seventy-two?

Are you focused on the temporary or eternal?

Last time: "Everyone who acknowledges me before men, the Son of Man also will acknowledge before the angels of God, but the one who denies me before men will be denied before the angels of God."

What have you said in the dark? What have you whispered in private rooms? What have you shouted from the rooftops? And does anyone in this crowd know?

PRAY WITH ME

Jesus, I want to confess You. Here and now. And before men—always. I acknowledge You as the Savior of the world. The Lamb of God who has taken away our sin. And it is Your blood and Your blood alone that washes me white as snow. I don't want to ever deny You. Please forgive me if I ever have or do in the future. I'm so sorry. I repent and turn back. At root is my fear of man, of which I am guilty many times over. In truth, I make a really good Pharisee, and when You spoke these words, You were then and are now speaking to me. Jesus, for the joy set before You, You endured the Cross and despised the shame and did not deny me. You accepted a baptism in my place and finished what I could not. Lord, I receive Your admonition. Your warning. Your words. Please receive mine. I acknowledge You, King Jesus.

AND GOD RESPONDS

"Because, if you confess with your mouth that Jesus is Lord and believe in your heart that God raised him from the dead, you will be saved. For with the heart one believes and is justified, and with the mouth one confesses and is saved."[14]

"I tell you this, brothers: flesh and blood cannot inherit the kingdom of God, nor does the perishable inherit the imperishable. Behold! I tell you a mystery. We shall not all sleep, but we shall all be changed, in a moment, in the twinkling of an eye, at the last trumpet. For the trumpet will sound, and the dead will be raised imperishable, and we shall be changed. For this perishable body must put on the imperishable, and this mortal body must put on immortality. When the perishable puts on the imperishable, and the mortal puts on immortality, then shall come to pass the saying that is written: 'Death is swallowed up in victory.' 'O death, where is your victory? O death, where is your sting?' The sting of death is sin, and the power of sin is the law. But thanks be to God, who gives us the victory through our Lord Jesus Christ."[15]

DAY 26

"Jesus, Son of David, have mercy on me!"

MARK 10:47

"And they came to Jericho. And as he was leaving Jericho with his disciples and a great crowd, Bartimaeus, a blind beggar, the son of Timaeus, was sitting by the roadside. And when he heard that it was Jesus of Nazareth, he began to cry out and say, 'Jesus, Son of David, have mercy on me!'"[1]

"Son of David" is a messianic claim. By saying it, Bartimaeus is broadcasting for all to hear that he believes Jesus is the long-awaited Messiah. This vocal proclamation could get him killed on several fronts—by the Pharisees who we already know consider this heresy, or by the Romans who have their kings and don't like competition.

"And many rebuked him, telling him to be silent."

But Bartimaeus doesn't care.

Now he's jumping up and down and waving his arms. "He cried out all the more, 'Son of David, have mercy on me!'"[2]

The contradiction between the crowd and Bartimaeus is striking. The crowd is following blindly while Bartimaeus is about to lose his mind. Why? What does the blind man see that they don't?

Seven hundred fifty years earlier, the prophet Isaiah encountered preincarnate Jesus. This is what he said:

"In the year that King Uzziah died I saw the Lord sitting upon a throne, high and lifted up; and the train of his robe filled the temple. Above him stood the seraphim. Each had six wings: with two he covered his face, and with two he covered his feet, and with two he flew. And one called to another and said: 'Holy, holy, holy is the LORD of hosts; the whole earth is full of his glory!' And the foundations of the thresholds shook at the voice of him who called and the house was filled with smoke."[3]

As a writer, I wonder if Isaiah isn't wrestling to find words to describe what he's seeing. I sense the same thing when I read John's revelation. Isaiah continued, "And I said: 'Woe is me! For I am lost; for I am a man of unclean lips, and I dwell in the midst of a people of unclean lips; for my eyes have seen the King, the Lord of hosts!'"[4]

Isaiah didn't know he was lost and unclean until he saw the Lord. Something about that revelation opened his eyes (and heart) to the truth of the King on the throne, Jesus. This seems like the prevailing reaction in Scripture.

Job loses everything. Family. Fortune. Even his health. And at the end of his trial, after all the conversations and the back-and-forth and the friends who aren't much help and don't speak rightly concerning the Lord, God spends two chapters asking Job if he really knows God. Does Job have any idea who he's talking to? Does he know all God has done and can do? When God finishes speaking, Job says:

"I know that you can do all things, and that no purpose of yours can be thwarted [withheld from you]. 'Who is this who hides counsel without knowledge?' [In this question, Job is speaking of himself.] Therefore I have uttered what I did not understand, things too wonderful for me, which I did not know. 'Hear, and I will speak: I will question you, and you make it known to me.' I had heard of you by the hearing of the ear, but now my eye sees you; therefore I despise myself and repent in dust and ashes."[5]

When did Job despise himself and repent? When he saw God for who He is.

The apostle John, called "the one whom Jesus loved,"[6] spent years in friendship with Jesus. The best of friends. So much that Jesus entrusted John with the care of His mother, Mary, as He was dying. It's safe to say, they hung out. Knew each other. Cut up. Laughed. Notice his body posture at the Last Supper as he and Peter try to determine who is soon to betray Jesus: "One of his disciples, whom Jesus loved, was reclining at table at Jesus' side, so Simon Peter motioned to him to ask Jesus of whom he was speaking. So that disciple, leaning back against Jesus, said to him, 'Lord, who is it?'"[7] Notice the familiarity. The casualness. The closeness. He might as well be saying, "Bro." Now fast-forward to John's revelation.

John has been exiled to the island of Patmos where he has a vision and hears a voice: "Then I turned to see the voice that was speaking to me, and on turning I saw seven golden lampstands, and in the midst of the lampstands one like a son of man, clothed with a long robe and with a golden sash around his chest. The hairs of his head were white, like white wool, like snow. His eyes were like a flame of fire, his feet were like burnished bronze, refined in a furnace, and his voice was like the roar of many waters. In his right hand he held seven stars, from his mouth came a sharp two-edged sword, and his face was like the sun shining in full strength. When I saw him, I fell at his feet as though dead."[8]

When did he fall at His feet? When he saw Him. What changed? Jesus' divinity had been uncloaked, and John saw Jesus as He is. He saw the embodiment and fulfillment of Daniel's vision: the King ruling the kingdom, sitting on the throne.[9]

Saul was a state-sponsored terrorist, killing Christians. Dragging them out of their homes and running a sword through their chests while their kids watched. When Stephen was being stoned—martyred—Saul watched and held everyone's clothes. Heartily joining the murder posse. Then he requested and had been granted orders to move north up the Damascus road. On the way, he encounters Jesus. So what does the arrogant butcher do? Confronted with the same Jesus that John details in his revelation, Saul falls on his face. Paralyzed. Blinded. Until Ananias arrives and prays for him. And Saul becomes Paul. In the years that follow, Paul transforms into the greatest evangelist and writer the world has ever known. Eventually, he is beheaded in a Roman prison, but not before writing two-thirds of the New Testament. The greatest defender of the faith, and the one who used his pen to point to the Cross more than any other in the history of the written word, is Paul.

How did murderer Saul become apostle Paul?

He came face-to-face with resurrected Jesus.

Moses fled Egypt after killing one of his own and then wandered in the desert forty years, shepherding sheep until a voice sounded behind a burning bush. From that moment, God uses Moses to free His chosen people through the greatest signs and wonders the world had ever known. Once free, the nation wanders in the wilderness, while this voice speaks to Moses. A cloud by day and fire by night. Moses knows God as the voice who declares, "I am who I am,"[10] but he's never seen Him. Has no idea what He looks like. So he asks the most normal of questions: "Please show me your glory."[11] This is, "What do You look like?" God says, "I will make all my goodness pass before you and will proclaim before you my name, 'The Lord.'

And I will be gracious to whom I will be gracious, and will show mercy on whom I will show mercy. But . . . you cannot see my face, for man shall not see me and live."[12]

The holiness of God, divinity uncloaked, is too much for us. It would be like staring at the sun. Times ten thousand.

Throughout Scripture, people who have encountered Jesus share a common reaction. A common posture. They are undone. They repent. They fall on their face because they know, maybe for the very first time, their own unworthiness in the sight of such perfect holiness.

Back to Bartimaeus. "And Jesus stopped and said, 'Call him.' And they called the blind man, saying to him, 'Take heart. Get up; he is calling you.' And throwing off his cloak, he sprang up and came to Jesus. And Jesus said to him, 'What do you want me to do for you?' And the blind man said to him, 'Rabbi, let me recover my sight.' And Jesus said to him, 'Go your way; your faith has made you well.' And immediately he recovered his sight and followed him on the way."[13]

The crowd saw a circus show. A prophet with a posse. A guru with a following. Bartimaeus saw the Son of God. Big difference.

When did the thief on the cross understand with his heart, turn, and be healed? Or saved? When he hung three feet from crucified Jesus. What about the centurion? Same answer. Paul would later write the church in Thessalonica about the last days and the destruction of the antichrist: "And then the lawless one will be revealed, whom the Lord Jesus will kill with the breath of his mouth and bring to nothing by the appearance of his coming."[14] The NKJV reads, "will consume with the breath of His mouth and destroy with the brightness of His coming." All Jesus needs do to is appear and speak. That's all.

No one can stand in His presence. No one can continue to be who they were. All are transformed when He appears. Even the worst—and most blind—among us.

WALK WITH ME BACK TO THE CROSS

What if you and I had a right revelation of Jesus? What if we stood here and saw Jesus for who He really is? The only begotten Son of God, Savior of the world, King of all kings, high and lifted up, ransoming mankind. Our problem is that we have an enemy who has worked really hard to obscure our view of Jesus. To lessen this Cross. To lessen Jesus.

But what if we, like Bartimaeus, cried out, "Son of David, have mercy on me. I want to see"?

PRAY WITH ME

King Jesus, please heal my eyes. Please let me see You for who You are. Let me hear You when You speak. Let my heart understand You when You call and speak to me. Please turn me, turn my heart, turn my affections, turn my mind, turn me physically toward You. And yes, I need healing. I ask for that. But, Jesus, more than anything, I need You. I need a right revelation of who You are. I need to encounter You like Bartimaeus, Isaiah, Job, Moses, and Paul. Please take these scales off my eyes. Please let me see Your glory. Over the course of my life, I have allowed the enemy to reduce You. To blind me to the truth of who You are. And as a result, I've become indifferent. Even cavalier. I've taken You for granted. I've taken this Cross for granted.

Jesus, I'm so sorry. The prophet Isaiah said we hear but don't understand, we see but we don't perceive.[15] *Our hearts are fat, ears heavy, and eyes blind. Jesus, please let me see You with my eyes, hear You with my ears, and understand You with my heart so that I might turn toward You and be healed. Son of David, have mercy on me. I want to see. In Jesus' name.*

AND GOD RESPONDS

"And he [Jesus] answered them, 'To you it has been given to know the secrets of the kingdom of heaven, but to them it has not been given. For to the one who has, more will be given, and he will have an abundance, but from the one who has not, even what he has will be taken away. This is why I speak to them in parables, because seeing they do not see, and hearing they do not hear, nor do they understand. Indeed, in their case the prophecy of Isaiah is fulfilled that says: "'You will indeed hear but never understand, and you will indeed see but never perceive.' For this people's heart has grown dull, and with their ears they can barely hear, and their eyes they have closed, lest they should see with their eyes and hear with their ears and understand with their heart and turn, and I would heal them." But blessed are your eyes, for they see, and your ears, for they hear. For truly, I say to you, many prophets and righteous people longed to see what you see, and did not see it, and to hear what you hear, and did not hear it.'"[16]

DAY 27

"The things that make for peace!"

LUKE 19:42

Jesus walks out of Jericho, twenty miles uphill, toward Jerusalem. In His wake, Bartimaeus is dancing, singing, screaming, "Son of David! Son of David!" Jesus just turned total darkness into light. He just turned stumbling down the street to running full speed. Bartimaeus was blind; now he can see. And not only can he see, but he has seen Jesus.

Face-to-face.

Having healed the son of Timaeus, Jesus sets His face like a flint toward Jerusalem and walks twenty miles uphill for the Passover.[1] The Lamb of God who takes away the sin of the world is about to go and do just that. He knows well the words of Isaiah because He first spoke them to Isaiah seven hundred years prior: "I gave my back to those who strike, and my cheeks to those who pull out the beard; I hid not my face from disgrace and spitting."[2] And not only does He know the words, but He knows what they point to: Rods. Fists. Beard plucked out. Crown of thorns. A cat-o'-nine-tails. Nails. "Like a lamb that is led to the slaughter, and like a sheep that before its shearers is silent, so he opened not his mouth."[3]

The crowd is enormous. They are here because they saw what He did with Lazarus. How He called him out. Raised him to life. And no one can deny it. Lazarus had been stone-cold dead and stinking. Four days in the tomb. Prompting the jealous Pharisees to say to one another, "You are gaining nothing. Look, the world has gone after him."[4]

When Jesus arrives, the fickle crowd puts Him on a donkey and parades Him into the city. Thronging the streets, they lay down their clothes and spread palm fronds, demanding to install Him as king. He can raise the dead, walk on water, make the blind see, make the lame walk. Even the demons believe and obey. What can He *not* do? Surely, He can take on Rome. With their voices they cry out, "Hosanna! Blessed is he who comes in the name of the Lord, even the King of Israel!"[5] Others shout, "Blessed is the King who comes in the name of the Lord! Peace in heaven and glory in the highest!"[6] The excitement reaches such a fever pitch that the religious rulers scold Jesus and tell Him to tell His followers to tone it down. "Teacher, rebuke your disciples."[7]

They call Him "Teacher," while the people call Him "King."

In effect, the Pharisees scold Him: "Young man, are You crazy?" Then they point to the road outside town. Dotted with crosses. "You don't want to mess with them. Have You seen what they do to rebels?"

Jesus studies the crowd, then the massive stones of Herod's temple mount, shakes His head, and gestures. "I tell you, if these were silent, the very stones would cry out."[8]

What did the rocks know that the crowd did not?

In the weeks prior, His conversation with the Pharisees had ramped up. They seemed both amused and somewhat frightened by Him. Worried that He might usurp the authority that they'd worked so hard to ensure, they feign to care about Him and warn, "Get away from here, for Herod wants to kill you." Jesus isn't bothered. Herod's predecessor tried the same. "And he said to them, 'Go and tell that fox, "Behold, I cast out demons and perform cures today and tomorrow, and the third day I finish my course."'"[9]

Another translation says, "And the third day I shall be perfected."[10] Perfected.

Jesus draws near, takes one look at the city, and weeps. The word Luke used for "weep" means to sob or wail out loud. To mourn for the dead. The writer of Hebrews said it this way: "In the days of his flesh, Jesus offered up prayers and supplications, with loud cries and tears."[11] Staring at the city where He's placed His name forever, Jesus cries so hard His shoulders shake. Through tears, He says, "Would that you, even you, had known on this day the things that make for peace! But now they are hidden from your eyes."[12]

Jesus' understatement strikes me. What are the "things that make for peace"? They're many, but they culminate with His shed blood on a criminal's splintery cross.

Why is He crying? Jesus whispers out across the city, "For the days will come upon you, when your enemies will set up a barricade around you and surround you and hem you in on every side and tear you down to the ground, you and your children within you. And they will not leave one stone upon another in you, because you did not know the time of your visitation."[13]

Whose visitation? The Son of God. The Savior of the world. And yet most of them missed Him entirely.

The feast is ramping up. The town is filling. Some who had come up to worship ask the disciples to speak with Jesus, but Jesus refuses, knowing the time for talking has ended. "The hour has come for the Son of Man to be glorified."[14]

Since He turned water to wine at the wedding in Cana, Jesus has been telling His followers, "My hour is not yet come." And yet, three years later, here it is. The hour.

Then Jesus tells a story. A parable. With all that awaits Him, He's still discipling the disciples. Training the Twelve. And us. "Unless a grain of wheat falls into the earth and dies, it remains alone; but if it dies, it bears much fruit." This is the Bread of Life speaking of Himself. "Whoever loves his life loses it, and whoever hates his life in this world will keep it for eternal life. If anyone serves me, he must follow me; and where I am, there will my servant be also. If anyone serves me, the Father will honor him."[15]

Look closely at Jesus' next words. "Now is my soul troubled. And what shall I say? 'Father, save me from this hour'? But for this purpose I have come to this hour. Father, glorify your name."

There it is a second time. The Son's motivation. To glorify the Father.

Then an amazing thing happens. So amazing that many questioned whether it was real. The heavens rumble; a voice thunders and answers the Son. "I have glorified it, and I will glorify it again."[16]

WALK WITH ME BACK TO THE CROSS

Jesus' hour came here. On this splintery tree. This Roman execution stake. Out here, outside the city walls on a common, everyday road where they burn the trash. Where passersby laughed, spit in His face, and called Him names—all while He was making payment on our behalf. Redeeming mankind. Satisfying the wrath of God. So that none should perish.[17] So that all should come to the knowledge of God.[18] So that you and I might know the love with which the

Father loves the Son and the Son loves the Father.[19] The moment Jesus uttered the word *tetelestai*, the earth shook, the sky turned dark, the heavens thundered—and a grain of wheat fell to the earth and died.

What will be the fruit of that death in you, and in me?

PRAY WITH ME

Jesus, like Bartimaeus, I am blind, and I want to see. Please let me see me as You see me. I wonder if when You wept over Jerusalem, You looked down through the ages. Through time. And You saw me. And You wept over me too. I tend to think You did. Please forgive me for the things I've done to cause You sorrow. Please forgive me where I am the cause of Your weeping. Please help me understand the things that have made for peace. Show me, Lord, the extent to which You went to save me—how far gone I was and how far You came to snatch me back.

I know that when Your hour came, You did not shy away. Did not run. With all the power of heaven at Your fingertips, You did not open Your mouth when You could have. And as a result, You suffered in my place. Jesus, You said, "Whoever loves his life loses it, and whoever hates his life in this world will keep it for eternal life. If anyone serves me, he must follow me; and where I am, there will my servant be also."[20] Lord, I want to serve You. Follow You. You've told me that where You are, there I'll be. That means I must follow You to an execution. Something in me must be put to death. Paul knew this. It's why he said, "I die daily"[21] and "I have been crucified with Christ."[22] Lord, I want to do the same. Give me courage, Lord.

Maybe this is why Paul said, "But far be it from me to boast except in the cross of our Lord Jesus Christ, by which the world has been cru-cified to me, and I to the world."[23] **Please forgive me for any boastful, arrogant, or prideful thought, word, or act where I've boasted in me and not in You. When You wept over Jerusalem, You said,** *"You did not know the time of your visitation."[24]* **Lord, please don't let me miss Your visitation. You are the Bread of Life. Only You satisfy. You're the kernel of wheat that fell to the earth and died in order to bear much fruit. Two things strike me about that: What rises up out of the ground does not look like what was put into it. And please bear fruit in and through me. In Jesus' name.**

AND GOD RESPONDS

"Therefore, if anyone is in Christ, he is a new creation. The old has passed away; behold, the new has come. All this is from God, who through Christ reconciled us to himself and gave us the ministry of reconciliation; that is, in Christ God was reconciling the world to himself, not counting their trespasses against them, and entrusting to us the message of reconciliation. Therefore, we are ambassadors for Christ, God making his appeal through us. We implore you on behalf of Christ, be reconciled to God. For our sake he made him to be sin who knew no sin, so that in him we might become the righteousness of God."[25]

DAY 28

". . . and anointed the feet of Jesus and
wiped his feet with her hair . . ."

JOHN 12:1–19

"Then Jesus, deeply moved again, came to the tomb. It was a cave, and a stone lay against it."[1]

Jesus is standing in Bethany. Weeping. His friend Lazarus is dead.

"Jesus said, 'Take away the stone.' Martha, the sister of the dead man, said to him, 'Lord, by this time there will be an odor, for he has been dead four days.'"[2]

Martha is trying to help Jesus save face. To spare Him the embarrassment. Not to mention the smell. But Jesus can smell Lazarus even with the stone in place. Jesus is about to confront her and everyone within the sound of His voice with the truth. The same truth with which He is currently confronting us. Lazarus is not the only dead man in the tomb. The truth is that all of us are dead and rotten to the core. Our eventual condition is to rot. Decay. Stink. No matter how much we work out, no matter how many supplements we take, no matter how much money we spend, every one of us will one day turn to worm food. Period. That may offend you, but Jesus offers a remedy:

"Jesus said to her, 'Did I not tell you that if you believed you would see the glory of God?' So they took away the stone. And Jesus lifted up his eyes and said, 'Father, I thank you that you have heard me. I knew that you always hear me, but I said this on account of the people standing around, that they may believe that you sent me.' When he had said these things, he cried out with a loud voice, 'Lazarus, come out.' The man who had died came out, his hands and feet bound with linen strips, and his face wrapped with a cloth. Jesus said to them, 'Unbind him, and let him go.'"[3]

Notice they rolled away the stone before Jesus called him out. What stone stands between you and Jesus? What needs rolling away in your life? What is preventing you from obeying His voice? And don't miss the obvious—Lazarus is us. And we are Lazarus.

Do you believe Jesus still raises the dead? Jesus is still speaking a word and bringing corpses back to life. It's just what He does.

Now jump forward. Closer to the end of the story. "Six days before the Passover, Jesus therefore came to Bethany, where Lazarus was, whom Jesus had raised from the dead."[4]

This means Jesus has just come up from Jericho having restored Bartimaeus's sight.

"So they gave a dinner for him there. Martha served, and Lazarus was one of those reclining with him at table. Mary therefore took a pound of expensive ointment made from pure nard, and anointed the feet of Jesus and wiped his feet with her hair. The house was filled with the fragrance of the perfume."[5]

This is a beautiful picture of worship—poured out on the feet of Jesus.

"But Judas Iscariot, one of his disciples (he who was about to betray him), said, 'Why was this ointment not sold for three hundred denarii and given to the poor?' He said this, not because he cared about the poor, but because he was a thief, and having charge of the moneybag he used to help himself to what was put into it. Jesus said, 'Leave her alone, so that she may keep it for the day of my burial. For the poor you always have with you, but you do not always have me.'"[6]

Does my worship of Him—does yours—spread throughout the whole house?

"When the large crowd of the Jews learned that Jesus was there, they came, not only on account of him but also to see Lazarus, whom he had raised from the dead. So the chief priests made plans to put Lazarus to death as well, because on account of him many of the Jews were going away and believing in Jesus."[7]

Lazarus had become a conundrum to the religious elite. Rather difficult to argue. He had been doornail dead. They all knew it. Then Jesus called him out, and out he walked wearing dead man's clothes. To which Jesus said, "Take off the grave clothes." How many of us, dead in our sins, having spent years in the tomb, have been called out of the tomb but have never taken off our grave clothes? How many of us weeks, months, or years later are still walking around draped in the mummy-wrappings of the old dead people we used to be?

But we are not those people. Seems silly to still be wearing those clothes.

"The next day the large crowd that had come to the feast heard that Jesus was coming to Jerusalem. So they took branches of palm trees and went out to meet him, crying out, 'Hosanna! Blessed is he who comes in the name of the Lord, even the King of Israel!' And Jesus found a young donkey and sat on it, just as it is written, 'Fear not, daughter of Zion; behold, your king is coming, sitting on a donkey's colt!' His disciples did not understand these things at first, but when Jesus was glorified, then they remembered that these things had been written about him and had been done to him. The crowd that had been with him when he called Lazarus out of the tomb and raised him from the dead continued to bear witness. . . . So the Pharisees said to one another, '. . . Look, the world has gone after him.'"[8]

Have we? Have we gone after Him? Or have we gone after something else? Someone else?

Walk with Me Back to the Cross

The truth is that all of us who are in Christ Jesus were once Lazarus. Doornail dead. Jesus wept over us. Then He rolled away the stone and called us out. If you've made it this far in this book and you have yet to respond to His call—to surrender to the lordship of Jesus Christ—listen carefully. He's calling you out. Right now. "Come out." I pray you listen and obey. And follow Him. Daily.

Then there are some of us who have heard Him, who've been raised to life in Christ, and yet we've never taken off our grave clothes. Or we put them back on from time to time. Because they're comfortable. Because we like to slip back into our old life. Because "sin dwells in us." Wretched people that we are, who will deliver us?

It's time for a permanent wardrobe change. To rip the grave clothes off and burn them. In a beautiful exchange, Jesus takes from us our dirty linens, the soiled stuff from our previous rotten life, and wraps us in His robe of righteousness. Rags for new. An inconceivable expression of unimaginable love.

What is your response at this Cross? A pile of dirty clothes at your feet? All your worship poured out on His? One of my spiritual heroes used to stand in church during the worship and wave a white handkerchief. A sea of people. One man with a white flag. I can still see it, and it's been forty years. When I asked him why, he said, "'For the eyes of the Lord run to and fro throughout the whole earth, to give strong support to those whose heart is blameless toward him.'"[9] I wonder if the Lord sees our worship? Does it catch His eye? Does our incense waft heavenward?

There is no place in Scripture that I can find where worship is not accompanied by an action of the body. That should challenge us and how we worship the only One worthy of our worship. The King of the universe stepped off His throne and gave Himself to ransom you and me. The exchange. Him for us. Jesus is worthy of our face-pressed-to-the-earth praise. Of our hands lifted high in worship. Of our dancing-like-David-danced worship. Of our handkerchief waving.

When He arrives and returns to judge the quick and the dead, I want Him to find me singing at the top of my lungs, hands raised, a white cloth in my hand, sweat on my brow, dressed in clothes He gave me.

So let me ask you: What are you wearing? Soiled grave clothes? Or a spotless robe of righteousness? Because here's the thing: Jesus looks down from this Cross and offers you new for old.

PRAY WITH ME

Lord Jesus, I want to wave the white flag. Both in surrender and praise. Surrender because You alone are King. And praise because You alone are King. In my heart of hearts, I make a really good Pharisee, and my knee-jerk is cynicism and unbelief. Mocking whispers. I tend to forget that I was Lazarus and You called me out. Which is crazy. How can I forget that? But I do. Constantly. I'm so sorry. Lord, I forget and I wander. A sheep led astray. But today, I want to lift up my white handkerchief and wave it. I pray You see me. And when You do, I pray You see someone whose heart is wholly Yours. Who has exchanged my rags for Your robe. In Jesus' name.

AND GOD RESPONDS

"And they sang a new song, saying, 'Worthy are you to take the scroll and to open its seals, for you were slain, and by your blood you ransomed people for God from every tribe and language and people and nation, and you have made them a kingdom and priests to our God, and they shall reign on the earth.' Then I looked, and I heard around the throne and the living creatures and the elders the voice of many angels, numbering myriads of myriads and thousands of thousands, saying with a loud voice, 'Worthy is the Lamb who was slain, to receive power and wealth and wisdom and might and honor and glory and blessing!' And I heard every creature in heaven and on earth and under the earth and in the sea, and all that is in them, saying, 'To him who sits on the throne and to the Lamb be blessing and honor and glory and might forever and ever!' And the four living creatures said, 'Amen!' and the elders fell down and worshiped."[10]

DAY 29

"When I am lifted up . . ."

JOHN 12:27–32

"Now is my soul troubled. And what shall I say? 'Father, save me from his hour'? But for this purpose I have come to this hour. Father, glorify your name." Then a voice came from heaven: "I have glorified it, and I will glorify it again." Then the crowd that stood there and heard it said that it had thundered. Others said, "An angel has spoken to him." Jesus answered, "This voice has come for your sake, not mine. Now is the judgment of this world; now will the ruler of this world be cast out. And I, when I am lifted up from the earth, will draw all people to myself."[1]

This is third time Jesus has spoken of being "lifted up." Those listening to Him know full well Isaiah's prophecy regarding the **Suffering Servant**: "Behold, my servant shall act wisely; he shall be high and lifted up, and shall be exalted. As many were astonished at you—his appearance was so marred, beyond human semblance, and his form beyond that of the children of mankind."[2] But I wonder how many of them are starting to put the pieces together. Do they know that they have a front-row seat to the redemption of the world?

Jesus telegraphed this lifting up early in His ministry when he told Nicodemus, "You must be born again."[3] Nicodemus then asked his famous question: "How can a man be born when he is old? Can he enter a second time into his mother's womb and be born?"[4] Nicodemus would have been familiar with Moses and the exodus and would understand the coming reference; he just had no idea what Jesus meant by His response: "And as Moses lifted up the serpent in the wilderness, so must the Son of Man be lifted up, that whoever believes in him may have eternal life."[5]

The nation of Israel had been wandering in the desert almost forty years. Moses' older siblings, Miriam and Aaron, are both dead. He now knows he will not lead the nation into the promised land because he struck the rock at Meribah rather than speak to it. The people are weary and complaining. "From Mount Hor they set out by the way to the Red Sea, to go around the land of Edom. And the people became impatient on the way. And the people spoke against God and against Moses, 'Why have you brought us up out of Egypt to die in the wilderness? For there is no food and no water, and we loathe this worthless food.'"[6]

That worthless food was manna that fell from the sky.

"Then the LORD sent fiery serpents among the people, and they bit the people, so that many people of Israel died. And the people came to Moses and said, 'We have sinned, for we have spoken against the LORD and against you. Pray to the LORD, that he take away the serpents from us.' So Moses prayed for the people. And the LORD said to Moses, 'Make a fiery serpent and set it on a pole, and everyone who is bitten, when he sees it, shall live.' So Moses made a bronze serpent and set it on a pole. And if a serpent bit anyone, he would look at the bronze serpent and live."[7]

Moses wraps the snake around the pole and lifts it high. The people walk forward, look up—admitting their guilt—and God spares them.

The second time Jesus speaks of being lifted up, He's in the temple. The Pharisees have just brought in a woman caught in adultery and tried to trap him. Jesus kneels, writes in the dirt, and speaks, "Let him who is without sin among you be the first to throw a stone at her."[8] Scripture does not record what He wrote, but the men looking at Him know the Torah. Verbatim. And they know that in Exodus 31, "He [God] gave to Moses, when he had finished speaking with him on Mount Sinai, the two tablets of the testimony, tablets of stone, written with the finger of God."[9] The Pharisees walk in set to accuse the woman and trap Jesus. Instead, they watch the finger of God doodle in the sand. One by one, they drop their stones, exit, and leave Jesus alone with the woman. "Neither do I condemn you; go, and from now on sin no more."[10]

Further evidence that there is more mercy in Jesus than sin in us.

But the Pharisees keep hounding Him, so they later find Him in the treasury and attempt to engage Him in mental jousting. Jesus says, "'I am going away, and you will seek me, and you will die in your sin. Where I am going, you cannot come.' So the Jews said, 'Will he kill himself, since he says, "Where I am going, you cannot come"?' He said to them, 'You are from below; I am from above. You are of this world; I am not of this world. I told you that you would die in your sins, for unless you believe that I am he you will die in your sins.' So they said to him, 'Who are you?'"[11]

Which, incidentally, is the most important question any of us will ever ask.

"Jesus said to them, 'Just what I have been telling you from the beginning. I have much to say to you and much to judge, but he who sent me is true, and I declare to the world what I have heard from him.' They did not understand that he had been speaking to them about the Father. So Jesus said to them, 'When you have lifted up the Son of Man, then you will know that I am he, and that I do nothing on my own authority, but speak just as the Father taught me. And he who sent me is with me. He has not left me alone, for I always do the things that are pleasing to him.'"[12]

Later, these same men will kill Jesus for calling God His Father and claiming to be His Son. Which will cause Him to be lifted up before their eyes.

The passage ends with this: "As he was saying these things, many believed in him."[13]

Do you see the word?

The third and last time Jesus speaks of being lifted up, the people are arguing whether it was a voice from heaven, an angel, or thunder. Jesus responds with, "Now is the judgment of this world; now will the ruler of this world be cast out. And I, when I am lifted up from the earth, will draw all people to myself."[14]

As much as I study this, I am struck by one thing—in order for Jesus to be lifted up, He had to first step down off His throne. Willingly.

And while this was Jesus' selfless response, this was not the posture of everyone in heaven. And the contrast is striking. We get insight into this when Ezekiel prophesied over Tyre. In his prophesy, he spoke of two people—a prince and a king. The prince was an earthly man; the king was not. The king was a principality. A power. And his name was lucipher.

"Moreover, the word of the LORD came to me: 'Son of man, raise a lamentation over the king of Tyre, and say to him, Thus says the Lord GOD: "You were the signet of perfection, full of wisdom and

218

perfect in beauty. You were in Eden, the garden of God; every precious stone was your covering, sardius, topaz, and diamond, beryl, onyx, and jasper, sapphire, emerald, and carbuncle; and crafted in gold were your settings and your engravings. On the day that you were created they were prepared. You were an anointed guardian cherub. I placed you; you were on the holy mountain of God; in the midst of the stones of fire you walked. You were blameless in your ways from the day you were created, till unrighteousness was found in you. In the abundance of your trade you were filled with violence in your midst, and you sinned; so I cast you as a profane thing from the mountain of God, and I destroyed you, O guardian cherub, from the midst of the stones of fire. Your heart was proud because of your beauty; you corrupted your wisdom for the sake of your splendor. I cast you to the ground; I exposed you before kings, to feast their eyes on you. By the multitude of your iniquities, in the unrighteousness of your trade you profaned your sanctuaries; so I brought fire out from your midst; it consumed you, and I turned you to ashes on the earth in the sight of all who saw you. All who know you among the peoples are appalled at you; you have come to a dreadful end and shall be no more forever."'"[15]

WALK WITH ME BACK TO THE CROSS

Notice two phrases from Ezekiel's prophesy: "Till unrighteousness was found in you"[16] and "by the multitude of your iniquities."

Iniquity is *the* problem. My problem. Your problem. It's the venom that runs in our veins. But God knew this. Let me help make the connection. Let's return to the Suffering Servant in Isaiah 53. "But he was pierced for our transgressions; he was crushed for our iniquities;" and "the Lord has laid on him the iniquity of us all."[17] On the Cross, when He was lifted up, Jesus took on Himself all of the evil due to us, our iniquity—our guilt and all of the consequences due us for that sin—and gave us, in return, all the good that was due to Him. "Upon him was the chastisement that brought us peace, and with his wounds we are healed."[18]

Isaiah described lucifer's fall (remember, I don't capitalize his name) and gave us insight into his motivation:

"Your pomp is brought down to Sheol, the sound of your harps; maggots are laid as a bed beneath you, and worms are your covers. 'How you are fallen from heaven, O Day Star, son of Dawn! How you are cut down to the ground, you who laid the nations low! You said in your heart, "I will ascend to heaven; above the stars of God, I will set my throne on high; I will sit on the mount of assembly in the far reaches of the north; I will ascend above the heights of the clouds; I will make myself like the Most High." But you are brought down to Sheol, to the far reaches of the pit.'"[19]

Five times, lucifer says "I will":

I will ascend to heaven.
I will set my throne on high.
I will sit on the mount of assembly.
I will ascend above.
I will make myself like the Most High.

This is anti-Christ.

So lucifer looks to the Father and says, "*I will*" while Jesus looks to the Father and says, "*Your will* be done." Derek Prince liked to say, "lucifer reached up and fell. Jesus stooped down and God raised Him up." There is an undeniable principle at work here. As undeniable as gravity: Jesus humbled Himself—bowed down—and God lifted Him up: "For everyone who exalts himself will be humbled, and he who humbles himself will be exalted."[20]

How then should we respond when we walk to this Cross? Swagger or limp? Paul explained it this way to the Philippians:

"Have this mind among yourselves, which is yours in Christ Jesus, who, though he was in the form of God, did not count equality with God a thing to be grasped, but emptied himself, by taking the form of a servant, being born in the likeness of men. And being found in human form, he humbled himself by becoming obedient to the point of death, even death on a cross. Therefore God has highly exalted him and bestowed on him the name that is above every name, so that at the name of Jesus every knee should bow, in heaven and on earth and under the earth, and every tongue confess that Jesus Christ is Lord, to the glory of God the Father."[21]

When you look at this Cross, what is your response? *I will*, or *Your will?*

Pray with Me

Lord, I'm an arrogant, prideful mess. I've reached up more times than I can count, sat on a throne only meant for You, and the thought of humbling myself has never entered my mind. When Ezekiel and Isaiah prophesied about lucipher, they could very well have been speaking of me: "Unrighteousness was found in me. My heart was filled with violence. I sinned. My heart was proud. By the multitude of my iniquities . . ." That same pride is in me. That same rebellion. That ugly arrogance that wants to reach up and glorify me over You. That venom flows in my veins.

God have mercy. Forgive me, please. I am so sorry. I've exalted me and my will over You and Yours. I've thumbed my nose at You, said, "I got this," when I don't and never have. I know me. I know my prideful thoughts. My selfish and self-serving intentions. And how, at the end of the day, what I want takes precedence over what You want ninety-nine times out of one hundred. Jesus have mercy. Today, I choose to humble myself. You've got this. You must increase, and I must decrease. Today, I bow my face to the ground and enthrone You in my heart. You alone are King, and I desire to serve You. I clothe myself with humility, a bondservant by choice.

My sin is more than I can count, but today, I want to address my pride—my rebellion—I want to crucify that here today. At Your Cross. Please drive a stake today through the heart of my pride. Lord, I give it to You. Here, take it all. I don't want it anymore. And when I wake up tomorrow and find that somewhere in the night I draped it around my neck like a prize, please let me come back here and take it off again. Every day. I want to die daily. Thank You for Your mercy. For Your blood that speaks a better word than that of Abel. For Your forgiveness. I don't deserve it, and I have no claim on it, but I receive it. Let it rain down. Let it wash over me. Baptize me today, fresh and anew. At Your name, I bow. Face to the carpet. I bow before You and You alone. In Jesus' name.

AND GOD RESPONDS

"And you were dead in the trespasses and sins in which you once walked, following the course of this world, following the prince of the power of the air, the spirit that is now at work in the sons of disobedience—among whom we all once lived in the passions of our flesh, carrying out the desires of the body and the mind, and were by nature children of wrath, like the rest of mankind. But God, being rich in mercy, because of the great love with which he loved us, even when we were dead in our trespasses, made us alive together with Christ—by grace you have been saved—and raised us up with him and seated us with him in the heavenly places in Christ Jesus, so that in the coming ages he might show the immeasurable riches of his grace in kindness toward us in Christ Jesus. For by grace you have been saved through faith. And this is not your own doing; it is the gift of God, not a result of works, so that no one may boast. For we are his workmanship, created in Christ Jesus for good works, which God prepared beforehand, that we should walk in them."[22]

DAY 30

"I am he."

JOHN 18:3–6

"And when he came, he went up to him at once and said, 'Rabbi!' And he kissed him. And they laid hands on him and seized him."[1] Under cover of night, in a garden, Jesus is betrayed with a kiss from one of his closest followers. A man who had lived, eaten, slept, and laughed with Him for the last three years. Everything Jesus did for and said to the other eleven, He did and said to Judas. Following the kiss, as if that weren't bad enough, He is then abandoned by everyone. He stands alone. Seeing Jesus bound by the soldiers and their captain and the officers of the Jews, "they all left him and fled."[2]

They lead Him to Annas, the father-in-law of Caiaphas, the high priest, who questions Jesus about His disciples and His teaching. "Jesus answered him, 'I have spoken openly to the world. I have always taught in the synagogues and in the temple, where all Jews come together. I have said nothing in secret. Why do you ask me? Ask those who have heard me what I said to them; they know what I said.' When he had said these things, one of the officers standing by struck Jesus with his hand, saying, 'Is that how you answer the high priest?'"[3]

Pause. Let this settle. Watch it happen. Someone standing close to Jesus made a fist and threw a haymaker at the Son of God.

Jesus is then led to Caiaphas's house where the scribes and elders are gathered to determine not if Jesus is the Son of God but *if He claimed to be*. They want to trap Him by His words. The chief priests and the whole council were envious and seeking false testimony against Jesus so they could put Him to death.[4] Two false witnesses have come forward and recalled how Jesus had said, "I am able to destroy the temple of God, and to rebuild it in three days."[5]

A marvel of the first-century world, Herod's temple had taken forty-six years to complete, so Caiaphas, in his infinite wisdom, stands up in dramatic and chest-pounding fashion and says to Jesus, "'Have you no answer to make? What is it that these men testify against you?' But Jesus remained silent." Further angered, Caiaphas demands, "I adjure you by the living God, tell us if you are the Christ, the Son of God." Which is interesting since the living God is standing three feet away and the soldiers who brought Him in couldn't stand in His presence when they tried to arrest Him in the garden. Jesus responds by referencing Daniel's prophecy, which Caiaphas would have known by heart. "You have said so. But I tell you, from now on you will see the Son of Man seated at the right hand of Power and coming on the clouds of heaven."[6] Jesus' response is akin to, "I am the One of whom Daniel spoke, and not only am I the Son of God, but I am returning to my Father in heaven where I will sit at His right hand and exercise the full power of God."

Caiaphas tears His clothes and shouts, "'He has uttered blasphemy. What further witnesses do we need? You have now heard his blasphemy. What is your judgment?' They answered, 'He deserves death.' Then they spit in his face and struck him. And some slapped him, saying, 'Prophesy to us, you Christ! Who is it that struck you?'"[7]

The Gospel of Mark records, "And some began to spit on him and to cover his face and to strike him, saying to him, 'Prophesy!' And the guards received him with blows."[8] The margin notes of the NASB say, "treated him with blows inflicted by rods."[9]

Spit, mock, punch, or bow—what determines the difference? Both are aimed at the same Jesus, so what does the bowing group possess that the punching group does not? What would cause someone to press their face to the dirt rather than throw a right hook?

Maybe the key lies with Solomon in Proverbs 2: "My son, if you receive my words and treasure up my commandments with you, making your ear attentive to wisdom and inclining your heart to understanding; yes, if you call out for insight and raise your voice for understanding, if you seek it like silver and search for it as for hidden treasures, then you will understand the fear of the Lord and find the knowledge of God."[10]

The difference? The fear of the Lord.

But what kind of fear is this when we know He has not given us a spirit of fear?[11] As I mentioned earlier, the fear of the Lord is not the same as being scared. Scared, or the healthy emotion of fear, is a response God gave us for our good—to warn us of danger. In contrast, the fear of the Lord is reverence. Awe. Mind-blowing, unable-to-wrap-your-head-around-it amazement.

What does the Bible say about this fear?

Moses commanded the people, "Let the fear of the Lord be upon you" and "Thus you shall do in the fear of the Lord, in faithfulness, and with your whole heart."[12] Job said, "Behold, the fear of the Lord, that is wisdom, and to turn away from evil is understanding."[13] King David said, "The fear of the Lord is clean, enduring forever," "Listen to me; I will teach you the fear of the Lord" and "The fear of the Lord is the beginning of wisdom."[14] Solomon said, "The fear of the Lord is the beginning of knowledge" and "The fear of the Lord is hatred of evil." "The fear of the Lord is a fountain of life" and "By the fear of the Lord one turns away from evil."[15]

Isaiah, in his prophecy regarding the Messiah, said, "And the Spirit of the Lord shall rest upon him, the Spirit of wisdom and understanding, the Spirit of counsel and might, the Spirit of knowledge and the fear of the Lord. And his delight shall be in the fear of the Lord."[16] After Jesus' crucifixion and resurrection, Luke wrote of the church in Acts, "And walking in the fear of the Lord and in the comfort of the Holy Spirit, it [the church] multiplied."[17] Lastly, Paul told the Corinthians in his second letter, "Therefore, knowing the fear of the Lord, we persuade others."[18] In other words, because of the fear of the Lord, we do what we do.

And God Himself said, "Then they will call upon me, but I will not answer; they will seek me diligently but will not find me. Because they hated knowledge and did not choose the fear of the Lord."[19] And in one of the most astounding statements in Scripture, "The fear of the Lord leads to life, and whoever has it rests satisfied; he will not be visited by harm."[20] The NASB reads, "untouched by evil." The NKJV says, "not be visited with evil."

Walk with Me Back to the Cross

Return now to the moment of His arrest. "Judas then, having received the Roman cohort and officers from the chief priests and the Pharisees, came there with lanterns and torches and weapons. So Jesus, knowing all the things that were coming upon Him, went forth and said to them, 'Whom do you seek?' They answered Him, 'Jesus the Nazarene.' He said to them, 'I am He.' And Judas also, who was betraying Him, was standing with them. So when He said to them, 'I am He,' they drew back and fell to the ground."[21]

The God of the universe, the One who made all things, in whom all things hold together, and at whose name every knee will one day bow—is speaking: "I am He." Which, incidentally, are the same words He spoke to Moses when He called to him out of the bush: "I am who I am."[22] And when Jesus speaks these words, even those who don't believe, who don't walk in the fear of Him, fall flat on their faces.

We have come to the end of day 30 in our pilgrimage. Tomorrow, we begin the final push up Mount Calvary. It will not be easy and will require something from you. As the sun sets on the Son, sit here with me. Lean against the post. Like the soldiers who were confronted with "I am" in the flesh, we face a choice: mock, spit, punch, betray . . . or bow. Either rebellion, defiance, and all-out mutiny, or total surrender. There is no in-between. Now look up. He is here. Will you punch Him? Or bow?

Pray with Me

King Jesus, more often than not, my knee-jerk reaction to who You are and what You say is to shake my head. Find some wiggle room. Make a defiant fist and punch You in the teeth. To mock and argue the words coming out of Your mouth. I may not do this openly, but I know my heart, and my reaction is closer to the servant of the high priest and his cronies than I'd like to admit. Please help me today to choose to walk in the fear of You, and only the fear of You. Please teach me the fear of the Lord. Let my heart's response be to fall flat on my face and worship. To cry out, "My Lord and my God."

The tax collector had a right fear of You. The Pharisee did not. I want that. With so much good promised from walking in the fear of the Lord, please teach me, and let me not be visited with evil. Please forgive me when I don't walk in fear of You. Judas did not walk in the fear of You, and yet he knew You intimately. Walked with You. Ate with You. Talked with You. Please, dear Jesus, let me first walk in fear and reverence of You and then, through that, intimacy with You. Please don't let me sin against You in my arrogance and pride. Don't let me think I'm part of Your inner circle when, in fact, I'm quick to betray You with a kiss rather than revere You. Jesus, I know if I walk in a right fear of You, then I will bear fruit worthy of repentance. Please help me do this all the days of my life starting with today. In Jesus' name.

AND GOD RESPONDS

"Follow me."

PART FOUR

What Was
Exchanged at
the Cross?

DAY 31

"What shall I do with Jesus who is called Christ?"

MATTHEW 27:1–23

"When morning came, all the chief priests and the elders of the people took counsel against Jesus to put him to death. And they bound him and led him away and delivered him over to Pilate the governor."[1] It is here, in Pilate's praetorium, or headquarters, that an amazing conversation occurs.

Jesus stands before the governor, and Pilate asks Him, "Are you the King of the Jews?" Jesus says, "You have said so." Pilate continues to press Him, "Do you not hear how many things they testify against you?"[2] Translation? "Don't You hear what they're saying? They want to kill You." But Jesus gives no answer. Not a single one. Which amazes Pilate.[3]

Pilate is uncertain, so in accordance with tradition, he offers to release one prisoner: Barabbas, a murderer who led an insurrection, or Jesus who is called Christ—for Pilate knew they had delivered Him up out of envy.[4] The crowd responds, "Give us Barabbas." While Pilate is sitting in the judgment seat, his wife sends word to have nothing to do with this righteous man, "for I have suffered much because of him today in a dream."[5] Pilate is looking for a way out, so while the chief priests and elders continue their scheming games, Pilate asks again, "Which of the two do you want me to release for you?"

And the crowd responds, "Barabbas."[6]

Then Pilate asks the most important question ever asked in the history of the world: "Then what shall I do with Jesus who is called Christ?"[7] Mark's gospel records it this way: "And Pilate again said to them, 'Then what shall I do with the man you call the King of the Jews?'"[8]

This is *the* question.

The crowd cries out, "'Let him be crucified!' And he said, 'Why? What evil has he done?' But they shouted all the more, 'Let him be crucified!'"[9]

Pilate finds an out when he hears that Jesus is a Galilean—which places Jesus under Herod's jurisdiction. So Pilate sends Jesus to be judged by Herod, who just happens to be in Jerusalem on that Thursday. Herod is glad to see Jesus, hoping to see Him perform a sign, but when he questions Jesus, Jesus makes no response. He stands silently as Herod treats Him with contempt and mocks Him, even dressing Him in "splendid clothing."[10] The gospel writers Matthew, Mark, and John described Jesus as being dressed in purple clothing, with a reed placed in His right hand and a crown of thorns twisted and beaten onto His brow with rods.[11] Then they kneel before Him, mocking Him, saying, "Hail, King of the Jews!"[12] Interestingly, Herod and Pilate—who had never been too friendly—became friends that day, over the death of the Son of God.

Pilate sees he can gain nothing and that a riot is beginning, so he calls for water, washes his hands in front of the crowd, and proclaims, "I am innocent of this man's blood; see to it yourselves." And it is here that the people answer with some of the worst and most painful words ever spoken in human history: "'His blood be on us and on our children!' Then he released for them Barabbas, and having scourged Jesus, delivered him to be crucified."[13]

Following Pilate's decision, Mark recorded possibly the saddest and most painful words ever written: "And when they had mocked him, they stripped him of the purple cloak and put his own clothes on him. And they led him out to crucify him."[14]

Back to Pilate's question. It's the most important question you and I will ever ask. Due to the grace and mercy of God our answer determines where we spend eternity. Either damnation in the fires of hell where we long for God while living eternally in His absence, or total and complete acceptance with the Father as a child of God living eternally in His presence. The contrast could not be more striking.

WALK WITH ME BACK TO THE CROSS

Over to our left, the soldiers gamble for His clothes. Nearby in the palace, Pilate and Herod lift a glass and slap each other's backs. Along the road, people spit, curse, and laugh. Above us hangs Jesus.

The question remains: What will you do with this man Jesus?

PRAY WITH ME

King Jesus, I'm so sorry that my sin separated me from You and that there was, and is, so much of it that I could never atone for it. Never pay the total penalty for my own sin. But You in Your mercy, due to a depth of love that I may never understand this side of the grave, chose to do for me what I could never do for myself, and for that I am eternally grateful. I know unexpressed gratitude is no gratitude at all, so please hear me when I cry out, "My Lord and My God." Your Word says, *"For the eyes of the Lord move to and fro throughout the earth that He may strongly support those whose heart is completely His."[15]* I pray that when You see me, You find a heart that is completely Yours.

And as for Pilate's question, I'd like to answer it. I'd like to go on record. Here and now. With all that I am, all that I have, with all the breath in my lungs, I bow and declare You Jesus. You and You alone are my Lord and my God. My King. Please rule and reign this day and let Your kingdom come and Your will be done. In all things. In Jesus' name.

AND GOD RESPONDS

"So Moses cut two tablets of stone like the first. And he rose early in the morning and went up on Mount Sinai, as the LORD had commanded him, and took in his hand two tablets of stone. The LORD descended in the cloud and stood with him there, and proclaimed the name of the LORD. The LORD passed before him and proclaimed, 'The LORD, the LORD, a God merciful and gracious, slow to anger, and abounding in steadfast love and faithfulness, keeping steadfast love for thousands, forgiving iniquity and transgression and sin, but who will by no means clear the guilty, visiting the iniquity of the fathers on the children and the children's children, to the third and the fourth generation.' And Moses quickly bowed his head toward the earth and worshiped. And he said, 'If now I have found favor in your sight, O Lord, please let the Lord go in the midst of us, for it is a stiff-necked people, and pardon our iniquity and our sin, and take us for your inheritance.' And he said, 'Behold, I am making a covenant. Before all your people I will do marvels, such as have not been created in all the earth or in any nation. And all the people among whom you are shall see the work of the LORD, for it is an awesome thing that I will do with you.'"[16]

DAY 32

"Jesus, remember me when you come into your kingdom."

LUKE 23:32–43

"Two others, who were criminals, were led away to be put to death with him. And when they came to the place that is called The Skull, there they crucified him, and the criminals, one on his right and one on his left. And Jesus said, 'Father, forgive them, for they know not what they do.' And they cast lots to divide his garments. And the people stood by, watching, but the rulers scoffed at him, saying, 'He saved others; let him save himself, if he is the Christ of God, his Chosen One!' The soldiers also mocked him, coming up and offering him sour wine and saying, 'If you are the King of the Jews, save yourself!' There was also an inscription over him, 'This is the King of the Jews.' One of the criminals who were hanged railed at him, saying, 'Are you not the Christ? Save yourself and us!' But the other rebuked him, saying, 'Do you not fear God, since you are under the same sentence of condemnation? And we indeed justly, for we are receiving the due reward of our deeds; but this man has done nothing wrong.' And he said, 'Jesus, remember me when you come into your kingdom.'"[1]

Two thieves bookend Jesus. One on His right, one on His left.

Below them, the soldiers seem to be enjoying themselves. They spit on Jesus. Roll dice. And one of the soldiers takes a sponge on a stick, called a *tersorium*, dips it in feces-laced vinegar, and shoves it into His mouth. Jesus doesn't like it. He's struggling to remain conscious as the weight of the world hangs on His shoulders.

Jesus' mother approaches, and when He says something to her, she cries on John's shoulder. While His hands and feet are nailed to the cross, it's her heart that is pierced. She is inconsolable.

In between breaths, Jesus prays. Talks to God. Calls Him Father.

The second criminal is indignant. Railing. "Are you not the Christ? Save yourself and us!"

The first criminal rebukes the second. "Do you not fear God, since you are under the same sentence of condemnation? And we indeed justly, for we are receiving the due reward of our deeds." His words tell us much about him.

To begin with, he's telling the truth. He got what he deserved. But for some reason, he looks to Jesus and says, "Jesus, remember me when you come into your kingdom." Two words reveal the thief's heart: "your kingdom."

Why does he say this? What happened? Both criminals are looking at the same Jesus. The One who said: "As Moses lifted up the serpent in the wilderness, so must the Son of Man be lifted up, that whoever believes in him may have eternal life."[2]

Eye level. The two humans closest to the crucifixion of the Son of God. How does one believe and one not? What happens to move one heart from not believing to believing?

We have no idea what he thought or believed about Jesus prior to now, but in this moment, He believes Jesus is who the sign above His head declares Him to be. The Son of God. The King with a kingdom. And that today, after being away, He's returning to it.

This belief that Jesus is who He says He is, is probably not the thinking that landed the thief on that cross. But of all the people in Scripture, of all the saints, we know something about this criminal that cannot be said of any other saint or person in Scripture. We know, beyond a shadow of a doubt, that He is with Jesus. Right this second. "Truly, I say to you, today you will be with me in paradise."[3]

What has the thief done to earn this?

He hasn't gone to church. He hasn't mended his ways or paid back all he owes. He hasn't studied great theological truths. He hasn't responded to an altar call or joined a discipleship group. He hasn't served at his local church. He hasn't visited any prisoners. He hasn't fed the poor. He hasn't prayed for the sick or preached the gospel of the kingdom. He hasn't taken care of widows and orphans. He hasn't tithed or fasted, and as far as we know, he hasn't prayed. He can't even lift his hands in worship because they're tied to the crossbar. This dude hasn't done squat—not one single thing—and yet, according to Jesus, this criminal is in heaven as I write this.

What's the difference between the two criminals? One's heart is puffed up. Angry. Arrogant. Reviling. The other's heart is bowed down. A posture of submission. Of yieldedness. Of total surrender. And Jesus, who can see all things, sees it. Plain as day.

So, rewind the tape. What happened? Just yesterday, the criminal was . . . a criminal. He got caught, had a trial, was convicted, marched out of town, and unceremoniously hung on this tree. And by his own admission, he deserves what he is getting. What happened between yesterday and right now?

I think the answer lies in the criminal's view. His perspective. Look through his eyes. Watch what he's watching. The man on the middle cross is drowning in his own lung fluid. Now listen with his ears. "Father, forgive them." "I thirst."[4] "Mother, behold your son."[5]

Now smell with his nose. He's outside the town, out where they burn the trash. He's also close enough to smell Jesus' sweat and blood. And to see His naked and shredded body.

Free of the veil, the thief hangs on the cross, wishes he could scratch his head, and realizes, maybe for the first time, "I'm a sinner, and judging by the marks on His mutilated body, the problem is worse than I think. I couldn't fix me in ten thousand lifetimes. I don't need a self-help book or a life coach, and no amount of money will pay my debt. I can't save me! I'm powerless to do anything about anything! There is only one way out of this mess alive. I need a savior. Period."

Does the thief know that Jesus said these words: "This is the work of God, that you believe in him whom he has sent"?[6] Highly unlikely. Does he know that when Jesus returned to Bethany, after Lazarus had died, He was met by Martha, who said, "Lord, if you had been here, my brother would not have died. But even now I know that whatever you ask from God, God will give you"?[7] And Jesus said to her, "I am the resurrection and the life. Whoever believes in me, though he die, yet shall he live, and everyone who lives and believes in me shall never die. Do you believe this?"[8] Doubtful. Does he know that just a short while later, Jesus said, "I have come into the world as light, so that whoever believes in me may not remain in darkness"?[9] Probably not.

Has the thief heard what Peter will later tell the Gentiles: "To him all the prophets bear witness that everyone who believes in him receives forgiveness of sins through his name"?[10] Or does he somehow know what Paul will later preach in the synagogue in Antioch: "And by him everyone who believes is freed from everything from which you could not be freed by the law of Moses"?[11]

Has the thief ever heard any of these words? Does he know that belief in Jesus is the singular requirement? We have no idea. I tend to doubt it.

And yet, he believes.

There is in every one of us the religion of Cain—the idea or the desire to bring to God an offering, a work, a something out of our own doing that makes us somehow better able to stand in His presence. That entitles us. Gives us access. Gets us back inside the gate. We operate on the fundamental assumption that something *we* can *do* grants us a right standing before Him. The same thinking that motivated the Philippian jailer when he thought Paul had escaped, only to find out he had not: "And the jailer called for lights and rushed in, and trembling with fear he fell down before Paul and Silas. Then he brought them out and said, 'Sirs, what must I do to be saved?'"[12]

You can hear it in his question. The pronoun gives it away. While his heart is in the right place, his paradigm is upside down. "Sirs, what must I do?" is the wrong question. The right question is: "Wretched man that I am! Who will deliver me from this body of death?"[13] The jailer's question looks inside himself for his salvation. Paul's question looks outside.

The truth of the Cross is that there is nothing you or I can *do*. That's the point. It's *been done*. Finished. He—*Jesus*—did it. To suggest otherwise mocks this Cross. What remains is to believe that He did, and that what He did—as inconceivable as it is—counted and is still counting and will forever count on our behalf. This is why Paul tells the jailer: "Believe in the Lord Jesus, and you will be saved, you and your household."[14]

Paul will later explain it this way to the Romans: "That is why his faith was 'counted to him as righteousness.' But the words 'it was counted to him' were not written for his sake alone, but for ours also.

It will be counted to us who believe in him who raised from the dead Jesus our Lord, who was delivered up for our trespasses and raised for our justification."[15]

Jesus has fully obeyed and satisfied the law on our behalf. The work is finished: "Christ is the end of the law for righteousness to everyone who believes."[16] The "doing" is done.[1] "He has delivered us from the domain of darkness and transferred us to the kingdom of his beloved Son."[17] And notice who did the delivering and transferring and who got delivered and transferred. Did we play any part in our own deliverance?

I've mentioned this once, but let me come at it from a slightly different angle. In Daniel's vision, he describes the throne room. The place where God, the Ancient of Days, sits. His clothing is like white snow, hair like pure wool, and His throne is on fire. Continually. There is a river that flows from underneath His throne and millions upon millions of angels are serving and tending and singing and standing before Him. When God takes His seat, Daniel says that "the books were opened."[18] As a writer, I love the thought that there are books, or scrolls, in heaven. That somehow, the written word endures.

That said, these books are a little different. Not the kind you want to read. They record every deed ever committed by us. Either good or bad. These books are our debt ledger. They record every

---

1. Note: I am not arguing against good works. I believe James when he said, "Show me your faith apart from your works, and I will show you my faith by my works" (2:18). Jesus said, "If you love me, you will keep my commandments" (John 14:15). The distinction I am making is that doing those "works" comes out of a heart that now believes. That obeys. That loves. "Doing" is the by-product of our love for Him, not the source of our belief in Him. Nor the thing that gets us to Him. Works are the fruit, not the root. We "work" because we love Him, because He has freed us from our chains, and because we want to do what He did and is doing. Period.

time we sinned against the Ancient of Days. The sum of what we owe. And it's more than we can ever repay. What's more, God is not indifferent to the words in those books. The total record of our sin. He hates it. His wrath is stored up against it. He won't simply overlook it. He won't brush it under the rug.

With court in session, Daniel continues looking. The boastful beast is slain, its body destroyed, thrown into the fire; and the rest of the beasts are reduced to nothing. But that doesn't clear the debt. Payment has to be made. The books are still open. How will the sin of all mankind be atoned for? Paid for? Who is worthy to clear the slate?

Remember when John the Baptist said, "Behold, the Lamb of God who takes away the sin of the world"?[19] This is the moment that that happens, and both criminals are watching it unfold. One on Jesus' left, one on His right.

Daniel records that the clouds part and "there came one like a son of man, and he came to the Ancient of Days and was presented before Him."[20] We don't know what was said, because Daniel can't hear that. I tend to think Jesus presented His wounds, the holes, His stripes, then poured out every last drop of His blood and said, "*Tetelestai*," but that's just a guess. Whatever is done and said, the Father accepts the Son's payment. In full. Before Daniel's very eyes, the blood of Jesus wipes the slate clean for everyone who believes in—trusts in—the Son. This is why John said, "The blood of Jesus cleanses us from all unrighteousness."[21] In recognition of the Son's perfect sacrifice, God gives His Son "dominion and glory and a kingdom, that all peoples, nations, and languages should serve him; his dominion is an everlasting dominion, which shall not pass away, and his kingdom one that shall not be destroyed."[22]

Jesus uses the title "Son of Man" to refer to Himself almost eighty times in the Gospels; and every time He does, He is referencing this moment. Driving a stake in this earth and in the ears of the kingdom of darkness and saying, "I am the Son of God. I am ransoming mankind with My blood. I am returning to My Father, and I am taking a host with me." The religious rulers of the day milling about the foot of the Cross, spitting on Jesus, are mocking Him because He said this. Because He claimed to be the Son of God. But His claim is even stronger than that. By calling Himself "Son of Man," He is saying, "I am the fulfillment of Daniel's vision, presented before the throne and accepted by the Father. All rule and authority and dominion is given to Me. And My kingdom is never ending."

Were it not true, it would be the most ridiculous claim in the history of history. And most everyone staring at Jesus is laughing at Him.

Save this criminal.

WALK WITH ME BACK TO THE CROSS

Somewhere in those six hours on that Friday, our thief watches the redemption of mankind unfold. Under a darkened sky, listening to Jesus gurgle and suffocate under the weight of his and your and my sin, the lightbulb is turned on. The blindfold is removed. With only a few breaths remaining in Jesus' body, the thief watches Jesus, lifted up, drawing all men to Himself. Literally. He is watching Jesus pay for sin, all sin, throughout all eternity—past, present, future—for all mankind. Billions of slates wiped clean before his eyes. Propitiation. Debt ledgers paid in full. Making Jesus both just and justifier.[23]

Can one sentence turn an entire life around? Can one statement alter eternity? According to Jesus, yes.

"Jesus, when you come into your kingdom . . ." It's a beautiful confession. A beautiful surrender. An eternal salvation.

This is the mystery, the majesty, and the I-just-can't-wrap-my-head-around-it wonder of the Cross. I can't prove it, but I think our thief on the cross comes to understand this. By the grace of God, the veil is lifted, and he sees Jesus. The Lamb of God. For who He is. When he does, he can't bow, can't lift his hands, can't do anything about anything. All he can do is surrender and speak, "Please remember me."

This inexplicable thing that Jesus does, this unmerited mercy, this salvation, this snatching-back-out-of-the-hand-of-the-devil, this grace upon grace, is a gift beyond measure.

Paul described the same transaction this way to the Romans: "Because, if you confess with your mouth that Jesus is Lord and believe in your heart that God raised him from the dead, you will be saved. For with the heart one believes and is justified, and with the mouth one confesses and is saved. For the Scripture says, 'Everyone who believes in him will not be put to shame.' For there is no distinction between Jew and Greek; for the same Lord is Lord of all, bestowing his riches on all who call on him. For 'everyone who calls on the name of the Lord will be saved.'"[24]

The thief brought nothing, save belief and confession. What do you bring?

Pray with Me

King Jesus, please remember me when You come into Your kingdom. I am so unworthy of You, and yet I believe You are who You say You are, the only begotten Son of God. And for reasons I'll not soon understand, because You love me with a love I just can't fathom, You left

Your throne and came here on a rescue mission, a prisoner swap—You for me. You willingly and knowingly died my death. Paid my debt. Wiped my slate. But, once dead, while Your work was finished, You weren't. You didn't just leave me floating in the ether tending to myself. You wrap me in Your arms and bring me to Your Father. But You don't bring me stained with sin. You bring me soaked in crimson. Washed. Clean. Spotless. Which shreds me because I know me, and I'm so unworthy. I don't belong. And yet, here I am. I'm at a loss. I know now that this is the unmerited grace of the Ancient of Days who sent His Son to do what I could not. Proof there is more grace in Jesus than sin in me.

Even now, after all I've confessed and believed and prayed, I can't wrap my head around the inconceivability of a God who made me, the Milky Way, and the hippopotamus, sent His only, perfect, and beloved Son to trade His infinitely valuable life for mine. And it's not like I'm a model citizen—I'm a wretched, black-hearted rebel, hellbent on mutiny. Despite this, the sinless Son lays down His life for me and makes payment for my sin. Why? "That the love with which you have loved me may be in them, and I in them."[25]

My response is to fall on my face, surrender wholeheartedly, and cry out, "Lord, have mercy. Remember me when You come into Your kingdom." Lord Jesus, when I was dead, You made me alive. So please, Lord, do what only You can do, and make me alive. Right now. Let me see what the criminal saw. Give me a front-row seat. To You. To the blood dripping off Your toes. To the mercy pouring out Your lips. God Most High, please use this road sign to point me to You, today, tomorrow, and the next. So that I don't take my eyes off You. So that I, like him, hear these words: "Truly you will be with me today in paradise." I pray this in the matchless, magnificent, undefeated, and grace-filled name of Jesus, Son of God and Son of Man. Amen.

AND GOD RESPONDS

"And you were dead in the trespasses and sins in which you once walked, following the course of this world, following the prince of the power of the air, the spirit that is now at work in the sons of disobedience—among whom we all once lived in the passions of our flesh, carrying out the desires of the body and the mind, and were by nature children of wrath, like the rest of mankind. But God, being rich in mercy, because of the great love with which he loved us, even when we were dead in our trespasses, made us alive together with Christ—by grace you have been saved—and raised us up with him and seated us with him in the heavenly places in Christ Jesus, so that in the coming ages he might show the immeasurable riches of his grace in kindness toward us in Christ Jesus. For by grace you have been saved through faith. And this is not your own doing; it is the gift of God, not a result of works, so that no one may boast. For we are his workmanship, created in Christ Jesus for good works, which God prepared beforehand, that we should walk in them."[26]

DAY 33

"Sin no more."

JOHN 8:2–11

"Early in the morning he came again to the temple. All the people came to him, and he sat down and taught them. The scribes and the Pharisees brought a woman who had been caught in adultery, and placing her in the midst they said to him, 'Teacher, this woman has been caught in the act of adultery. Now in the Law, Moses commanded us to stone such women. So what do you say?' This they said to test him, that they might have some charge to bring against him. Jesus bent down and wrote with his finger on the ground. And as they continued to ask him, he stood up and said to them, 'Let him who is without sin among you be the first to throw a stone at her.' And once more he bent down and wrote on the ground. But when they heard it, they went away one by one, beginning with the older ones, and Jesus was left alone with the woman standing before him. Jesus stood up and said to her, 'Woman, where are they? Has no one condemned you?' She said, 'No one, Lord.' And Jesus said, 'Neither do I condemn you; go, and from now on sin no more.'"[1]

We explored in day 15 how the Pharisees bring in this woman and attempt to trap Jesus. Here in day 33, I want to see this from a different angle. They throw the woman at Jesus, who kneels and writes in the dirt. I love everything about this because these self-righteous men, who know well the Law, watch the very finger of God who wrote the Law on stone for Moses, doodle in the sand. One by one, they drop their stones, exit, and leave Jesus alone with the woman. "Neither do I condemn you; go, and from now on sin no more." Let me say again what I said earlier because it's worth repeating—you cannot out-sin the grace and mercy of Jesus. To believe otherwise is to mock this Cross. Paul said it this way: "Where sin increased, grace abounded all the more."[2]

Now look at Jesus' final words to the woman. "Sin no more." This is an impossible commandment. It can't be done. Not in this life. Not in ten thousand lives to come. So what's the solution? Is there a get-out-of-jail-free card?

There *is* a remedy. A single solution. But you're not going to like it. To "sin no more," we must kill the sinner. Put him or her to death.

So, how big a problem is our sin? Like, really? I mean, if Jesus died and paid for my sins (which He absolutely did), then why are we still talking about this? Yes, Jesus' blood cleanses us from all unrighteousness, and He paid the complete penalty. When He said, "It is finished," He wasn't kidding. I get it. Point made. I'm a sinner. Why're you browbeating me with this whole sin thing?

Jesus then tells them He is the Light of the World, and the deaf Pharisees totally miss the point. Instead, they begin to argue the fact that He is bearing witness about Himself, thereby stating His testimony is not true.

"So he said to them again, 'I am going away, and you will seek me, and you will die in your sin. Where I am going, you cannot come.' So the Jews said, 'Will he kill himself,' since he says, 'Where I am going, you cannot come'?' He said to them, 'You are from below;

I am from above. You are of this world; I am not of this world. I told you that you would die in your sins, for unless you believe that I am he you will die in your sins.'"[3]

The Pharisees already hate Him. Being told "you are from below" and "you will die in your sin" doesn't change that. In fact, it only makes it worse. Jesus ends the conversation with this: "Jesus answered them, 'Truly, truly, I say to you, everyone who practices sin is a slave to sin.'"[4]

They especially don't like being told they are slaves.

Before He goes to the Cross, Jesus will look at His closest friends and say, "I have said all these things to you to keep you from falling away."[5] Notice the words "falling away." The NASB translates it this way: "These things I have spoken to you so that you will not be led into sin."[6]

There is a fine line, or tension, here where we stay so focused on our sin that we never see or receive or experience the grace of Jesus and never live in the reality that we are, in fact, forgiven. The flip side is also true: we so focus on the grace that we miss or deny the enormity of our sin. Not realizing our deep need for forgiveness. And so we take the Cross for granted.

Here is the truth of us: we aren't good people who happen to do bad things. There was only one good person. We are all sinners who sin. There's nothing inherently good in us. That may offend you, but your offense is proof.

Adam and Eve had no children inside the garden. When they sinned, God removed them from the garden, and Eve soon gave birth—outside the gate. That means that sin—rebellion—was passed to all mankind. To us. Hence, we're all snakebitten. It's part of our DNA.

Paul explained it this way: "Therefore, as one trespass led to condemnation for all men, so one act of righteousness leads to justification and life for all men. For as by the one man's disobedience the many were made sinners, so by the one man's obedience the many will be made righteous. Now the law came in to increase the trespass, but where sin increased, grace abounded all the more, so that, as sin reigned in death, grace also might reign through righteousness leading to eternal life through Jesus Christ our Lord."[7]

Through one trespass and one man's disobedience, the many were made sinners. This is our condition at birth. When we open our eyes.

Paul continued: "For when you were slaves of sin, you were free in regard to righteousness. But what fruit were you getting at that time from the things of which you are now ashamed? For the end of those things is death. But now that you have been set free from sin and have become slaves of God, the fruit you get leads to sanctification and its end, eternal life. For the wages of sin is death, but the free gift of God is eternal life in Christ Jesus our Lord."[8]

Once slaves of sin. Owned by something more powerful than us. A master who controlled us. And the cost for that sin was and is death. Our death.

But . . . then Jesus and the Cross.

"Likewise, my brothers, you also have died to the law through the body of Christ, so that you may belong to another, to him who has been raised from the dead, in order that we may bear fruit for God. For while we were living in the flesh, our sinful passions, aroused by the law, were at work in our members to bear fruit for death. But now we are released from the law, having died to that which held us captive, so that we serve in the new way of the Spirit and not in the old way of the written code."[9]

This begs two questions: What held us captive, and how do we die to it?

Paul continued:

"What then shall we say? That the law is sin? By no means! Yet if it had not been for the law, I would not have known sin. For I would not have known what it is to covet if the law had not said, 'You shall not covet.' But sin, seizing an opportunity through the commandment, produced in me all kinds of covetousness. For apart from the law, sin lies dead. I was once alive apart from the law, but when the commandment came, sin came alive and I died. The very commandment that promised life proved to be death to me. For sin, seizing an opportunity through the commandment, deceived me and through it killed me."[10]

Look at the verbs. Sin seizes, produces, came alive, deceived, and killed me.

"So the law is holy, and the commandment is holy and righteous and good. Did that which is good, then, bring death to me? By no means! It was sin, producing death in me through what is good . . ."

Notice, sin produces death in us.

"In order that sin might be shown to be sin, and through the commandment might become sinful beyond measure. For we know that the law is spiritual, but I am of the flesh, sold under sin."[11]

Remember this phrase, "sold under sin." I'm coming back to it.

From here, Paul went into his famous I-do-what-I-don't-want-to-do-and-don't-do-what-I-want-to-do statement. "For I do not understand my own actions. For I do not do what I want, but I do the very thing I hate. Now if I do what I do not want, I agree with the law, that it is good. So now it is no longer I who do it, but sin that dwells within me."[12]

Here it is in four words: sin dwells within me.

Dwells. Meaning, it's alive. We are not just good people who do bad things. We are sinners who must crucify—put to death—the sin.

253

"For I know that nothing good dwells in me, that is, in my flesh."[13]

Don't skim over that. "Nothing good dwells in me." This should humble us.

"For I have the desire to do what is right, but not the ability to carry it out."[14]

"Not the ability." If you've ever thought, *I got this*, the truth is, you don't. And you can't.

"For I do not do the good I want, but the evil I do not want is what I keep on doing. Now if I do what I do not want, it is no longer I who do it, but sin that dwells within me."[15]

Here it is again. "Sin dwells within me."

"So I find it to be a law that when I want to do right, evil lies close at hand. For I delight in the law of God, in my inner being, but I see in my members another law waging war against the law of my mind and making me captive to the law of sin that dwells in my members."[16]

That's three times. Bringing Paul to this realization that he, and we, are captive to sin. And the only way to deal with sin is not to pacify, appease, or convince it to act good. But to kill it. Crucify it.

Which brings Paul to this conclusion: "Wretched man that I am! Who will deliver me from this body of death? Thanks be to God through Jesus Christ our Lord! So then, I myself serve the law of God with my mind, but with my flesh I serve the law of sin."[17]

Let's go back to that earlier phrase: "Sold under sin." A strange phrase. What does Paul mean?

Through the prophet Ezekiel, God gave this warning:

"As I live, declares the Lord GOD, surely with a mighty hand and an outstretched arm and with wrath poured out I will be king over you. I will bring you out from the peoples and gather you out of the countries where you are scattered, with a mighty hand and an outstretched arm, and with wrath poured out. And I will bring you into the wilderness of the peoples, and there I will enter into judgment with you face to face. As I entered into judgment with your fathers in the wilderness of the land of Egypt, so I will enter into judgment with you, declares the Lord God. I will make you pass under the rod, and I will bring you into the bond of the covenant. I will purge out the rebels from among you, and those who transgress against me. I will bring them out of the land where they sojourn, but they shall not enter the land of Israel. Then you will know that I am the Lord."[18]

The picture Ezekiel painted is one of a shepherd separating the herd with his rod, or shepherd's staff.

Then in Leviticus, God gave this command: "And every tithe of herds and flocks, every tenth animal of all that pass under the herdsman's staff, shall be holy to the Lord."[19]

Finally, Jesus said this in Matthew: "Before him will be gathered all the nations, and he will separate people one from another as a shepherd separates the sheep from the goats. And he will place the sheep on his right, but the goats on the left."[20]

These three scriptures point to a shepherd and his staff.

The second possibility comes from the descriptions of a slave market during and prior to Jesus' day. When the kings of conquering tribes would capture their enemies, they would sell them in a slave market. And to reinforce the fact that the enemy had been captured and enslaved, each slave was placed on a block standing beneath a horizontal spear hung above their head. The same spear used to defeat them. Meaning, they have come under the dominion of the hand that wielded that spear.

Whatever the meaning, whether the shepherd's staff or the slave master's spear, "to pass under the rod" means to pass under the hand that has conquered you and now has dominion over you.

WALK WITH ME BACK TO THE CROSS

Jesus' words to the woman caught in adultery were "sin no more." The truth is, we are all that woman. Every one of us has loved someone other than Jesus. Many times over. Given our condition, and the fact that sin is not only wrapped around our DNA but also infused into it, it is impossible to sin no more. We are incapable of not sinning. We can sin less. (And I pray that we do as Jesus sanctifies us. And I pray that we want to because He said, "If you love me, obey my commandments.") But we were born sinners, and we will die sinners.

To suggest otherwise is to mock the Cross of Jesus.

The remedy is to kill the sinner. Which is exactly what we do when we put our faith, our belief, in Christ Jesus and His atoning work on this Cross. This is why Paul said (and it's one of my favorite scriptures in the Bible): "I have been crucified with Christ. It is no longer I who live, but Christ who lives in me. And the life I now live in the flesh I live by faith in the Son of God, who loved me and gave himself for me."[21] It's also why he said, "I die daily."[22] Because every morning we wake up a sinner. And our only hope—the only way out of this alive—is the sanctifying, justifying, redeeming, ransoming, rescuing, atoning, snatching-back-out-of-the-hand-of-the-devil blood of Jesus that cleanses us from all sin.

For me, this is the really difficult part of my walk with Jesus. Dying daily. Crucifying myself, picking up His Cross, and following Him. Your will be done. But sometimes, like now, I look (in my mind's eye) into the face of Jesus here on this Cross, and I am reminded what it cost Him, what it cost me (nothing), and what He so selflessly offers me in exchange.

And I am undone.

Pray with Me

Jesus, I know You paid for my sin. All of it. And I know that doing so cost You everything. That said, I don't think I've had, or do have, an accurate view of the true enormity of my own sin. I've bought into this idea that I'm basically a good person. Not as bad as so-and-so or that person in the news or that person in prison. Truth is, I'm as bad as all of them. Equal sinners. I'm the woman caught in adultery. I'm guilty of loving any and everyone but You. I'm sick at the sight of my own stuff. It's horrible. I echo Paul: "Wretched man that I am. Who will deliver me from this body of death?"

Jesus, You're the only One. You alone, who knew no sin, became sin for me so that I might become the righteousness of God. Such news is too much. Too wonderful. Too utterly unbelievable. And yet it is true. You did that. You did this. For me. For us. Jesus, I am so sorry. Please forgive all my sin. I'm not just praying the sinner's prayer; I'm praying because my heart is pierced again, and You in Your mercy have shown me an accurate picture of me; and because you have done so, I now have a clearer picture of You and what I cost You. And it's a lot more than I had previously thought. Like the woman, I receive Your words, "Sin no more." But, Jesus, the only way that's possible is if You take my place. Which You did. An unbelievable exchange.

Thank You. Thank You for buying me back. For purchasing me when I could not. When I was dead. For ransoming me when I had been sold under sin. A slave to sin. For rescuing me. Jesus, I am torn amid the crushing weight of my own sin and the limitless joy of knowing that You did all this and that when You said, "It is finished," You were thinking of me too. In Jesus' name.

AND GOD RESPONDS

"And you, who were dead in your trespasses and the uncircumcision of your flesh, God made alive together with him, having forgiven us all our trespasses, by canceling the record of debt that stood against us with its legal demands. This he set aside, nailing it to the cross. He disarmed the rulers and authorities and put them to open shame, by triumphing over them in him."[23]

"You were bought with a price."[24]

DAY 34

—◆◆◆—

"Love one another: just as I have loved you."

JOHN 13:30–35

"When Jesus had finished all these sayings, he said to his disciples, 'You know that after two days the Passover is coming, and the Son of Man will be delivered up to be crucified.'"[1]

I wonder if the disciples can really process what He's saying?

"Then the chief priests and the elders of the people gathered in the palace of the high priest, whose name was Caiaphas, and plotted together in order to arrest Jesus by stealth and kill him. But they said, 'Not during the feast, lest there be an uproar among the people.'"[2]

"Then Satan entered into Judas called Iscariot, who was of the number of the twelve."[3]

"Then one of the twelve, whose name was Judas Iscariot, went to the chief priests and said, 'What will you give me if I deliver him over to you?' And they paid him thirty pieces of silver. And from that moment he sought an opportunity to betray him."[4]

Yesterday I said Jesus walks into a slave market and buys our freedom. Why did I say that? Because according to Exodus—in the law of Moses—thirty shekels is the price for a slave. "If the ox gores

a slave, male or female, the owner shall give to their master thirty shekels of silver, and the ox shall be stoned."[5]

"During supper, when the devil had already put it into the heart of Judas Iscariot, Simon's son, to betray him, Jesus, knowing that the Father had given all things into his hands, and that he had come from God and was going back to God, rose from supper. He laid aside his outer garments, and taking a towel, tied it around his waist. Then he poured water into a basin and began to wash the disciples' feet and to wipe them with the towel that was wrapped around him."[6]

Could you wash Judas's feet? Because Jesus did.

"When he had washed their feet and put on his outer garments and resumed his place, he said to them, 'Do you understand what I have done to you? You call me Teacher and Lord, and you are right, for so I am. If I then, your Lord and Teacher, have washed your feet, you also ought to wash one another's feet. For I have given you an example, that you also should do just as I have done to you. Truly, truly, I say to you, a servant is not greater than his master, nor is a messenger greater than the one who sent him. If you know these things, blessed are you if you do them. I am not speaking of all of you; I know whom I have chosen. But the Scripture will be fulfilled, "He who ate my bread has lifted his heel against me." I am telling you this now, before it takes place, that when it does take place you may believe that I am he. Truly, truly, I say to you, whoever receives the one I send receives me, and whoever receives me receives the one who sent me.' After saying these things, Jesus was troubled in his spirit, and testified, 'Truly, truly, I say to you, one of you will betray me.' The disciples looked at one another, uncertain of whom he spoke. One of his disciples, whom Jesus loved, was reclining at table at Jesus' side, so Simon Peter motioned to him to ask Jesus of whom he was speaking.

"So that disciple, leaning back against Jesus, said to him, 'Lord, who is it?' Jesus answered, 'It is he to whom I will give this morsel of bread when I have dipped it.' So when he had dipped the morsel, he gave it to Judas, the son of Simon Iscariot."[7]

The Bread of Life extending mercy to the betrayer.

"Then after he had taken the morsel, Satan entered into him. Jesus said to him, 'What you are going to do, do quickly.'"[8]

"So, after receiving the morsel of bread, he immediately went out. And it was night."[9]

I hate everything about this moment. Except for the fact that without it, there's no Cross.

"When Jesus had spoken these words, he went out with his disciples across the brook Kidron, where there was a garden, which he and his disciples entered. Now Judas, who betrayed him, also knew the place, for Jesus often met there with his disciples. So Judas, having procured a band of soldiers and some officers from the chief priests and the Pharisees, went there with lanterns and torches and weapons. Then Jesus, knowing all that would happen to him, came forward and said to them, 'Whom do you seek?' They answered him, 'Jesus of Nazareth.' Jesus said to them, 'I am he.' Judas, who betrayed him, was standing with them. When Jesus said to them, 'I am he,' they drew back and fell to the ground. So he asked them again, 'Whom do you seek?' And they said, 'Jesus of Nazareth.'"[10]

"And the man called Judas, one of the twelve, was leading them. He drew near to Jesus to kiss him, but Jesus said to him, 'Judas, would you betray the Son of Man with a kiss?' And when those who were around him saw what would follow, they said, 'Lord, shall we strike with the sword?' And one of them struck the servant of the high priest and cut off his right ear. But Jesus said, 'No more of this!' And he touched his ear and healed him. Then Jesus said to the chief priests and officers of the temple and elders, who had come out against him, 'Have you come out as against a robber, with swords and clubs? When I was with you day after day in the temple, you did not lay hands on me. But this is your hour, and the power of darkness.'"[11]

"When morning came, all the chief priests and the elders of the people took counsel against Jesus to put him to death. And they bound him and led him away and delivered him over to Pilate the governor."[12]

"Then when Judas, his betrayer, saw that Jesus was condemned, he changed his mind and brought back the thirty pieces of silver to the chief priests and the elders, saying, 'I have sinned by betraying innocent blood.'"[13]

Innocent blood. Even His betrayer knew He wasn't guilty.

The NASB translates it this way: "Then when Judas, who had betrayed Him, saw that He had been condemned, he felt remorse and returned the thirty pieces of silver to the chief priests and elders."[14]

What did Judas feel? Remorse. Which exposes the problem. Remorse is not repentance. Remorse is regret and even guilt, coupled with shame. While repentance turns to Jesus and confesses.

"They said, 'What is that to us? See to it yourself.' And throwing down the pieces of silver into the temple, he departed, and he went and hanged himself. But the chief priests, taking the pieces of silver, said, 'It is not lawful to put them into the treasury, since it is blood money.' So they took counsel and bought with them the potter's field as a burial place for strangers. Therefore that field has been called the Field of Blood to this day. Then was fulfilled what had been spoken by the prophet Jeremiah, saying, 'And they took the thirty pieces of silver, the price of him on whom a price had been set by some of the sons of Israel, and they gave them for the potter's field, as the Lord directed me.'"[15]

Look back to the moment Judas betrays Jesus. He has just left the room. It's night. And Jesus turns to the eleven: "When he had gone out, Jesus said, 'Now is the Son of Man glorified, and God is glorified in him. If God is glorified in him, God will also glorify him in himself, and glorify him at once. Little children, yet a little while I am with you. You will seek me, and just as I said to the Jews, so now I also say to you, "Where I am going you cannot come."'"[16]

I think this broke their hearts.

Then He says this: "A new commandment I give to you, that you love one another: just as I have loved you, you also are to love one another. By this all people will know that you are my disciples, if you have love for one another."[17]

I don't think they have any idea what He's talking about until about twenty-four hours later as they watch His lifeless body drip blood on the street and the back slapping soldiers shove a spear into His chest cavity and listen as the blood and water splatter on the road. And somewhere in there, I think His words echoed: "Love one another, as I have loved you."

Walk with Me Back to the Cross

This picture of Judas is one of the most painful in all of Scripture. And yet, I—and you—are Judas. We've betrayed Him in our thoughts, words, and deeds, ten thousand times over. We've not loved Him with our whole heart. We've not loved each other as He loved us. We've felt remorse yet not confessed in repentance. We are Judas. And yet, when they drove in the nails, Jesus said, "Father, forgive them."

This is unmerited mercy poured out. Grace upon grace.

Forgiveness is the signature of the Messiah. It's the reason for the mushroom cloud rising out of hell.

To take away sin, He forgave.

Here's my point: an unforgiving disciple is a disciple, just not a disciple of Jesus. To follow Jesus means to do what He does. And Jesus forgave those who killed Him—as they were killing Him. We cannot love like Jesus without forgiveness. It's step one. It's the threshold.

Without this Cross, there is no forgiveness. We are all still dead in our sin. With this Cross, we are forgiven. He has made us alive. And by and because of and through the blood shed on this Cross, we get to forgive people who don't deserve it.

Unforgiveness is the poison we drink thinking it will kill someone else. And Jesus will never make you forgive anyone. Just as He chose to forgive us while we were still sinners, He lets us choose. So let me ask you—do you really want to follow Jesus? Because forgiven people forgive people. How can we not?

Straight up—who do you need to forgive?

PRAY WITH ME

Jesus, I can't do this on my own. Help. I know that I am Judas. I have betrayed You. Not loved You with my whole heart. Ten thousand times over. And while I am remorseful and know the weight and pain of guilt and regret, I want to repent. Forgive me, please. I'm so sorry. And in asking You to forgive me, I know I need to forgive others. You command it. You tell us in Your Word: "But if you do not forgive others their trespasses, neither will your Father forgive your trespasses."[18] **And again You tell us:** *"In anger his master delivered him to the jailers, until he should pay all his debt. So also my heavenly Father will do to every one of you, if you do not forgive your brother from your heart."*[19]

Jesus, this is one of the most difficult things I've ever done, but I want to be obedient. So, hard as it is, I forgive (name each one):

_____

_____

_____

I give them to You to do with them as You will. I give justice to You. And I tear up the IOU that I carry in my pocket. I give it all to You. I repent for harboring that. It's been like a bitter stone, eating me from the inside out. So, today, I put it all down here at Your Cross. I'm done with it. I forgive them. Outright and completely. In the same way You forgave me—which I did not deserve—and yet You in Your mercy offer it, and I not only receive it but offer it to others in return. Jesus, please, by the power of Your Holy Spirit, heal the wound in me that was created when (name them) sinned against me. Hurt me. Rejected me. Abandoned me. Betrayed me. Come into me now and heal that wounded place in me. I can't do it. You alone are my Healer. Come, Lord Jesus. In Jesus' name.

AND GOD RESPONDS

MATTHEW'S GOSPEL: "Then Jesus told his disciples, 'If anyone would come after me, let him deny himself and take up his cross and follow me.'"[20]

MARK'S GOSPEL: "And calling the crowd to him with his disciples, he said to them, 'If anyone would come after me, let him deny himself and take up his cross and follow me.'"[21]

LUKE'S GOSPEL: "And he said to all, 'If anyone would come after me, let him deny himself and take up his cross daily and follow me.'"[22]

DAY 35

"You will deny me three times."

MATTHEW 26:30–35

"And when they had sung a hymn, they went out to the Mount of Olives. Then Jesus said to them, 'You will all fall away because of me this night. For it is written, "I will strike the shepherd, and the sheep of the flock will be scattered."'"[1]

This is one of my least favorite and most painful records in all of Scripture.

Then He says this: "But after I am raised up, I will go before you to Galilee."[2]

I have often wondered if He said this primarily for Peter's benefit. Peter's going to need it.

Peter answers him, "'Though they all fall away because of you, I will never fall away.' Jesus said to him, 'Truly, I tell you, this very night, before the rooster crows, you will deny me three times.' Peter said to him, 'Even if I must die with you, I will not deny you!' And all the disciples said the same."[3]

Jesus turns to Peter: "Simon, Simon, behold, Satan demanded to have you, that he might sift you like wheat, but I have prayed for you that your faith may not fail. And when you have turned again, strengthen your brothers."[4]

Read that slowly. Jesus just told Peter that satan is going to sift him. But Peter need not worry because Jesus prayed that Peter's faith won't fail. Wait, what? If I'm Peter, I have a few questions: What about delivering me from the evil one? What about crushing satan under the sole of Your foot? What about slinging lightning bolts from on high?

Undeterred, Peter doubles down. "Peter said to him, 'Lord, I am ready to go with you both to prison and to death.' Jesus said, 'I tell you, Peter, the rooster will not crow this day, until you deny three times that you know me.'"[5]

We know Jesus dearly loves Peter. He will give His life for him in the days ahead. So why does He do this? And if He prayed for Peter this way, what about us? Does Jesus pray that our faith might not fail? Why? Wouldn't it make more sense to just crush our enemy? To rip his head off his shoulders and post it on a stake outside the city walls? Jesus spent thirty years in private life, three years in public ministry, and, ever since, has spent over two thousand years seated at the right hand of God interceding for us. Right this very second, He has the Father's ear, and He is speaking to Him about us. This tells me that our faith matters a great deal to the Lord.

"Simon Peter said to him, 'Lord, where are you going?' Jesus answered him, 'Where I am going you cannot follow me now, but you will follow afterward.' Peter said to him, 'Lord, why can I not follow you now? I will lay down my life for you.' Jesus answered, 'Will you lay down your life for me? Truly, truly, I say to you, the rooster will not crow till you have denied me three times.'"[6]

Let's be honest, just as we're all Judas, we're all Peter. How many times have I denied Jesus? More than I can count. I'm the most deceitful, backstabbing person I know. No one has lied to me more than I have and no one has let me down more than I have. And what's more, Jesus knows this about me. About you. All our worst stuff, long before we do it. Including our denials.

"Simon Peter followed Jesus, and so did another disciple. Since that disciple was known to the high priest, he entered with Jesus into the courtyard of the high priest, but Peter stood outside at the door. So the other disciple, who was known to the high priest, went out and spoke to the servant girl who kept watch at the door, and brought Peter in. The servant girl at the door said to Peter, 'You also are not one of this man's disciples, are you?' He said, 'I am not.' Now the servants and officers had made a charcoal fire, because it was cold, and they were standing and warming themselves. Peter also was with them, standing and warming himself."[7]

Remember the charcoal fire.

"Now Simon Peter was standing and warming himself. So they said to him, 'You also are not one of his disciples, are you?' He denied it and said, 'I am not.' One of the servants of the high priest, a relative of the man whose ear Peter had cut off, asked, 'Did I not see you in the garden with him?' Peter again denied it, and at once a rooster crowed."[8]

In the three previous years, Peter had stood in Caesarea Philippi and affirmed Jesus as the Messiah—"You are the Christ."[9] And Jesus told him, "On this rock [your proclamation], I will build my church."[10] Peter saw Jesus transfigured alongside Elijah and Moses and heard the Father's voice affirming the Son. He saw Jesus heal the blind, lame, and sick. He saw demons cast out. He saw the dead raised to life. He saw wind and waves calmed with a word. Peter had a front-row seat to the life, work, and ministry of the only begotten Son of God. He laughed with Jesus. Joked with Jesus. Fished with

Jesus. Walked hundreds of miles with Jesus. And yet, when pushed, his response was, "I am not."

How these words must have pierced Peter.

"And he said to them, 'Do not be alarmed. You seek Jesus of Nazareth, who was crucified. He has risen; he is not here. See the place where they laid him. But go, tell his disciples and Peter that he is going before you to Galilee. There you will see him, just as he told you.' And they went out and fled from the tomb, for trembling and astonishment had seized them, and they said nothing to anyone, for they were afraid."[11]

Interesting, how the angel singles out Peter. I don't hear it as condemnation, as in: "Peter, your reckoning is coming." I hear it as mercy. The restoration of a dear brother. Jesus knew this about Peter. It's why He said, "And when you have turned again, strengthen your brothers."[12] Jesus knew Peter would turn back. Which proves Peter's faith didn't fail. Remember this. It matters.

"Simon Peter said to them, 'I am going fishing.' They said to him, 'We will go with you.' They went out and got into the boat, but that night they caught nothing."[13]

Simon is draped in shame. He betrayed and denied his best friend. He's good for nothing. So he returns to his former life because he doesn't feel worthy to follow his King. But the deepest, single desire of his heart is to be restored. Forgiven. Welcomed back in. Made worthy. The weight of the memory of "I am not" is soul crushing. Made worse by the fact that he lives in an agrarian society where multiple roosters crow every morning.

"Just as day was breaking, Jesus stood on the shore; yet the disciples did not know that it was Jesus. Jesus said to them, 'Children, do you have any fish?' They answered him, 'No.' He said to them, 'Cast the net on the right side of the boat, and you will find some.'"[14]

These are professional fishermen. They've been doing this a minute. They probably think, *Who does this guy think He is? We've been out here all night.*

"So they cast it, and now they were not able to haul it in, because of the quantity of fish. That disciple whom Jesus loved therefore said to Peter, 'It is the Lord!' When Simon Peter heard that it was the Lord, he put on his outer garment, for he was stripped for work, and threw himself into the sea."[15]

Who puts on clothes when they jump in the water? Someone draped in shame.

"The other disciples came in the boat, dragging the net full of fish, for they were not far from the land, but about a hundred yards off. When they got out on land, they saw a charcoal fire in place, with fish laid out on it, and bread."

Uh-oh. This does not bode well for Peter.

"Jesus said to them, 'Bring some of the fish that you have just caught.' So Simon Peter went aboard and hauled the net ashore, full of large fish, 153 of them. And although there were so many, the net was not torn."[16]

There are a lot of theories about the number 153. My favorite has to do with numbers and letters. In the Hebrew alphabet, every letter is also assigned a number, which allowed the Hebrews to use their alphabet both for words and as a numbering system. This meant each Hebrew word also held within its letters a numerical total (or the sum of all the letters added up to a numerical value). The Hebrew word *ani Elohim* written in numerical format is: $1+50+10 =$ ani. And $1+30+6+5+10+40 =$ Elohim. Or, 61 and 92. Which, added together, equals 153. Translated, "ani Elohim" means "I am God."

Peter is swimming to shore. The other disciples are counting fish. 149. 150 . . . 153. Wait. What? Once more Jesus is blowing their minds.

A minute ago, they—all of them—could not move the net. Now, one ashamed man moves it by himself. This mighty work of the flesh is Peter's heart, saying again, "Give me a second chance. I'm ready to die for You." But there's the fire. Which Peter can see and smell. And the memory of the slave girl and her words causes his heart to race.

"Jesus said to them, 'Come and have breakfast.' Now none of the disciples dared ask him, 'Who are you?' They knew it was the Lord. Jesus came and took the bread and gave it to them, and so with the fish."[17]

Again, the Bread of Life, extending life.

"This was now the third time that Jesus was revealed to the disciples after he was raised from the dead."[18]

In the meantime, Peter is sitting with his hair draped down over his eyes. Inside he is dying. Cracking down the middle. Afraid to look at Jesus.

"When they had finished breakfast, Jesus said to Simon Peter, 'Simon, son of John, do you love me more than these?'"

I've heard this taught as a finger-pointing, poke-in-the-chest condemnation of Peter. I don't agree. I believe it is the most merciful and perfect restoration. The most beautiful do-over in the history of do-overs.

"He said to him, 'Yes, Lord; you know that I love you.' He said to him, 'Feed my lambs.'"[19]

I've also heard this taught that Jesus stares down at Peter. Deep voice. Commanding. I don't think so. I think He's seated, side to side, one arm wrapped around Peter's shoulder. Why? Because Jesus loves Peter. Jesus knew what was going to happen. He's not ashamed of Peter. And He's bringing him back into the fold. Putting him back on the front lines.

"He said to him a second time, 'Simon, son of John, do you love me?' He said to him, 'Yes, Lord; you know that I love you.' He said to him, 'Tend my sheep.'"

This time, I think Jesus leans in. Presses His forehead to Peter's. Eye to eye. Whispering. Just between the two of them. One pal to another.

"He said to him the third time, 'Simon, son of John, do you love me?' Peter was grieved because he said to him the third time, 'Do you love me?' and he said to him, 'Lord, you know everything; you know that I love you.'"[20]

"You know everything." Peter is undone. All he wants is a chance to be restored, to be considered worthy when his recent betrayal is evidence that he is not. Peter wants another chance after so massively blowing the last. So Jesus, in perfect mercy-filled fashion, leans in again. Maybe even placing a palm on Peter's cheek or the back of his head, pulling him to Jesus.

"Jesus said to him, 'Feed my sheep.'"[21] And in my mind, Jesus does this forehead to forehead. Eye to eye. A smile on His face. A whisper on His tongue.

He has said it three times—one for each denial. Probably because He needed to get through Peter's thick head. And about here, Peter understands that only a shepherd can feed and tend sheep. "He's calling me a shepherd." Peter is not disqualified. He's being welcomed back in. His faith did not fail.

"'Truly, truly, I say to you, when you were young, you used to dress yourself and walk wherever you wanted, but when you are old, you will stretch out your hands, and another will dress you and carry you where you do not want to go.' (This he said to show by what kind of death he was to glorify God.)"[22]

Jesus knows all things, and He has seen Peter's end. And to Peter, they are some of the best and greatest words he's ever heard.

Why? Because he learns from Jesus that he will finish this race and glorify God.

But Jesus isn't finished. He pauses, locks eyes with Peter, and says the two most beautiful words Peter has ever heard. The two singular words his heart is dying to hear. Why? Because he needs to know he is worthy to follow his Lord.

"And after saying this he said to him, 'Follow me.'"[23]

WALK WITH ME BACK TO THE CROSS

Just as Jesus was not ashamed of Peter, He's not ashamed of us. At all. Our sin doesn't disqualify us. No sin. Hear that. No sin can separate us from Him. He loves us because He loves us, and He has never loved us less or more because of what we've done in this life. Our actions, whether public proclamation or denial, don't bring us closer to Him or push us further from Him. He never moves. No matter what we do, He will never leave us or forsake us. This is tough for us to wrap our heads around. As it was tough for Peter. But here's the truth: nothing—not one single thing—can ever separate us from Him and His love. Period. And right this second, knowing the truth of our lying, backstabbing ways, He is praying for us. Building our faith. Because, without faith, it is impossible to please Him.[24]

PRAY WITH ME

Jesus, I've got some shame. A lot actually. I'm draped in it, and it's dripping off my face. I've denied You like Peter. A thousand times over. I'm so sorry. I don't want to be like this. I hate the thought of my own sin, my own betrayal, my own denial. When I had the chance to stand up and boldly speak Your name or acknowledge You or confess You, I didn't. I hate that. I hate the fact that I cowered under pressure. Under the fear of man. Under the fear of what might happen to me. When I had the chance to choose holiness over sin, I chose sin. When I had the chance to choose purity over sin, I chose sin. When I had the chance to choose Your kingdom over mine, I chose mine. When I had the chance to choose You over me, I chose me. Jesus, I can't even lift my face off the floor. I am undone. Please restore me. Speak the words my heart needs to hear. Please let me follow You again. Jesus, my heart's desire is to follow You, to walk with You, to serve You in faithfulness and truth, and like the psalmist said in Psalm 45, to make Your great name known to the nations. Please forgive me when I don't. When I haven't. When I will fail in the future—a thought that causes me to cringe. Please put Your words in my mouth. And put Your fire in me.

Jesus, please sit next to me, wrap Your arm around my shoulder, press Your forehead to mine, and speak the words my heart needs to hear. The words that let me know You're not ashamed of me. The two words that are the DNA cry of my heart: "Follow me." And then help me do it. Jesus, I am a wretched human. Please deliver me. Help me not only run but finish this race. And finish well. Serving You with my whole heart. My whole life. All that I am. In Jesus' name.

AND GOD RESPONDS

(These are some of my favorite words in all of Scripture.)

"What then shall we say to these things? If God is for us, who can be against us? He who did not spare his own Son but gave him up for us all, how will he not also with him graciously give us all things? Who shall bring any charge against God's elect? It is God who justifies. Who is to condemn? Christ Jesus is the one who died—more than that, who was raised—who is at the right hand of God, who indeed is interceding for us. Who shall separate us from the love of Christ? Shall tribulation, or distress, or persecution, or famine, or nakedness, or danger, or sword? As it is written, 'For your sake we are being killed all the day long; we are regarded as sheep to be slaughtered.' No, in all these things we are more than conquerors through him who loved us. For I am sure that neither death nor life, nor angels nor rulers, nor things present nor things to come, nor powers, nor height nor depth, nor anything else in all creation, will be able to separate us from the love of God in Christ Jesus our Lord."[25]

DAY 36

———◆◆◆———

"And he will give you another Helper."

JOHN 14:15–16:15

"Truly, truly, I say to you, whoever believes in me will also do the works that I do; and greater works than these will he do, because I am going to the Father. Whatever you ask in my name, this I will do, that the Father may be glorified in the Son. If you ask me anything in my name, I will do it."[1]

Judas has left the room. The end has come. Time is short. Jesus is speaking final words to His friends. I doubt they understand, "greater works than these will you do." Then He says this: "If you love me, you will keep my commandments."[2]

Jesus lived a sinless life and fulfilled the law of God. Completely and perfectly. Meaning, He never sinned. When we *pisteuo* in Him, believing in, trusting in, and putting our faith in Him and His atoning sacrifice, we get credit for His obedience. His perfect score. And in exchange, His righteousness is credited to us. An inconceivable exchange.

So what does He require of us who follow Him? Who love Him? An obedience to His Word motivated *not* by the compulsion of a slave but by the love of an adopted child. Bondservants by choice.

He continues, "And I will ask the Father, and he will give you another Helper, to be with you forever, even the Spirit of truth, whom the world cannot receive, because it neither sees him nor knows him. You know him, for he dwells with you and will be in you. I will not leave you as orphans; I will come to you."[3]

Everyone in the room knows the difficulty in obedience. It's tough. Sin dwells in every one of them. Thus far in their lives, it's been a losing battle. But Jesus promises help. His Spirit. This is why the apostle John, late in his life, wrote this: "You are from God, little children, and have overcome them; because greater is He who is in you than he who is in the world."[4] How did they overcome? The Spirit of Christ—who lives in them.

But at the moment, as Jesus is speaking, they haven't yet learned this. All they know at this point is that Jesus is going somewhere they cannot follow. Which saddens them greatly. And who is this "Helper"? Everyone listening to the sound of His voice knows well the words of the prophet Joel: "And it shall come to pass afterward, that I will pour out my Spirit on all flesh; your sons and your daughters shall prophesy, your old men shall dream dreams, and your young men shall see visions. Even on the male and female servants in those days I will pour out my Spirit."[5]

But what does it mean to "pour out my Spirit"? And does Jesus have to leave in order for this pouring to happen?

"And I will show wonders in the heavens and on the earth, blood and fire and columns of smoke. The sun shall be turned to darkness, and the moon to blood, before the great and awesome day of the Lord comes. And it shall come to pass that everyone who calls on the name of the Lord shall be saved."[6] The KJV says, "delivered."

We know for certain that Peter knew this scripture because he would later quote it on the southern steps of the temple in Acts 2 on the day of Pentecost, but at this moment, does he understand? Does anyone? I doubt it.

Standing in the garden of Gethsemane, do they remember the words of John the Baptist some three years prior:

"The next day he saw Jesus coming toward him, and said, 'Behold, the Lamb of God, who takes away the sin of the world! This is he of whom I said, "After me comes a man who ranks before me, because he was before me." I myself did not know him, but for this purpose I came baptizing with water, that he might be revealed to Israel.' And John bore witness: 'I saw the Spirit descend from heaven like a dove, and it remained on him. I myself did not know him, but he who sent me to baptize with water said to me, "He on whom you see the Spirit descend and remain, this is he who baptizes with the Holy Spirit. And I have seen and have borne witness that this is the Son of God."'"[7]

John is standing in the water, baptizing people. He's wet. So is everyone else. What does he mean, "baptize with the Holy Spirit"? How does one do that? And when would the disciples remember these words? My guess is sometime after Jesus died.

Those listening aren't quite sure, but this idea of giving and pouring out the Spirit is not new. Two chapters later, John spoke again of the Spirit: "For he whom God has sent utters the words of God, for he gives the Spirit without measure. The Father loves the Son and has given all things into his hand. Whoever believes in the Son has eternal life; whoever does not obey the Son shall not see life, but the wrath of God remains on him."[8]

There's a lot here. Belief leads to life. Disbelief, and hence disobedience, leads to death and eternal wrath. But what about the Spirit? Who is He? And what does He mean, "gives the Spirit without measure"? And why would Jesus send Him rather than remain Himself? Certainly it's better for Jesus to be here. Right?

Back in the garden of Gethsemane, with only moments remaining, Jesus says this: "These things I have spoken to you while I am still with you. But the Helper, the Holy Spirit, whom the Father will send in my name, he will teach you all things and bring to your remembrance all that I have said to you."[9]

As soldiers muster outside the city walls, Jesus says this: "Nevertheless, I tell you the truth: it is to your advantage that I go away."[10]

How many of the remaining eleven scratched their heads at this and asked themselves, *Whoa! Hold it! Hold it! What, or who, could be better than You, Lord?*

Jesus doesn't stop to explain. "But when the Helper comes, whom I will send to you from the Father, the Spirit of truth, who proceeds from the Father, he will bear witness about me."[11]

At this point, each of them knows something is about to happen they won't like, but they have yet to make the connection between Jesus' words and the words of the prophets telling of the Messiah's death. And they haven't made the connection between the bodily absence of Jesus and the indwelling presence of His Spirit.

Jesus is signaling an imminent exchange, the likes of which this world has never seen. Jesus—the Anointed One, God with us, the promised Messiah, the King of all kings, who came on a rescue mission—is going away. Leaving. Returning to the Father. His work on the Cross is soon to be finished.[1] And in exchange, He is sending His Spirit.

Then, just to make sure they heard Him, He says it again: "For if I do not go away, the Helper will not come to you. But if I go, I will send him to you. And when he comes, he will convict the

---

1. Note: While His work on the Cross is finished, His work in us is not.

world concerning sin and righteousness and judgment: concerning sin, because they do not believe in me; concerning righteousness, because I go to the Father, and you will see me no longer; concerning judgment, because the ruler of this world is judged."[12]

Years later, John, as an older man, while writing his gospel, put the pieces together—with the help of the very Spirit Jesus promised: "Now this he said about the Spirit, whom those who believed in him were to receive, for as yet the Spirit had not been given, because Jesus was not yet glorified."[13]

But standing in the garden, listening to the sound of approaching footsteps and angry shouts and clanking swords and shields, the eleven have no idea what's coming. As the soldiers exit the east gate and descend into the valley and cross the brook Kidron, Jesus utters these words: "I still have many things to say to you, but you cannot bear them now. When the Spirit of truth comes, he will guide you into all the truth, for he will not speak on his own authority, but whatever he hears he will speak, and he will declare to you the things that are to come. He will glorify me, for he will take what is mine and declare it to you. All that the Father has is mine; therefore I said that he will take what is mine and declare it to you."[14]

After this horrible crucifixion, Jesus makes good on His promise. He pours out His Spirit. Baptizing the children of God. The book of Acts records what happens next. They did greater works. They preached the gospel of the kingdom. Word got out. The church spread like wildfire. The lame walked. The blind saw. The dead were raised to life. The lepers were cleansed. And demons were cast out. The believers in Jesus performed miracles, like Jesus. In fact, they did so in every chapter in the book of Acts. Take the miracles out of Acts and you must remove every chapter. There is no Acts without the "signs and wonders" that followed those who believed.

Which attracted a lot of attention. Everyone wanted this.

In Acts 8, Simon, a magician who actively practiced witchcraft, saw the great signs and miracles performed by Philip as he preached the good news about the kingdom of God and the name of Jesus Christ. Simon himself believed and was baptized. Peter and John heard that Samaria had received the word of God, so they came down and prayed that "they might receive the Holy Spirit, for he had not yet fallen on any of them, but they had only been baptized in the name of the Lord Jesus. Then they laid their hands on them and they received the Holy Spirit."[15] Simon saw this and offered them money. Why? He saw the power and wanted it.

"Now when Simon saw that the Spirit was given through the laying on of the apostles' hands, he offered them money, saying, 'Give me this power also, so that anyone on whom I lay my hands may receive the Holy Spirit.' But Peter said to him, 'May your silver perish with you, because you thought you could obtain the gift of God with money! You have neither part nor lot in this matter, for your heart is not right before God. Repent, therefore, of this wickedness of yours, and pray to the Lord that, if possible, the intent of your heart may be forgiven you. For I see that you are in the gall of bitterness and in the bond of iniquity.' And Simon answered, 'Pray for me to the Lord, that nothing of what you have said may come upon me.'"[16]

Since the Holy Spirit was poured out, people have seen the power He exercises and wanted it for themselves. We see this in Simon's own words—he wanted the power, not a relationship with the One who empowers. This desire is not new and started with lucipher's fall. But while that desire and the accompanying abuses do very much exist, do they nullify either the offer or the power?

Not according to Scripture. The disciples, including Paul, saw the abuses and yet continued to lay hands on people and pray that they might receive the Holy Spirit.

Without this Cross, there is no exchange. No redemption. And no sending of His Spirit.

But with, by, and through this Cross, Jesus returns and sends His Spirit. Who, in turn, reveals Jesus to us, makes Him known, glorifies Him, and dwells in us. An inconceivable thought. The Spirit of Christ living in my chest. In yours.

But it doesn't end there. According to Scripture, when He—the Spirit of Christ, the same Spirit who raised Christ Jesus from the dead—does dwell in those who believe and receive, things happen in the lives of those who have received Him. The blind see. The lame walk. Demons are cast out. The dead are raised to life. Miracles happen. Real power—sent from the throne room of God—is possible.

The Spirit of God heals the sick, raises the dead, casts out demons, prophesies, and preaches the gospel of the kingdom. He even speaks in tongues through the mouths of those He fills. Does He do these things in you? Do these describe or reflect your walk with, your following of, Jesus? Does your life look like the lives of those who believed in Acts?

Why not?[2]

In Mark 7, Jesus chastises the Pharisees by saying, "You leave the commandment of God and hold to the tradition of men."

Notice what they leave and what they hold to.

Jesus continues, "And he said to them, 'You have a fine way

---

2. I realize there are those who believe this "signs and wonders" power of the Holy Spirit died with the last apostles. I'm not in that camp and find no scriptural basis for that. Further, while my experience does not define my theology, it has confirmed it. I feel like Peter when he and John were arrested: "How can we but speak of what we've seen and heard?" (Acts 4:20, my paraphrase). I've seen and heard, so I am speaking—and writing.

of rejecting the commandment of God in order to establish your tradition!'"[17]

Now notice what they reject and what they establish in its place.

Jesus again continues, "Thus making void the word of God by your tradition that you have handed down. And many such things you do."[18]

The only thing on planet Earth that makes "void the word of God" is the tradition of man. The NASB says, "Invalidating the word of God by your tradition which you have handed down."

Does your tradition make void this Word of God? Does it invalidate or affirm? Let me ask it this way: Do you believe, have faith in, your tradition or His Word?

In Acts 2, Jesus makes good on His promise and "pours out His Spirit on all flesh." This prompts the question: Are you "all flesh"?

From that moment, the Spirit of God, working in, to, and through the people of God, did things. All to the glory of Jesus and to reveal Jesus as the resurrected only begotten Son of God. The reason signs and wonders followed those who believed was and is because He sent His Spirit.

And the people received Him.

WALK WITH ME BACK TO THE CROSS

An inexplicable exchange is happening. Jesus offers us His Spirit. To dwell inside us. The Spirit of God living in our chest.

While His work on the Cross is finished, is completed, is perfected, His work in, to, and through us is not. He's still working. How? According to Jesus, through His Spirit.

Because sin also dwells in us, there is a danger that we chase signs and wonders like Simon. God forbid. I know the abuses. I've seen them. Experienced them. I, too, cringe. We are caught in a cross fire. But pause a second and look through the eyes of the enemy. If you were your enemy, what would you do to prevent you from receiving the Spirit of God and all that He intends?

Let me ask it this way: What would you not do?

In Luke 18, Jesus is surrounded by "some who trusted in themselves that they were righteous, and treated others with contempt."[19] Then He tells the parable of the Pharisee and the tax collector. Speaking of their need for humility. As He is talking, people are bringing their children for Jesus to touch. "Now they were bringing even infants to him that he might touch them. And when the disciples saw it, they rebuked them. But Jesus called them to him, saying, 'Let the children come to me, and do not hinder them, for to such belongs the kingdom of God. Truly, I say to you, whoever does not receive the kingdom of God like a child shall not enter it.'"[20]

"Like a child" is one who hears the words of Jesus and does them. Period. No argument. No rebuttal. No negotiation. Just simple, first-time obedience. How would a child respond to the Holy Spirit?

Let me turn the mirror: Have you received the Holy Spirit and given Him unfettered access and license to do with you as He wills? No matter what that looks like? Even if you look foolish? Or, in agreement with some church tradition rooted in unbelief, have you received Him only to give Him guardrails, explain His limits, sit Him in a chair in the corner, and tell Him to hush and don't make a scene?

Straight up, do signs and wonders follow you?

If we follow Jesus, are surrendered to His lordship, and have received His Spirit, then why wouldn't our lives mirror the first believers'? Is Jesus not speaking to us when He promises to pour out His Spirit? Has His Spirit changed? Did Jesus change His mind?

What if, right this second, Jesus baptized you in and with His Spirit just like He did with the early church? Would you let Him?

PRAY WITH ME

Lord Jesus, You who baptize with fire and Spirit, if I'm honest, I've limited You. Put You in a box. Told You where to sit and be quiet. For whatever reason, whether tradition or abuse or lack of belief, I've said I believe in Your atoning work on the Cross and I believe You are who You say You are and You did what Scripture records You as having done, and yet I've rejected the work of Your Spirit in, to, and through me. Or, like Simon, I've lusted after the power and not yearned for a relationship with You. Lord, I am so sorry. Please forgive me. That is honestly the last thing I want to do.

Here and now, I repent, wholeheartedly and completely, for whatever reason has kept me from truly receiving Your Spirit. Peter said in Acts 2:38 on the southern steps of the temple, "Repent and be baptized every one of you in the name of Jesus Christ for the forgiveness of your sins, and you will receive the gift of the Holy Spirit." He then said, "For the promise is for you and for your children and for all who are far off, everyone whom the Lord our God calls to himself." Jesus, that "all" and that "everyone" includes me. Today, in this moment, I lay down all my excuses. Cut myself free from any tradition that would hinder me from receiving the promise of Your Spirit. And the release of Your Spirit in, to, and through me. I refuse to be influenced by the abuses of those who've come before me.

Jesus, I believe and I receive. I receive Your Holy Spirit. As You intend. Have Your way. And any power of darkness, any demonic spirit, any generational curse, and any power of witchcraft that would seek to hinder or inhibit Your Spirit baptizing me, I rebuke, bind, and cast down and out of my life in the magnificent and undefeated name of Jesus. My desire, my will, is to be Your temple. Filled with and empowered by Your Spirit because that's Your will for me. Let Your kingdom come. You poured out Your Spirit on all flesh, and You are pouring still. Today. Lord Jesus, please pour out on me. Come, Lord Jesus. Come, Holy Spirit. In Jesus' name.

AND GOD RESPONDS

"[He] was declared to be the Son of God in power according to the Spirit of holiness by his resurrection from the dead, Jesus Christ our Lord."[21]

"You, however, are not in the flesh but in the Spirit, if in fact the Spirit of God dwells in you. Anyone who does not have the Spirit of Christ does not belong to him. But if Christ is in you, although the body is dead because of sin, the Spirit is life because of righteousness. If the Spirit of him who raised Jesus from the dead dwells in you, he who raised Christ Jesus from the dead will also give life to your mortal bodies through his Spirit who dwells in you."[22]

"For all who are led by the Spirit of God are sons of God."[23]

DAY 37

*"And his sweat became like great drops of
blood falling down to the ground."*

LUKE 22:44

"And he withdrew from them about a stone's throw, and knelt down and prayed, saying, 'Father, if you are willing, remove this cup from me. Nevertheless, not my will, but yours, be done.' And there appeared to him an angel from heaven, strengthening him."[1]

Jesus' blood vessels have burst, and He is bleeding through His pores. One of the more painful ways to bleed. Is this really necessary? Why drag it out? Why not just kill Him and be done with it? I don't know that I can answer that, but I think there's more going on here than first meets the eye. And in order to understand it, we need to back up a few years. When John the Baptist saw Jesus coming toward him, he said, "Behold, the Lamb of God, who takes away the sin of the world!"[2]

Why a lamb? Why not a velociraptor? Why not someone so powerful that all He does is leave carnage, mayhem, and a trail of bodies in His wake? Because that's not the kingdom of God. That day will come, but this is not it.

Standing in the water, John the Baptizer is looking through the lens of the promises in the written Word of God. And he knows this:

"And he [the high priest] shall take some of the blood of the bull and sprinkle it with his finger on the front of the mercy seat on the east side, and in front of the mercy seat he shall sprinkle some of the blood with his finger seven times. Then he shall kill the goat of the sin offering that is for the people and bring its blood inside the veil and do with its blood as he did with the blood of the bull, sprinkling it over the mercy seat and in front of the mercy seat. . . . And he shall sprinkle some of the blood on it with his finger seven times, and cleanse it and consecrate it from the uncleannesses of the people of Israel. . . . For on this day shall atonement be made for you to cleanse you. You shall be clean before the LORD from all your sins."[3]

In the kingdom of God, cleansing and consecration from uncleanness (sin) requires the sprinkling of blood. Sprinkling. Blood must be sprinkled to make atonement. But where does that start?

Seven hundred fifty years before Jesus appeared in this garden, Isaiah prophesied the coming Suffering Servant. I want to look at one verse in chapter 53: "But he was pierced for our transgressions; he was crushed for our iniquities; upon him was the chastisement that brought us peace, and with his wounds we are healed."[4]

Crushed. The Hebrew word is *daka*. It means "to crumble, beat to pieces, to be crushed, broken, shattered."

Jesus is currently kneeling in the garden of Gethsemane before anyone has laid a hand on Him, and yet His blood vessels are bursting. The Hebrew word for Gethsemane is *gat shemanim*, which means "oil press." The place where the olives are crushed by great weight. As Jesus prays with the Father, asking, "If there be any other way . . .," the weight of all the world's sin for all time begins to crush the Son of Man. It's as if the Father pulls back the veil that separates eternity from right now, and He allows the sum total of the accumulated wrath of God to drip like an IV into the Son of Man. How does Jesus' body respond?

Drip. Drip. Drip.

In response to sin, the sinless body of the Son of God bursts. And drops of blood paint the earth below. Sin in. Blood out. An inexplicable exchange. The first recorded sin outside the garden of Eden occurred when one brother killed another. Cain spilled Abel's blood. To which God said, "The voice of your brother's blood is crying to me from the ground."[5] What's he crying? "Guilty!"

But what about us? The diagnosis and message of the Cross is that we're all as guilty as Cain. And yet, here we are, standing on Mount Zion crying out for mercy. This is the writer of Hebrews: "But you have come to Mount Zion and to the city of the living God, the heavenly Jerusalem, and to innumerable angels in festal gathering, and to the assembly of the firstborn who are enrolled in heaven, and to God, the judge of all, and to the spirits of the righteous made perfect, and to Jesus, the mediator of a new covenant, and to the sprinkled blood that speaks a better word than the blood of Abel."[6]

What is that "better word"?

Innocent. Righteous. Forgiven. Ransomed. Redeemed. Snatched back out of the hand of the devil. Righteous men made perfect.

How is this possible?

Tetelestai.

In the place where the olives are crushed, Jesus accepts our sin and all the evil consequences due to us and, in return, gives us His blood. It is here that He stares across eternity and says to us: "Me for you."

Years ago, on my first trip to Jerusalem, I stood in that garden. The Judean desert just a couple hundred yards behind me.

Somewhere in that awestruck moment, it hit me: He could have disappeared. He didn't have to stay. And yet, He did. I remember staring at my feet and thinking, *Right here, the shedding began. The willful shedding of the most precious blood in the history of blood.* It was too much then, and it is still too much now. I simply can't take it in.

What kind of King is this?

Jesus' body was physically in the garden here on earth, but spiritually, I think it is here that He walks into the prison that held all of us. Shackled. Chained. Dead in our sin. Prisoners serving an eternal sentence in the kingdom of darkness. Maggots. Rotting flesh. Death all around. And makes a ridiculous offer. Peter described it this way: "For Christ also suffered once for sins, the righteous for the unrighteous, that he might bring us to God, being put to death in the flesh but made alive in the spirit, in which he went and proclaimed to the spirits in prison, because they formerly did not obey, when God's patience waited in the days of Noah, while the ark was being prepared, in which a few, that is, eight persons, were brought safely through water."[7]

In my storytelling mind, Jesus walks into the dungeon, surveys all of us, and says to the slave master, "I'll buy them all."

The slave master shakes his head. "You can't afford them."

To which Jesus responds by holding out His hand and squeezing. One drop. A second. Then a third . . .

A flow that does not stop until Jesus pushes up on His nail-pierced feet and declares, "*Tetelestai.*"

"Paid in full."

Through the crushing of the Son, we are blood-bought, blood-washed, and blood-redeemed. Where does this begin? In a garden, amid the olive trees.

WALK WITH ME BACK TO THE CROSS

On this bloody, splintery execution stake, Jesus bought us. Made payment. Hanging in our place. Seems like an awful waste had God not ordained it fifteen hundred years prior: "For the life of the flesh is in the blood, and I have given it for you on the altar to make atonement for your souls, for it is the blood that makes atonement by the life."[8] This tree is where God the Father made good on that promise.

As an old man, looking back on that moment, the disciple—and Jesus' beloved friend—John, said this: "In this is love, not that we have loved God but that he loved us and sent his Son to be the propitiation for our sins."[9]

"In this is love . . ." Let that sink in. "In this . . ."

If you have ever felt unloved, ever been made to feel you're insignificant, that you don't matter, forgotten, thrown away, disqualified, too far gone, beyond the grasp of God, that you'd be better off dead, let me say this to you: you are loved. Please hear that—you are loved. How do I know? Look up. He loves you more than you can fathom. Need proof? Follow the trail. It leads from here, makes a serpentine path through the city, then out across the brook Kidron and into a garden. And He did that for you. In fact, He calls you "beloved." That's you. Beloved. What does it mean? It means "to be loved." Where do we do that? Right here.

PRAY WITH ME

King Jesus, I have heard these words before, but now they mean a bit more: "And as Moses lifted up the serpent in the wilderness, so must the Son of Man be lifted up, that whoever believes in him may have eternal life. For God so loved the world, that he gave his only Son, that whoever believes in him should not perish but have eternal life. For God did not send his Son into the world to condemn the world, but in order that the world might be saved through him. Whoever believes in him is not condemned, but whoever does not believe is condemned already, because he has not believed in the name of the only Son of God."[10]

I just had no idea. I thank You, as much as I am able, that You took all the evil due to me and gave me all the good due to You from Your and my Father. That You took my place. That You paid my debt. That You did what I could not. Jesus, when I think what the Cross cost You, I am undone. When I see how Your Father crushed You for me, my heart is torn. I bring nothing to my own redemption except the sin that causes me to need it and You. So, Lord . . . here. Here's all my sin. All I am. And everything I will be. Laid at Your feet. I'm nothing without You. I cry out for mercy. For forgiveness. For atonement. And I receive this unmerited and unearned gift with my face to the floor in gratitude. You alone are God and worthy of all praise. In Jesus' name.

AND GOD RESPONDS

"Who has believed what he has heard from us? And to whom has the arm of the Lord been revealed? For he grew up before him like a young plant, and like a root out of dry ground; he had no form or majesty that we should look at him, and no beauty that we should desire him. He was despised and rejected by men, a man of sorrows and acquainted with grief; and as one from whom men hide their faces he was despised, and we esteemed him not. Surely he has borne our griefs and carried our sorrows; yet we esteemed him stricken, smitten by God, and afflicted. But he was pierced for our transgressions; he was crushed for our iniquities; upon him was the chastisement that brought us peace, and with his wounds we are healed. All we like sheep have gone astray; we have turned—every one—to his own way; and the Lord has laid on him the iniquity of us all. He was oppressed, and he was afflicted, yet he opened not his mouth; like a lamb that is led to the slaughter, and like a sheep that before its shearers is silent, so he opened not his mouth. By oppression and judgment he was taken away; and as for his generation, who considered that he was cut off out of the land of the living, stricken for the transgression of my people? And they made his grave with the wicked and with a rich man in his death, although he had done no violence, and there was no deceit in his mouth. Yet it was the will of the Lord to crush him; he has put him to grief; when his soul makes an offering for guilt, he shall see his offspring; he shall prolong his days; the will of the Lord shall prosper in his hand. Out of the anguish of his soul he shall see and be satisfied; by his knowledge shall the righteous one, my servant, make many to be accounted righteous, and he shall bear their iniquities. Therefore I will divide him a portion with the many, and he shall divide the spoil with the strong, because he poured out his soul to death and was numbered with the transgressors; yet he bore the sin of many, and makes intercession for the transgressors."[11]

"Therefore, since we are surrounded by so great a cloud of witnesses, let us also lay aside every weight, and sin which clings so closely, and let us run with endurance the race that is set before us, looking to Jesus, the founder and perfecter of our faith, who for the joy that was set before him endured the cross, despising the shame, and is seated at the right hand of the throne of God."[12]

DAY 38

———◆•◆———

"Then Pilate took Jesus and flogged him."

JOHN 19:1

The end is within reach. Just over that hill. Two days from the end of our pilgrimage, I feel as if we've reached Holy ground. "Shoes off, face to the floor" kind of stuff. Sitting here, I'm wrestling with tone. With how best to end. And how to revere. If I'm honest, I'm hesitant. I know what's coming, and it's going to hurt. Tears are close to the surface. Pushing me onward is the knowledge that it hurt Him far worse. So how do I write—really—the execution of the innocent Son of God? How do I faithfully—without adding to or detracting from—tell of the last few hours of Jesus' life? How do I get us, you and me, next to the Cross where we can hear that singular word spoken? Somewhere in here, I'm reminded of the words of John the Baptist: "The one who has the bride is the bridegroom. The friend of the bridegroom, who stands and hears him, rejoices greatly at the bridegroom's voice. Therefore this joy of mine is now complete. He must increase, but I must decrease."[1]

So let's do that. Let me step back. And let's ask the bridegroom to tell the story in His own voice.

How will He do this? Well, He already did. Long ago. The Old

Testament writers, speaking through the power of the Holy Spirit, have far more to say about the crucifixion of Jesus than the New Testament. The Gospels say simply, "They crucified Him." But how? What was the process? And what was Jesus thinking? Why say so little about the most significant event in all of human history? To help answer this, I've cut and pasted the last twenty-four hours of Jesus' life from the Gospels while also inserting what the Old Testament writers prophesied or foretold.[2]

For reasons I can't comprehend, Jesus filled men—real people like you and me—with His Spirit and then gave them words to describe His Cross. His passion. His thoughts. His suffering. And His joy. So let's read their words and see this through their eyes.

WALK WITH ME BACK TO THE CROSS

"And Peter said, 'See, we have left our homes and followed you.' And he said to them, 'Truly, I say to you, there is no one who has left house or wife or brothers or parents or children, for the sake of the kingdom of God, who will not receive many times more in this time, and in the age to come eternal life.' And taking the twelve, he said to them, 'See, we are going up to Jerusalem, and everything that is written about the Son of Man by the prophets will be accomplished. For he will be delivered over to the Gentiles and will be mocked and shamefully treated and spit upon. And after flogging him, they will kill him, and on the third day he will rise.' But they understood none of these things. This saying was hidden from them, and they did not grasp what was said."[3]

"Then he said to them, 'My soul is very sorrowful, even to death; remain here, and watch with me.' And going a little farther he fell on his face and prayed, saying, 'My Father, if it be possible, let this cup pass from me; nevertheless, not as I will, but as you will.'"[4]

"Then Simon Peter, having a sword, drew it and struck the high priest's servant and cut off his right ear. (The servant's name was Malchus.) So Jesus said to Peter, 'Put your sword into its sheath; shall I not drink the cup that the Father has given me?'"[5]

ISAIAH 51:22–23:

"Thus says your Lord, the Lord, your God who pleads the cause of his people: 'Behold, I have taken from your hand the cup of staggering; the bowl of my wrath you shall drink no more; and I will put it into the hand of your tormentors, who have said to you, "Bow down, that we may pass over"; and you have made your back like the ground and like the street for them to pass over.'"

"So the band of soldiers and their captain and the officers of the Jews arrested Jesus and bound him. First they led him to Annas, for he was the father-in-law of Caiaphas, who was high priest that year."[6]

ISAIAH 53:3:

"He was despised and rejected by men, a man of sorrows and acquainted with grief; and as one from whom men hide their faces he was despised, and we esteemed him not."

"The high priest then questioned Jesus about his disciples and his teaching. Jesus answered him, 'I have spoken openly to the world. I have always taught in synagogues and in the temple, where all Jews come together. I have said nothing in secret. Why do you ask me? Ask those who have heard me what I said to them; they know what I said.' When he had said these things, one of the officers standing by struck Jesus with his hand, saying, 'Is that how you answer the high priest?'"[7]

PSALM 33:6–9:

"By the word of the Lord the heavens were made, and by the breath of his mouth all their host. He gathers the waters of the sea as a heap; he puts the deeps in storehouses. Let all the earth fear the Lord; let all the inhabitants of the world stand in awe of him! For he spoke, and it came to be; he commanded, and it stood firm."

"Then they led Jesus from the house of Caiaphas to the governor's headquarters. It was early morning. They themselves did not enter the governor's headquarters, so that they would not be defiled, but could eat the Passover. So Pilate went outside to them and said, 'What accusation do you bring against this man?' They answered him, 'If this man were not doing evil, we would not have delivered him over to you.' Pilate said to them, 'Take him yourselves and judge him by your own law.' The Jews said to him, 'It is not lawful for us to put anyone to death.'"[8]

ISAIAH 53:7:

"He was oppressed, and he was afflicted, yet he opened not his mouth; like a lamb that is led to the slaughter, and like a sheep that before its shearers is silent, so he opened not his mouth."

"So Pilate entered his headquarters again and called Jesus and said to him, 'Are you the King of the Jews?' Jesus answered, 'Do you say this of your own accord, or did others say it to you about me?' Pilate answered, 'Am I a Jew? Your own nation and the chief priests have delivered you over to me. What have you done?' Jesus answered, 'My kingdom is not of this world. If my kingdom were of this world, my servants would have been fighting, that I might not be delivered over to the Jews. But my kingdom is not from the world.' Then Pilate said to him, 'So you are a king?' Jesus answered, 'You say that I am a king. For this purpose I was born and for this purpose I have come into the world—to bear witness to the truth.

Everyone who is of the truth listens to my voice.' Pilate said to him, 'What is truth?' After he had said this, he went back outside to the Jews and told them, 'I find no guilt in him. But you have a custom that I should release one man for you at the Passover. So do you want me to release to you the King of the Jews?' They cried out again, 'Not this man, but Barabbas!' Now Barabbas was a robber."[9]

"Then Pilate took Jesus and flogged him."[10]

ISAIAH 52:14:

"As many were astonished at him—his appearance was so marred, beyond human semblance, and his form beyond that of the children of mankind." (The NASB says, "His appearance was marred beyond that of a man, and His form beyond the sons of mankind.")

"And the soldiers twisted together a crown of thorns and put it on his head and arrayed him in a purple robe. They came up to him, saying, 'Hail, King of the Jews!' and struck him with their hands. Pilate went out again and said to them, 'See, I am bringing him out to you that you may know that I find no guilt in him.' So Jesus came out, wearing the crown of thorns and the purple robe. Pilate said to them, 'Behold the man!' When the chief priests and the officers saw him, they cried out, 'Crucify him, crucify him!' Pilate said to them, 'Take him yourselves and crucify him, for I find no guilt in him.' The Jews answered him, 'We have a law, and according to that law he ought to die because he has made himself the Son of God.'"[11]

MICAH 5:1:

"With a rod they strike the judge of Israel on the cheek."

ISAIAH 50:6:

"I gave my back to those who strike, and my cheeks to those who pull out the beard; I hid not my face from disgrace and spitting."

"Now it was the day of Preparation of the Passover. It was about the sixth hour. He said to the Jews, 'Behold your King!' They cried out, 'Away with him, away with him, crucify him!' Pilate said to them, 'Shall I crucify your King?' The chief priests answered, 'We have no king but Caesar.' So he delivered him over to them to be crucified. So they took Jesus."[12]

ISAIAH 53:4–6:

"Surely he has borne our griefs and carried our sorrows; yet we esteemed him stricken, smitten by God, and afflicted. But he was pierced for our transgressions; he was crushed for our iniquities; upon him was the chastisement that brought us peace, and with his wounds we are healed. All we like sheep have gone astray; we have turned—every one—to his own way; and the Lord has laid on him the iniquity of us all."

"And as they led him away, they seized one Simon of Cyrene, who was coming in from the country, and laid on him the cross, to carry it behind Jesus. And there followed him a great multitude of the people and of women who were mourning and lamenting for him. But turning to them Jesus said, 'Daughters of Jerusalem, do not weep for me, but weep for yourselves and for your children.'"[13]

ZECHARIAH 12:10:

"When they look on me, on him whom they have pierced, they shall mourn for him, as one mourns for an only child, and weep bitterly over him, as one weeps over a firstborn."

"And he went out, bearing his own cross, to the place called The Place of a Skull, which in Aramaic is called Golgotha. There they crucified him, and with him two others, one on either side, and Jesus between them."[14]

PSALM 22:1–2:

"My God, my God, why have you forsaken me? Why are you so far from saving me, from the words of my groaning? O my God, I cry by day, but you do not answer, and by night, but I find no rest."

PSALM 22:6–7:

"But I am a worm and not a man, scorned by mankind and despised by the people. All who see me mock me; they make mouths at me; they wag their heads."

"When the soldiers had crucified Jesus, they took his garments and divided them into four parts, one part for each soldier; also his tunic. But the tunic was seamless, woven in one piece from top to bottom."[15]

PSALM 22:11–18:

"Be not far from me, for trouble is near, and there is none to help. Many bulls encompass me; strong bulls of Bashan surround me; they open wide their mouths at me, like a ravening and roaring lion. I am poured out like water, and all my bones are out of joint; my heart is like wax; it is melted within my breast; my strength is dried up like a potsherd, and my tongue sticks to my jaws; you lay me in the dust of death. For dogs encompass me; a company of evildoers encircles me; they have pierced my hands and feet—I can count all my bones—they stare and gloat over me; they divide my garments among them, and for my clothing they cast lots."

ZECHARIAH 13:6:

"And if one asks him, 'What are these wounds on your back?' he will say, 'The wounds I received in the house of my friends.'"[1]

DEUTERONOMY 21:22–23:

"And if a man has committed a crime punishable by death and he is put to death, and you hang him on a tree, his body shall not

---

1. There is no small amount of discussion in theological circles as to whether this passage refers to Jesus or the false prophets in the previous verse. I can not settle that argument here, but I think it might, or could, refer to Jesus. I've included it because Jesus did receive His wounds in the house of His friends. He says so: "I have called you friends" (John 15:15).

remain all night on the tree, but you shall bury him the same day, for a hanged man is cursed by God."

"When Jesus had received the sour wine . . ."[16]

PSALM 69:20–21:

"Reproaches have broken my heart, so that I am in despair. I looked for pity, but there was none, and for comforters, but I found none. They gave me poison for food, and for my thirst they gave me sour wine to drink."

"He said, 'It is finished,' and he bowed his head and gave up his spirit."[17]

PSALM 31:5:

"Into your hand I commit my spirit; you have redeemed me, O Lord, faithful God."

PSALM 22:30–31:

"Posterity shall serve him; it shall be told of the Lord to the coming generation; they shall come and proclaim his righteousness to a people yet unborn, that he has done it."

That he has done it—it is finished.

"But when they came to Jesus and saw that he was already dead, they did not break his legs. But one of the soldiers pierced his side with a spear, and at once there came out blood and water. He who saw it has borne witness—his testimony is true, and he knows that he is telling the truth—that you also may believe. For these things took place that the Scripture might be fulfilled: 'Not one of his bones will be broken.' And again another Scripture says, 'They will look on him whom they have pierced.'"[18]

PSALM 34:19–20:

"Many are the afflictions of the righteous, but the Lord delivers him out of them all. He keeps all his bones; not one of them is broken."

PRAY WITH ME

Jesus, Psalm 22, written by David and spoken in and through the inspiration of the Holy Spirit, ends with the words "that he has done it." And You did. You did it. You paid the price. Made atonement. Stood in our place. Ransomed mankind with Your very own blood. Said another way, "It is finished." The totality of Scripture is well beyond my ability to encapsulate it all. I can grasp parts, but the whole is amazing. It's like a diamond with ten trillion facets, and each facet has ten trillion facets, and so on. Your Word is perfect. And nothing, not a single jot or tittle, is wasted. Jesus, thank You for Your precious and unbroken and absolutely true Word. In Jesus' name.

AND GOD RESPONDS

"God is our refuge and strength, a very present help in trouble. Therefore we will not fear though the earth gives way, though the mountains be moved into the heart of the sea, though its waters roar and foam, though the mountains tremble at its swelling. There is a river whose streams make glad the city of God, the holy habitation of the Most High. God is in the midst of her; she shall not be moved; God will help her when morning dawns. The nations rage, the kingdoms totter; he utters his voice, the earth melts. The Lord of hosts is with us; the God of Jacob is our fortress. Come, behold the works of the Lord, how he has brought desolations on the earth. He makes wars cease to the end of the earth; he breaks the bow and shatters the spear; he burns the chariots with fire. 'Be still, and know that I am God. I will be exalted among the nations, I will be exalted in the earth!' The Lord of hosts is with us; the God of Jacob is our fortress."[19]

DAY 39

"When the soldiers had crucified Jesus . . ."

JOHN 19:23

We've talked a lot about the Cross. Looked at it and He who died there from every angle. As we spend one final day looking at the crucifixion, I want to step back once again and let the eyewitness narratives tell the story. In their own words. To do this, I've included all four Gospels arranged in a chronological attempt to tell the story, beginning to end:

WALK WITH ME BACK TO THE CROSS . . . ONE LAST TIME

"A third time he said to them, 'Why? What evil has he done? I have found in him no guilt deserving death. I will therefore punish and release him.' But they were urgent, demanding with loud cries that he should be crucified. And their voices prevailed. So Pilate decided that their demand should be granted. He released the man who had been thrown into prison for insurrection and murder, for whom they asked, but he delivered Jesus over to their will."[1]

"And as they led him away, they seized one Simon of Cyrene, who was coming in from the country, and laid on him the cross, to carry it behind Jesus. And there followed him a great multitude of the people and of women who were mourning and lamenting for him. But turning to them Jesus said, 'Daughters of Jerusalem, do not weep for me, but weep for yourselves and for your children. For behold, the days are coming when they will say, "Blessed are the barren and the wombs that never bore and the breasts that never nursed!" Then they will begin to say to the mountains, "Fall on us," and to the hills, "Cover us." For if they do these things when the wood is green, what will happen when it is dry?'"[2]

"Two others, who were criminals, were led away to be put to death with him. And when they came to the place that is called The Skull, there they crucified him, and the criminals, one on his right and one on his left."[3]

"Men of Israel, hear these words: Jesus of Nazareth, a man attested to you by God with mighty works and wonders and signs that God did through him in your midst, as you yourselves know—this Jesus, delivered up according to the definite plan and foreknowledge of God, you crucified and killed by the hands of lawless men."[4]

"And Jesus said, 'Father, forgive them, for they know not what they do.' And they cast lots to divide his garments. And the people stood by, watching, but the rulers scoffed at him, saying, 'He saved others; let him save himself, if he is the Christ of God, his Chosen One!' The soldiers also mocked him, coming up and offering him sour wine and saying, 'If you are the King of the Jews, save yourself!' There was also an inscription over him, 'This is the King of the Jews.'"[5]

"When the soldiers had crucified Jesus, they took his garments and divided them into four parts, one part for each soldier; also his tunic. But the tunic was seamless, woven in one piece from top to bottom, so they said to one another, 'Let us not tear it, but cast lots for it to see whose it shall be.' This was to fulfill the Scripture which says, 'They divided my garments among them, and for my clothing they cast lots.' So the soldiers did these things."[6]

"But standing by the cross of Jesus were his mother and his mother's sister, Mary the wife of Clopas, and Mary Magdalene. When Jesus saw his mother and the disciple whom he loved standing nearby, he said to his mother, 'Woman, behold, your son!' Then he said to the disciple, 'Behold, your mother!' And from that hour the disciple took her to his own home."[7]

"One of the criminals who were hanged railed at him, saying, 'Are you not the Christ? Save yourself and us!' But the other rebuked him, saying, 'Do you not fear God, since you are under the same sentence of condemnation? And we indeed justly, for we are receiving the due reward of our deeds; but this man has done nothing wrong.' And he said, 'Jesus, remember me when you come into your kingdom.' And he said to him, 'Truly, I say to you, today you will be with me in paradise.'"[8]

"Now from the sixth hour there was darkness over all the land until the ninth hour. And about the ninth hour Jesus cried out with a loud voice, saying, 'Eli, Eli, lema sabachthani?' that is, 'My God, my God, why have you forsaken me?' And some of the bystanders, hearing it, said, 'This man is calling Elijah.' And one of them at once ran and took a sponge, filled it with sour wine, and put it on a reed and gave it to him to drink. But the others said, 'Wait, let us see whether Elijah will come to save him.'"[9]

"After this, Jesus, knowing that all was now finished, said (to fulfill the Scripture), 'I thirst.' A jar full of sour wine stood there, so they put a sponge full of the sour wine on a hyssop branch and held it to his mouth."[10]

"When Jesus had received the sour wine, he said, 'It is finished,' and he bowed his head and gave up his spirit."[11]

"It was now about the sixth hour, and there was darkness over the whole land until the ninth hour, while the sun's light failed. And the curtain of the temple was torn in two. Then Jesus, calling out with a loud voice, said, 'Father, into your hands I commit my spirit!' And having said this he breathed his last."[12]

"And behold, the curtain of the temple was torn in two, from top to bottom. And the earth shook, and the rocks were split. The tombs also were opened. And many bodies of the saints who had fallen asleep were raised, and coming out of the tombs after his resurrection they went into the holy city and appeared to many. When the centurion and those who were with him, keeping watch over Jesus, saw the earthquake and what took place, they were filled with awe and said, 'Truly this was the Son of God!'"[13]

"So the soldiers came and broke the legs of the first, and of the other who had been crucified with him. But when they came to Jesus and saw that he was already dead, they did not break his legs. But one of the soldiers pierced his side with a spear, and at once there came out blood and water. He who saw it has borne witness—his testimony is true, and he knows that he is telling the truth—that you also may believe. For these things took place that the Scripture might be fulfilled: 'Not one of his bones will be broken.'"[14]

"Now when the centurion saw what had taken place, he praised God, saying, 'Certainly this man was innocent!' And all the crowds that had assembled for this spectacle, when they saw what had taken place, returned home beating their breasts. And all his acquaintances and the women who had followed him from Galilee stood at a distance watching these things."[15]

PRAY WITH ME

King Jesus. All that I have, all that I am, all that I will be, is Yours.

AND GOD RESPONDS

"When Jesus had spoken these words, he lifted up his eyes to heaven, and said, 'Father, the hour has come; glorify your Son that the Son may glorify you, since you have given him authority over all flesh, to give eternal life to all whom you have given him. And this is eternal life, that they know you, the only true God, and Jesus Christ whom you have sent. I glorified you on earth, having accomplished the work that you gave me to do. And now, Father, glorify me in your own presence with the glory that I had with you before the world existed.

'I have manifested your name to the people whom you gave me out of the world. Yours they were, and you gave them to me, and they have kept your word. Now they know that everything that you have given me is from you. For I have given them the words that you gave me, and they have received them and have come to know in truth that I came from you; and they have believed that you sent me. I am praying for them. I am not praying for the world but for those whom you have given me, for they are yours. All mine are yours, and yours are mine, and I am glorified in them. And I am no longer in the world, but they are in the world, and I am coming to you. Holy Father, keep them in your name, which you have given me, that they may be one, even as we are one. While I was with them, I kept them in your name, which you have given me. I have guarded them, and not one of them has been lost except the son of destruction, that the

Scripture might be fulfilled. But now I am coming to you, and these things I speak in the world, that they may have my joy fulfilled in themselves. I have given them your word, and the world has hated them because they are not of the world, just as I am not of the world. I do not ask that you take them out of the world, but that you keep them from the evil one. They are not of the world, just as I am not of the world. Sanctify them in the truth; your word is truth. As you sent me into the world, so I have sent them into the world. And for their sake I consecrate myself, that they also may be sanctified in truth.

'I do not ask for these only, but also for those who will believe in me through their word, that they may all be one, just as you, Father, are in me, and I in you, that they also may be in us, so that the world may believe that you have sent me. The glory that you have given me I have given to them, that they may be one even as we are one, I in them and you in me, that they may become perfectly one, so that the world may know that you sent me and loved them even as you loved me. Father, I desire that they also, whom you have given me, may be with me where I am, to see my glory that you have given me because you loved me before the foundation of the world. O righteous Father, even though the world does not know you, I know you, and these know that you have sent me. I made known to them your name, and I will continue to make it known, that the love with which you have loved me may be in them, and I in them.'"[16]

"Even as the Son of Man came not to be served but to serve, and to give his life as a ransom for many."[17]

"All the ends of the earth shall remember and turn to the Lord, and all the families of the nations shall worship before you. For kingship belongs to the Lord, and he rules over the nations. All the prosperous of the earth eat and worship; before him shall bow all who go down to the dust, even the one who could not keep himself alive. Posterity shall serve him; it shall be told of the Lord to the coming generation; they shall come and proclaim his righteousness to a people yet unborn, that he has done it."[18]

NASB: "He has performed it."

KJV: "He hath done this."

NIV: "He has done it!"

Tetelestai. It is finished.

DAY 40

"He is not here, for he has risen."

MATTHEW 28:1–9

Our pilgrimage has come to a close, the last page, the final step; but thank God, the story doesn't end at a bloody Cross. Far from it. Everything up to now has been prologue. The Cross is a beginning. A birth. Represented by the blood and water that flowed out of His chest. I wonder sometimes about those first few heartbroken souls to reach the tomb. John, Peter, Mary. How their hearts must have ached. Burned. With their worlds upended, they poked their heads in. Looked around. But Jesus was nowhere to be found. Body gone. Imagine the shock. Anger. Frustration. What else could possibly go wrong? And then Mary meets the gardener, and light pierces the darkness. Oh, how I love that moment. Wish I had been there. I think Mary came unglued and lost her ever-loving mind. With this as the backdrop, I want to attempt to tell the story of the greatest moment in all of history through the eyes of those who saw it, lived it, and then did their best to recount it using these crazy little things God gave us. These things called *words.*

MATTHEW:

"Now after the Sabbath, toward the dawn of the first day of the week, Mary Magdalene and the other Mary went to see the tomb. And behold, there was a great earthquake, for an angel of the Lord descended from heaven and came and rolled back the stone and sat on it. His appearance was like lightning, and his clothing white as snow. And for fear of him the guards trembled and became like dead men. But the angel said to the women, 'Do not be afraid, for I know that you seek Jesus who was crucified. He is not here, for he has risen, as he said. Come, see the place where he lay. Then go quickly and tell his disciples that he has risen from the dead, and behold, he is going before you to Galilee; there you will see him. See, I have told you.' So they departed quickly from the tomb with fear and great joy, and ran to tell his disciples. And behold, Jesus met them and said, 'Greetings!' And they came up and took hold of his feet and worshiped him."[1]

MARK:

"When the Sabbath was past, Mary Magdalene, Mary the mother of James, and Salome bought spices, so that they might go and anoint him. And very early on the first day of the week, when the sun had risen, they went to the tomb. And they were saying to one another, 'Who will roll away the stone for us from the entrance of the tomb?' And looking up, they saw that the stone had been rolled back—it was very large. And entering the tomb, they saw a young man sitting on the right side, dressed in a white robe, and they were alarmed. And he said to them, 'Do not be alarmed. You seek Jesus of Nazareth, who was crucified. He has risen; he is not here. See the place where they laid him. But go, tell his disciples and Peter that he is going before you to Galilee. There you will see him, just as he told you.' And they went out and fled from the tomb, for trembling and astonishment had seized them, and they said nothing to anyone, for they were afraid."[2]

LUKE:

"But on the first day of the week, at early dawn, they went to the tomb, taking the spices they had prepared. And they found the stone rolled away from the tomb, but when they went in they did not find the body of the Lord Jesus. While they were perplexed about this, behold, two men stood by them in dazzling apparel. And as they were frightened and bowed their faces to the ground, the men said to them, 'Why do you seek the living among the dead? He is not here, but has risen. Remember how he told you, while he was still in Galilee, that the Son of Man must be delivered into the hands of sinful men and be crucified and on the third day rise.' And they remembered his words, and returning from the tomb they told all these things to the eleven and to all the rest. Now it was Mary Magdalene and Joanna and Mary the mother of James and the other women with them who told these things to the apostles, but these words seemed to them an idle tale, and they did not believe them. But Peter rose and ran to the tomb; stooping and looking in, he saw the linen cloths by themselves; and he went home marveling at what had happened."[3]

JOHN:

"But Mary stood weeping outside the tomb, and as she wept she stooped to look into the tomb. And she saw two angels in white, sitting where the body of Jesus had lain, one at the head and one at the feet. They said to her, 'Woman, why are you weeping?' She said to them, 'They have taken away my Lord, and I do not know where they have laid him.' Having said this, she turned around and saw Jesus standing, but she did not know that it was Jesus. Jesus said to her, 'Woman, why are you weeping? Whom are you seeking?' Supposing him to be the gardener, she said to him, 'Sir, if you have carried him away, tell me where you have laid him, and I will take him away.' Jesus said to her, 'Mary.' She turned and said to him in Aramaic, 'Rabboni!' (which means Teacher). Jesus said to her, 'Do not cling to me, for I have not yet ascended to the Father; but go to my brothers and say to them, "I am ascending to my Father and your Father, to my God and your God."' Mary Magdalene went and announced to the disciples, 'I have seen the Lord'—and that he had said these things to her."[4]

WALK INTO THE EMPTY TOMB WITH ME

In this tomb, used once for a total of three days, the angels spoke the seven most amazing, most fantastic, most inconceivably awesome and mind-blowing words ever uttered: "He is not here. He is risen." Try to hear those words through the ears of the disciples. Imagine the confusion as they wrestle with the words. As the hope stirs. Watch them shake their heads as the incredulity rises: "What? Wait a minute. What are you saying? We left His body right here . . ." In the Charles Martin translation, the angel lowers his eyes, stares over his sunglasses, and says, "Dude . . . He's alive. Death defeated. Jesus wins. Forever." Pause. A smirk. "And when He said, 'It is finished,' He wasn't kidding."

Rather than walk back to the Cross or stand in the empty tomb, let's just praise the risen King.

RAISE YOUR HANDS WITH ME

While we have spent forty days returning to the Cross, here's the truth. He is not still hanging here. And He's not in that tomb over there. This tomb is empty. This Cross is unmanned. Jesus Christ is risen. And He is alive. Right now.

Right this very moment, Jesus—the undefeated King of all kings—is seated at the right hand of God. An honor bestowed, given Him by the Father. He's the only One to ever sit there. The only One worthy. The Lion of the tribe of Judah has prevailed. To Him has been given all dominion and authority. And His kingdom shall never end. And notice that Jesus, the High Priest of our confession, is seated. Why? Because His work on the Cross is finished. That said, His work in us is not. Until His return on this mountain, we are all still works in progress. The finished work of the Cross, the blood of Jesus, is still working in us, to us, and through us. That's the beauty and wonder and majesty and I-just-can't-believe-it-ness of this Cross.

PRAY WITH ME

Jesus, I don't have any idea what to say. All I know is that I want to add my voice to the countless millions around Your throne who declare, "Worthy is the Lamb who was slain, to receive power and wealth and wisdom and might and honor and glory and blessing! . . . To him who sits on the throne and to the Lamb be blessing and honor and glory and might forever and ever!"[5]

Here's what I hope from this day forward: I want to live like You're alive. Like You really did walk out of that tomb. Like it really is finished. I want to live in the power of Your resurrection. I may not completely understand what that means, maybe not very much at all, but I want it. Not because I deserve it but because You died to give it to me. To bring me to Your and Our Father. I've read this scripture many times, and I thought I knew what it meant. It means a little more now: "*Therefore, since we are surrounded by so great a cloud of witnesses, let us also lay aside every weight, and sin which clings so closely, and let us run with endurance the race that is set before us, looking to Jesus, the founder and perfecter of our faith, who for the joy that was set before him endured the cross, despising the shame, and is seated at the right hand of the throne of God.*"[6]

I don't pretend to be the joy that was set before You, but I'd like to think I'm one part of the whole. And according to Your Word, I am. And because of that joy, You endured what no one else could. You prevailed. As long as I live, I'll never wrap my head around that fact. And I pray I never do. I pray that You and what You alone did on that Cross never gets old and I never take it for granted. Today, You're seated with Your Father. At His right hand. Perfect fellowship. Perfect love. Perfectly perfect. Something so amazing, so utterly unbelievable that You left heaven to bring us back to it and to Him. I look forward to that.

I pray that You would help me share Your story with others so that they might come to know You and that same love. From what You've told us, there's more than enough to go around. So come, Lord Jesus. Rule. Reign. Let Your kingdom come. Your will be done. Be magnified and lifted high. I pray that it is no longer I who live but You who live in and through me. And let me follow You all the days of my life having come to know You, Jesus Christ crucified, the power of the Cross, and the immeasurable glory and victory of Your resurrection. In the matchless, all-powerful, undefeated, limitless name of Jesus.

AND GOD RESPONDS

"He is risen."

EPILOGUE FROM JERUSALEM

At 3:00 P.M., a stone's throw away in the temple, the high priest has sharpened his knife, bound a spotless lamb, and slit its throat, catching the blood in a basin. As that warm blood dribbles over his hand and into a bowl, the man on the middle cross cries out. Then in His final act on earth, He bows His head and offers up His Spirit. Were He not dying in agony, it would look like an act of worship.

But then a strange thing happens. Were it not for hundreds of eyewitnesses, it'd be easy to argue its veracity. As His last breath exhales from His chest, darkness covers the earth, an earthquake rocks Jerusalem, the veil in the temple is torn in two—from top to bottom—and long-dead people get up out of their graves and walk through the city streets of Jerusalem visiting loved ones.

Hold it.

I write fiction for a living, have a rather vivid imagination, but this stretches the bounds of believability. Darkness? Earthquake? Dead people walking? As if they were somehow tied like a puppet string to this man's life? And what's this business about the veil? The thing was so thick you couldn't tear it with a truck. And yet, something did. Complicating matters, it tore from the top down. Almost as if God were sending a message.

After Jesus' death, His friends peeled His limp body off the cross and then hastily wrapped Him like a mummy and laid Him in a grave. A cave of sorts. Then the same soldiers who executed Him sealed the tomb and stood guard so nobody could rob the body and make up some myth about Him, further fueling the failed rebellion. Mind you, they've been given orders. Failure to obey is a death sentence. But on the morning of the third day, as His friends walked to His grave to mourn, they found no soldiers. Not a single one. Further, the iron spike used to seal the tomb had been snapped like a toothpick, and the huge stone, roughly half the size of a Volkswagen, had been rolled back. Out of the way. Stepping into the tomb, His followers found it empty save two angels who casually said, "Why do you seek the living among the dead? He is not here, but has risen."[1]

Try to hear this for the first time. As if you've never heard it. "He is not here, but has risen." What? How? Could it get any crazier?

Maybe the centurion was right. Maybe this man was the Son of God.[2]

Scripture records, almost as an aside, "And when they had crucified Him, they divided up His garments among themselves by casting lots."[3] "When they had crucified him." The most important event in human history gets five words in the annals of history.

Without the empty tomb, the Cross is just a cross and Jesus is just one more dead man. But because there is an empty tomb on the other side, *this* Cross, the Cross of Jesus Christ, is the centerpiece of human history. It matters more than anything.

The last time I was in Jerusalem, we walked down underground to a Herodian road that bordered the west side of the city and led from Caiaphas's house to Pilate's praetorium. Almost a direct shot. In studying the history of Jerusalem and the life of Jesus, there are many things we are not sure of. Some things we have to guess at. But we are pretty sure Jesus walked this road. Especially if they wanted to shame Him.

The stones are old, worn, smooth, and shiny. You can almost see your reflection in them.

Standing before the praetorium, with my feet on those stones, two things struck me. Over on the ground to my right, I saw something that looked like a tic-tac-toe game carved into the stone. Through much use, the multiple perpendicular lines had formed deep grooves in the stone. Here on these stones, beneath my feet, is where they would strip the condemned, and because he had no further use for his clothes, they'd gamble for them while someone swung the cat-o'-nine-tails. An executioner's perk.

To my left, a few feet away, sat a circular hole. Maybe eight inches in diameter. Soldiers would wedge a post into the hole, then lash a prisoner to it. Face to the pole. Then they'd whip him. Mercilessly.

Standing on those stones, it struck me. This was real. This really happened. They really gambled. They really beat Him. And He really bled—maybe right here. Splattered all around me. I knelt and traced the grooves with my fingers like a letter written in braille. In my ear I heard Isaiah saying, "His appearance was marred more than any man and His form more than the sons of men."[4] The NLT says it this way: "But many were amazed when they saw him. His face was so disfigured he seemed hardly human, and from his appearance, one would scarcely know he was a man."

I stared at the stones. Listening. Did it happen right here? Did Jesus become unrecognizable as a man on these smooth stones? Shaking my head, I whispered, "What kind of love is this? What kind of King does this?"

In my ear, I heard this echo: *The same King who says:* "[So] that the love with which you have loved me may be in them, and I in them."[5]

Perfect love.

I spent the next few minutes on my knees, palms to the stone, my tears falling into the grooves, mixing with the dust.

Inches from the stone, it struck me: I am blood-bought, blood-washed, and blood-redeemed. And I am so unworthy. And I am so grateful. And I wept.

And somewhere in there I had my first glimpse of this book—and at the time I didn't think I could write it. Honestly, I was scared to. Scared to try. Who am I? Further, who am I to lead such a pilgrimage?

And every day since, as I've sat in this chair, I have been simultaneously crushed by two things: First, the weight of me. My sin. My self. It's ugly. Much worse than I or you think. Paul was right. There is a sin that dwells in me that will not be appeased or satiated. It can't be improved, rehabbed, or talked off the ledge. And it won't compromise. Ever. It wants what it wants. Given that, the only solution is execution. The self in me must be crucified. Put to death. A stake must be driven through its chest. Daily. In these days, I have found the prayer of the tax collector to be much comfort: "Lord, have mercy. I'm a sinner." I've said it many times.

Second, I have been crushed by a joy I've never known. I can't explain that. I just have. These two have met me here every day. Sorrow and joy. And I am eternally grateful for both.

For the joy set before Him, and despising the shame, Jesus really did this. Redeemed mankind. With His very own blood. The most precious blood of any blood ever, and He shed it. For us. Emptied Himself. "We were bought with a price." And that price cost Him everything and me nothing. Even after all this time, I can't wrap my head around this. That He stood in my place. Brought me out from beneath the spear. Paid my sin-debt. Returned me to His, and now my own, Father. It's inconceivable. What kind of love is this? Better yet, what kind of King?

I hope I never get over this. Hope I never get used to the idea that Jesus literally paid it all. Willingly. Because I know me, and I'm not worth the life of the Son of God. And yet, to Him, I am.

An inconceivable exchange.

Most days, as I've sat here, I end up with one question, which He has answered several times. I won't tell you my answers. Those are between me and Him. But, fear not. He'll answer you as well. Just ask. The question is this: Lord, why me? Why would You do that, endure the Cross and despise the shame, for me? For Charles. Because being gut-level honest, I know me, and I'm not worth You.

Many days, I've ended my time writing with tears streaming down my face. Undone. It's been one of the most beautiful things He and I have ever done together. He has been faithful to meet me here every day. I show up with my coffee, still dark outside, and sit in this chair: "It's me, Lord. I'm back. Please help."

And we write.

I'm fifty-three. I've known the Lord for fifty years or better. That doesn't mean I've always been surrendered to Him or always obeyed Him in all that time, but I've known Him and walked with Him. The process of writing this book has been the single most profound and impacting thing I've ever done in that walk. Walking this journey, back to the Cross, for what was forty days for you but, for me, was more like eight or nine months, has been, well . . . significant on a level I've never known. I wouldn't trade it. These have been sweet, tender, mind-blowing, heart-rending times where He's peeled back the layers and revealed His Word to me. Himself. His heart. His joy.

Many times, when I write the end of a book, I'm ready for it to be over. "The end." But not this one. I don't want it to end. Maybe in the years ahead my publisher will let me come back and revise or add. Making other editions as I grow in maturity. In wisdom. And in stature. I'd like that. I pray it happens. People often ask me, What's your favorite book? I always shake my head. Don't have one. But this one falls into a different category. This one will have its own shelf. There's this one, and then there's everything else.

If readers could read only one of my twenty-five-plus books, I'd want them to read this one. Because in truth, it unashamedly points to the only thing on planet Earth that matters.

As I write these last words, I am in Jerusalem. Literally staring out across the Mount of Olives and the city where He has placed His name forever. The city of the great King. I love this place. I love these people. I love this mountain of God. This city where Abram raised his hand to God Most High after he met Melchizedek, who brought out bread and wine. This city where David returned the ark, dancing. This city where the prophets wept. Where Jesus the boy stood on the southern steps of the temple and astounded the aged leaders. This city where He healed. Cast out. Preached. And this city where He, Jesus, who knew no sin, became sin for us so that we might become the righteousness of God.

Beneath my feet is the mountain where Jesus drained the Father's cup of wrath, then extended—and continues to extend to us—His own cup. The cup of the new covenant. In His blood. An inconceivable exchange.

I used to wonder why Paul said this: "In the same way also he took the cup, after supper, saying, 'This cup is the new covenant in my blood. Do this, as often as you drink it, in remembrance of me.' For as often as you eat this bread and drink the cup, you proclaim the Lord's death until he comes."[6]

Why His death? Why not His sinless life? His ascension? His miracles? Because His life and the empty tomb only matter because He first died. No death? No redemption. No death? No transfer out of the kingdom of darkness. No death? No satisfying the wrath of God. No death? No debt payment. No death? No life. It is the death of Jesus, the sacrifice of the only begotten Son of God, the murder of the only sinless man to ever live, that finishes the work. That returns us to the Father. That allows us to become children of God.

Some things are just simple: the Son of Man came to seek and save the lost. That's us.

If Scripture is true—and I believe it is—He will return here. To this city. According to Zechariah, He will do so on that hillside right over there. The same hill where He prayed and sweated drops of blood. Where He was betrayed. Where He was arrested. Where He wept over Jerusalem. Where He wept over you and me. But this time, He's not returning to make payment. Not to drink the cup. Not to save. He's already done that. It is finished.

When He returns, He will do so as Judge, and He will hold court over the quick and the dead. When my time comes and I am called forth to the court of the ages, with all of heaven assembled in festal array, I hope He lets me bring this book—this record of my words—as evidence before the jury. So I can lay it at His feet. When I do, I pray He picks it up and reads it aloud. Not to make much of me. But because I believe these words make much of Him. They tell His story. What He did. What He finished. And who He purchased. These imperfect words are my attempt to lift high the only One who is perfectly perfect. In that moment, if I can speak, if I can breathe, if I can lift my face off the ground, and if I have any wits about me whatsoever, I hope to say, "My King, my Jesus, my Lord and my God, I believe these words are true. And I believe in You."

Charles Martin
Jerusalem
February 2023

NOTES

INTRODUCTION
1. John 19:28.
2. Psalm 69:21.
3. Psalm 69:12.
4. John 19:29.
5. John 19:29.
6. John 19:30.
7. 1 Corinthians 1:17–18, 22–24.
8. 1 Corinthians 2:2.
9. Galatians 3:1 NASB1995.
10. Romans 8:32.
11. Romans 4:24–25.
12. Galatians 6:14.
13. Luke 9:23; Matthew 16:24.
14. Galatians 2:20.
15. Galatians 5:11.
16. Isaiah 8:14.
17. 1 Corinthians 2:2.
18. Ephesians 1:17–24.
19. 1 Corinthians 1:18–31.

DAY 1
1. John 19:14–19.
2. Laura Geggel, "Jesus Wasn't the Only Man to Be Crucificed. Here's the History Behind This Brutal Practice," Live Science, April 19, 2019, https://www .livescience.com/65283 -crucifixion-history.html.
3. Francois Retief and Louise Cilliers, "The History and Pathology of Crucifixion," *South African Medical Journal* 93, no. 12 (December 2003): 938–41, https://pubmed.ncbi .nlm.nih.gov/14750495/.
4. Kristina Killgrove, "Heel Bone from Italy Is Only Second Example of Crucifixion Ever Found," *Forbes*, December 23, 2019, https://www.forbes.com /sites/kristinakillgrove/2019 /12/23/heel-bone-from-italy -is-only-second-example-of -crucifixion-ever-found; Gael F. Cooper, "Skeleton with Nail in Heel Offers Evidence of Roman Crucifixion," CNET, December 9, 2021, https://www

.cnet.com/science/skeleton
-with-nail-in-heel-offers
-evidence-of-roman
-crucifixion/.
5. Colossians 1:26.
6. Ephesians 3:8, 11.
7. Colossians 1:15–23.

DAY 2

1. John 9:1–6.
2. Russell Lazarus, "How Does
   the Eye Work?", Optometrists
   Network, October 11, 2020,
   https://www.optometrists.org
   /general-practice-optometry
   /guide-to-eye-health
   /how-does-the-eye-work.
3. John 9:6–7.
4. John 9:8–15 NIV.
5. Genesis 2:7.
6. John 17:20–26.
7. John 17:26.
8. Genesis 3:8.
9. Genesis 3:9.
10. John 3:16.
11. Colossians 1:13–14.
12. John 9:3.
13. John 14:18.
14. Psalm 139:13–18.

DAY 3

1. John 18:15–17.
2. John 18:18, 25–27.
3. John 1:17.
4. Genesis 1:26–28.
5. Genesis 3:1.
6. Genesis 3:7.

7. Genesis 3:10.
8. Genesis 3:11–12.
9. Genesis 3:14.
10. Ephesians 2:5.
11. Genesis 3:15.
12. Exodus 19:4.
13. John 6:40.
14. John 14:6.
15. Charles Simeon, *Horae
    Homileticae*
16. Romans 16:20.
17. Genesis 3:20–21.
18. Hebrews 9:22.
19. Isaiah 53:6.
20. Matthew 9:12–13.
21. Hebrews 4:16.
22. 2 Corinthians 5:19.
23. Colossians 1:21–23.
24. Ephesians 3:14–19.
25. Exodus 19:4.

DAY 4

1. John 1:29.
2. John 1:30–31.
3. Matthew 11:11.
4. John 1:32–34.
5. Exodus 19:4.
6. John 17:26.
7. John 14:6.
8. Hebrews 9:22.
9. Leviticus 17:11.
10. Hebrews 10:4.
11. Revelation 5:2.
12. Revelation 5:5.
13. Galatians 5:1.
14. 1 Corinthians 1:30.
15. John 17:22–23.

16. Revelation 5:1–14.
17. Romans 5:6–21.

DAY 5
1. John 17:25–26.
2. Genesis 3:23–24.
3. Romans 3:26.
4. Colossians 1:19.
5. 1 Corinthians 15:42–45.
6. Romans 6:23.
7. Numbers 6:24–26.
8. Job 9:32–35.
9. John 17:26.
10. 1 John 4:18.
11. Hebrews 10:14.

DAY 6
1. Matthew 26:39.
2. Luke 22:44.
3. John 18:11.
4. Genesis 3:22–24.
5. Ephesians 2:5.
6. 1 Corinthians 1:30.
7. 1 Peter 1:3.
8. 2 Peter 3:9.
9. Exodus 19:4.
10. John 1:12.
11. John 3:3; 1 Peter 1:3; Romans 8:17.
12. John 14:18.
13. 1 Corinthians 6:9.
14. Ephesians 2:3.
15. Colossians 1:13–14.
16. Luke 19:10.
17. Romans 8:1.
18. Isaiah 53:6.
19. Isaiah 64:6.

20. Isaiah 53:5–6.
21. Isaiah 53:11.
22. Isaiah 59:2.
23. John 8:34.
24. 1 Corinthians 6:19–20.
25. Matthew 1:21.
26. John 8:36.
27. Matthew 20:22.
28. Matthew 20:23.
29. John 6:53–57.
30. 1 Corinthians 11:25–26.

DAY 7
1. John 1:1–5.
2. Revelation 4:1–11.
3. Psalm 33:6–9.
4. Daniel 4:34–35, 37.
5. Revelation 19:14–16.
6. Colossians 1:15–20.
7. John 3:16.
8. 1 Corinthians 1:23–25.
9. 1 Corinthians 2:2.
10. 1 Corinthians 1:18.
11. John 3:17–21.
12. John 3:16.

DAY 8
1. Luke 7:1–6.
2. Luke 7:6–8.
3. Luke 7:9–10.
4. Luke 7:13–17.
5. 1 Corinthians 1:30.
6. Ephesians 2:4–8.
7. John 10:10.
8. 1 Corinthians 15:22.
9. 2 Corinthians 5:17.

DAY 9
1. Luke 4:1–2.
2. Luke 4:14–15.
3. Luke 4:16–21.
4. Luke 4:28–30.
5. Isaiah 53.
6. 1 John 4:9–10.
7. Romans 5:8.
8. John 17:26.
9. Luke 19:10.
10. Hebrews 12:1–2.
11. James 2:5.
12. 2 Corinthians 5:21.

DAY 10
1. Luke 2:41–47.
2. Matthew 12:34.
3. Luke 2:48.
4. Luke 2:49.
5. John 19:6.
6. John 19:7.
7. Luke 2:50.
8. John 17:25–26.
9. Matthew 5:17.
10. Romans 8:15.
11. Galatians 4:6.
12. John 14:6.
13. John 14:18.
14. John 1:12.
15. Galatians 3:27.
16. Romans 8:9–18.
17. Hebrews 4:16.
18. Romans 8:26–39.

DAY 11
1. John 1:6–7.
2. John 1:8–13.

3. John 2:11.
4. John 2:16.
5. John 2:19.
6. John 2:22.
7. John 2:23.
8. John 3:14–15.
9. John 3:16–18.
10. John 3:28, 35–36.
11. John 4:7.
12. John 4:21–26.
13. John 5:6 NASB1995.
14. John 5:7.
15. John 5:8 NIV.
16. John 5:18 NKJV.
17. John 5:24.
18. John 6:28.
19. John 6:29.
20. John 6:40.
21. Hebrews 12:2 NASB1995.
22. John 20:26–31.

DAY 12
1. Luke 18:10–14.
2. Hebrews 2:17.
3. Isaiah 64:6.
4. Proverbs 9:10.
5. Proverbs 19:23.
6. Isaiah 52:14.
7. Colossians 1:15–22.
8. "O soul, are you weary and troubled?" Helen Howarth Lemmel. 1922.
9. Hebrews 10:26–31.

DAY 13
1. John 3:1–3.
2. Hebrews 9:22.

3. Leviticus 16:14.

4. Leviticus 16:15, 19, 30.

5. Leviticus 17:11.

6. Hebrews 2:17.

7. 1 John 2:2.

8. 1 John 4:10.

9. The KJV says simply, "And they crucified him . . ." (Matthew 27:35).

10. John 3:16–18.

11. Galatians 2:19–20.

12. 1 Peter 2:23–25.

13. Philippians 2:6–8.

14. Romans 3:21–26.

DAY 14

1. Matthew 8:24–27.

2. John 11:3.

3. John 11:6.

4. John 11:4.

5. John 11:14–15.

6. John 11:21.

7. John 11:25–27.

8. Joshua 1:5–9.

9. John 14:1.

10. Luke 12:22.

11. Philippians 4:6.

12. 1 John 3:8.

13. Hebrews 2:14 NASB1995.

14. John 6:19.

15. John 6:20.

16. Hebrews 2:14–15.

17. Genesis 1:31.

18. Romans 8:31–39. (These are some of my favorite words in all of Scripture.)

DAY 15

1. John 8:1–6.

2. John 8:7–8.

3. Exodus 32:15–16.

4. John 8:10–11.

5. John 1:14,16–17.

6. John 8:12.

7. John 8:13.

8. John 8:15–16.

9. John 8:19.

10. John 8:21.

11. John 8:22.

12. John 8:23–24.

13. John 8:28–29.

14. John 8:30.

15. John 8:31–32.

16. John 8:33–36.

17. John 8:39.

18. Genesis 15:6.

19. John 8:40–41.

20. John 8:41–47.

21. John 8:56.

22. John 8:57–58.

23. John 8:59.

24. Galatians 5:1.

25. Romans 1:16–25.

DAY 16

1. Matthew 9:32–34.

2. Matthew 9:35–36.

3. Matthew 10:7–8.

4. Matthew 10:16.

5. Matthew 10:17–22.

6. Matthew 10:23–25.

7. Matthew 10:26–31.

8. Matthew 10:32–33.

9. Matthew 10:34–37.

10. Matthew 10:38–39.

11. John 14:12–14.

12. Galatians 2:20.

DAY 17

1. Matthew 5:1–3.

2. Matthew 4:19.

3. Matthew 4:17.

4. Isaiah 24:6.

5. Hebrews 11:13.

6. Psalm 19:7.

7. For a more complete list, see Deuteronomy 28.

8. Acts 15:10.

9. "The LORD descended in the cloud and stood with him there, and proclaimed the name of the LORD. The LORD passed before him and proclaimed, 'The LORD, the LORD, a God merciful and gracious, slow to anger, and abounding in steadfast love and faithfulness, keeping steadfast love for thousands, forgiving iniquity and transgression and sin, but who will by no means clear the guilty, visiting the iniquity of the fathers on the children and the children's children, to the third and the fourth generation'" (Exodus 34:5–7).

10. Exodus 20:5–6; 34:5–7; Numbers 14:18; Deuteronomy 5:8–10.

11. For a more detailed teaching on blessing and curse, see chapter 8 of my book *What If It's True*.

12. Galatians 3:10.

13. Deuteronomy 28:15.

14. Malachi 3:6.

15. Isaiah 24:5–6.

16. Matthew 5:3–12.

17. Matthew 8:16.

18. Matthew 9:1–2; Mark 2:5; Luke 5:20.

19. John 9:2.

20. Isaiah 52:14.

21. Galatians 3:13.

22. 2 Corinthians 5:21.

23. 1 John 1:7.

24. Matthew 12:37.

25. Romans 6:11.

26. Romans 6:14.

27. Romans 7:4.

28. Romans 7:6.

29. Romans 8:2.

30. Romans 8:1–4.

DAY 18

1. Luke 7:39.

2. Luke 7:40–43.

3. Luke 7:44–46.

4. Luke 7:47–48.

5. Luke 7:49–50.

6. Hebrews 9:26.

7. Hebrews 10:12–14.

8. 2 Corinthians 5:17–21.

9. Ephesians 2:13–16.

DAY 19

1. Matthew 8:1–4.

2. Matthew 8:16–17 NASB.

3. Psalm 9:13.

4. Psalm 22:24.

5. Psalm 25:18.
6. Psalm 31:7.
7. Psalm 34:19.
8. John 15:3.
9. Colossians 1:19–22.

DAY 20
1. Luke 10:25–28.
2. Luke 10:29–37.
3. Luke 18:18.
4. Luke 18:19–23.
5. Luke 18:24–25.
6. Luke 18:26–27.
7. Philippians 3:4–6.
8. Romans 7:24.
9. Philippians 3:7–8.
10. Ephesians 2:8–10.

DAY 21
1. John 5:18.
2. John 5:19–21.
3. John 5:22–24.
4. Exodus 6:9.
5. Exodus 15:26.
6. Deuteronomy 11:13 NASB1995.
7. Deuteronomy 18:15.
8. Deuteronomy 18:19.
9. Joshua 5:6.
10. John 5:25–27.
11. John 5:30.
12. John 5:38–42.
13. John 5:43–44.
14. John 5:45–47.
15. John 6:14.
16. Deuteronomy 6:4–6.
17. John 6:32–37.

DAY 22
1. John 6:22–25.
2. John 6:15.
3. John 6:26–27.
4. Daniel 7:13–14.
5. John 6:28.
6. John 6:29.
7. Numbers 21:5.
8. Numbers 21:7.
9. Numbers 21:9.
10. John 6:30–31.
11. John 6:32–34.
12. John 6:35–40.
13. John 17:12.
14. John 10:27–30.
15. Colossians 2:13–15.
16. Isaiah 1:18.
17. Hebrews 2:9–18.

DAY 23
1. John 6:38–40.
2. Daniel 12:1–4.
3. Philippians 2:10–11.
4. 2 Corinthians 5:10.
5. John 11:21–24.
6. John 12:36–43.
7. John 12:44.
8. John 12:44–46.
9. John 12:47–48.
10. John 6:39–40.
11. John 5:28–29.
12. 1 Corinthians 15:50–57.
13. Philippians 2:12–13, 15–16.

DAY 24
1. John 6:41–42.
2. John 6:43–45.

3. John 6:45–47.

4. John 6:48–51.

5. Deuteronomy 18:15.

6. Exodus 19; Matthew 5–7.

7. Hebrews 3:1–6.

8. John 6:52.

9. John 6:53–58.

10. John 6:59.

11. John 6:60–62.

12. John 6:63–65.

13. John 6:66.

14. John 6:67.

15. Matthew 7:14.

16. John 6:68–69.

17. John 6:53.

18. John 6:61–62.

19. Lewis, C. S., *Mere Christianity (Rough Cut).* (United Kingdom: HarperCollins, 2001), 52.

20. Colossians 1:26–27.

21. Colossians 2:1–3.

22. Colossians 2:9–15.

DAY 25

1. Luke 12:1–3.

2. 1 Corinthians 5:6–8.

3. Matthew 9:33–34.

4. Luke 10:17–20.

5. Genesis 3:15.

6. Luke 10:21–22.

7. Luke 11:20–23.

8. Luke 12:4–5.

9. Luke 12:8–10.

10. Luke 12:13.

11. Luke 12:50.

12. Psalm 88:7.

13. Romans 6:5.

14. Romans 10:9–10.

15. 1 Corinthians 15:50–57.

DAY 26

1. Mark 10:46–47.

2. Mark 10:48.

3. Isaiah 6:1–4.

4. Isaiah 6:5.

5. Job 42:2–6.

6. John 20:2.

7. John 13:23–25.

8. Revelation 1:12–17.

9. Daniel 7.

10. Exodus 3:14.

11. Exodus 33:18.

12. Exodus 33:19–20.

13. Mark 10:49–52.

14. 2 Thessalonians 2:8.

15. Isaiah 6:9–10.

16. Matthew 13:11–17.

DAY 27

1. Isaiah 50:7.

2. Isaiah 50:6.

3. Isaiah 53:7.

4. John 12:19.

5. John 12:13.

6. Luke 19:38.

7. Luke 19:39.

8. Luke 19:40.

9. Luke 13:31–32.

10. NKJV and NASB margin notes.

11. Hebrews 5:7.

12. Luke 19:41–42.

13. Luke 19:43–44.

14. John 12:23.

15. John 12:24–26.

16. John 12:27–28.

17. 2 Peter 3:9.

18. 1 Timothy 2:4.

19. John 17:26.

20. John 12:25–26.

21. 1 Corinthians 15:31 NASB1995.

22. Galatians 2:20.

23. Galatians 6:14.

24. Luke 19:44.

25. 2 Corinthians 5:17–21.

DAY 28

1. John 11:38.

2. John 11:39.

3. John 11:40–44.

4. John 12:1.

5. John 12:2–3.

6. John 12:4–8.

7. John 12:9–11.

8. John 12:12–17, 19.

9. 2 Chronicles 16:9.

10. Revelation 5:9–14.

DAY 29

1. John 12:27–32.

2. Isaiah 52:13–14.

3. John 3:7.

4. John 3:4.

5. John 3:14–15.

6. Numbers 21:4–5.

7. Numbers 21:6–9.

8. John 8:7.

9. Exodus 31:18.

10. John 8:11.

11. John 8:21–25.

12. John 8:25–29.

13. John 8:30.

14. John 12:31–32.

15. Ezekiel 28:11–19.

16. The NKJV translates "unrighteousness" as "iniquity."

17. Isaiah 53:5–6.

18. Isaiah 53:5.

19. Isaiah 14:11–15.

20. Luke 14:11.

21. Philippians 2:5–11.

22. Ephesians 2:1–10.

DAY 30

1. Mark 14:45–46.

2. Mark 14:50.

3. John 18:20–22.

4. Mark 14:55; 15:10.

5. Matthew 26:61.

6. Matthew 26:62–64.

7. Matthew 26:65–68.

8. Mark 14:65.

9. Mark 14:65 margin notes.

10. Proverbs 2:1–5.

11. 2 Timothy 1:7.

12. 2 Chronicles 19:7, 9.

13. Job 28:28.

14. Psalm 19:9; 34:11; 111:10.

15. Proverbs 1:7; 8:13; 14:27; 16:6.

16. Isaiah 11:2–3.

17. Acts 9:31.

18. 2 Corinthians 5:11.

19. Proverbs 1:28–29.

20. Proverbs 19:23.

21. John 18:3–6 NASB1995.

22. Exodus 3:14.

DAY 31

1. Matthew 27:1–2.

2. Matthew 27:11–13.

3. Matthew 27:14.

4. Matthew 27:17–18.

5. Matthew 27:19.

6. Matthew 27:21.

7. Matthew 27:22.

8. Mark 15:12.

9. Matthew 27:22–23.

10. Luke 23:1–12.

11. Matthew 27:29; Mark 15:17; John 19:2, 5.

12. Matthew 27:29.

13. Matthew 27:24–26.

14. Mark 15:20.

15. 2 Chronicles 16:9 NASB1995.

16. Exodus 34:4–10.

DAY 32

1. Luke 23:32–42.

2. John 3:14–15.

3. Luke 23:43.

4. John 19:28.

5. John 19:26.

6. John 6:29.

7. John 11:21–22.

8. John 11:25–26.

9. John 12:46.

10. Acts 10:43.

11. Acts 13:39.

12. Acts 16:29–31.

13. Romans 7:24.

14. Acts 16:31.

15. Romans 4:22–25.

16. Romans 10:4.

17. Colossians 1:13.

18. Daniel 7:10.

19. John 1:29.

20. Daniel 7:13.

21. 1 John 1:9.

22. Daniel 7:14.

23. Romans 3:26.

24. Romans 10:9–13.

25. John 17:26.

26. Ephesians 2:1–10.

DAY 33

1. John 8:2–11.

2. Romans 5:20.

3. John 8:21–24.

4. John 8:34.

5. John 16:1.

6. John 16:1 NASB.

7. Romans 5:18–21.

8. Romans 6:20–23.

9. Romans 7:4–6.

10. Romans 7:7–11.

11. Romans 7:12–14.

12. Romans 7:15–17.

13. Romans 7:18.

14. Romans 7:18.

15. Romans 7:19–20.

16. Romans 7:21–23.

17. Romans 7:24–25.

18. Ezekiel 20:33–38.

19. Leviticus 27:32.

20. Matthew 25:32–33.

21. Galatians 2:20.

22. 1 Corinthians 15:31 NASB1995.

23. Colossians 2:13–15.

24. 1 Corinthians 6:20.

DAY 34

1. Matthew 26:1–2.

2. Matthew 26:1–5.

3. Luke 22:3.
4. Matthew 26:14–16.
5. Exodus 21:32.
6. John 13:2–5.
7. John 13:12–26.
8. John 13:27.
9. John 13:30.
10. John 18:1–7.
11. Luke 22:47–53.
12. Matthew 27:1–2.
13. Matthew 27:3–4.
14. Matthew 27:3 NASB1995.
15. Matthew 27:3–10.
16. John 13:31–33.
17. John 13:34–35.
18. Matthew 6:15.
19. Matthew 18:34–35.
20. Matthew 16:24.
21. Mark 8:34.
22. Luke 9:23.

DAY 35

1. Matthew 26:30–31.
2. Matthew 26:32.
3. Matthew 26:33–35.
4. Luke 22:31–32.
5. Luke 22:33–34.
6. John 13:36–38.
7. John 18:15–18.
8. John 18:25–27.
9. Matthew 16:16.
10. Matthew 16:18.
11. Mark 16:6–8.
12. Luke 22:32.
13. John 21:3.
14. John 21:4–6.
15. John 21:6–7.

16. John 21:8–11.
17. John 21:12–13.
18. John 21:14.
19. John 21:15.
20. John 21:16–17.
21. John 21:17.
22. John 21:18–19.
23. John 21:19.
24. Hebrews 11:6.
25. Romans 8:31–39.

DAY 36

1. John 14:12–14.
2. John 14:15.
3. John 14:16–18.
4. 1 John 4:4 NASB1995.
5. Joel 2:28–29.
6. Joel 2:30–32.
7. John 1:29–34.
8. John 3:34–36.
9. John 14:25–26.
10. John 16:7.
11. John 15:26.
12. John 16:7–11.
13. John 7:39.
14. John 16:12–15.
15. Acts 8:15–17.
16. Acts 8:18–24.
17. Mark 7:8–9.
18. Mark 7:13.
19. Luke 18:9.
20. Luke 18:15–17.
21. Romans 1:4.
22. Romans 8:9–11.
23. Romans 8:14.

DAY 37
1. Luke 22:41–43.
2. John 1:29.
3. Leviticus 16:14–15, 19, 30.
4. Isaiah 53:5.
5. Genesis 4:10.
6. Hebrews 12:22–24.
7. 1 Peter 3:18–20.
8. Leviticus 17:11.
9. 1 John 4:10.
10. John 3:14–18.
11. Isaiah 53:1–12.
12. Hebrews 12:1–2.

DAY 38
1. John 3:29–30.
2. This is not exhaustive.
3. Luke 18:28–34.
4. Matthew 26:38–39.
5. John 18:10–11.
6. John 18:12–13.
7. John 18:19–22.
8. John 18:28–31.
9. John 18:33–40.
10. John 19:1.
11. John 19:2–7.
12. John 19:14–16.
13. Luke 23:26–28.
14. John 19:17–18.
15. John 19:23.
16. John 19:30.
17. John 19:30.
18. John 19:33–37.
19. Psalm 46:1–11.

DAY 39
1. Luke 23:22–25.

2. Luke 23:26–31.
3. Luke 23:32–33.
4. Acts 2:22–23.
5. Luke 23:34–38.
6. John 19:23–24.
7. John 19:25–27.
8. Luke 23:39–43.
9. Matthew 27:45–49.
10. John 19:28–29.
11. John 19:30.
12. Luke 23:44–46.
13. Matthew 27:51–54.
14. John 19:32–36.
15. Luke 23:47–49.
16. John 17:1–26.
17. Matthew 20:28.
18. Psalm 22:27–31.

DAY 40
1. Matthew 28:1–9.
2. Mark 16:1–8.
3. Luke 24:1–12.
4. John 20:11–18.
5. Revelation 5:12–13.
6. Hebrews 12:1–2.

EPILOGUE
1. Luke 24:5–6.
2. Mark 15:39.
3. Matthew 27:35 NASB1995.
4. Isaiah 52:14 NASB1995.
5. John 17:26.
6. 1 Corinthians 11:25–26.

ABOUT THE AUTHOR

Charles Martin is a *New York Times* and *USA Today* bestselling author of over fourteen books. Charles and his wife, Christy, live in Jacksonville, Florida. Learn more at charlesmartinbooks.com.